BERLITZ

HUNGARIAN
FOR TRAVELLERS

By the staff of Berlitz Guides

Library of Congress Catalog Card Number: 02-799880-0

8th printing 1989

Printed in Switzerland

Berlitz Guides
Avenue d'Ouchy 61
1000 Lausanne 6, Switzerland

Preface

You are about to visit Hungary. Our aim has been to produce a practical phrase book to help you on your trip.

In preparing this book we took into account a wealth of suggestions from phrase book users around the world. The accent is on helping the traveller in practical, every-day situations.

The contents are logically arranged so you can find the right phrase at the moment you need it.

Hungarian for Travellers features:

- all the phrases and supplementary vocabulary you'll need on your trip
- complete phonetic transcription throughout, enabling you to pronounce every word correctly
- special panels showing replies your listener might like to give you: just hand him the book and let him point to the appropriate phrase. This is particularly useful in certain difficult situations (trouble with the car, at the doctor's, etc.)
- a wide range of travel facts, hints and useful practical information, providing valuable insight into life in Hungary
- a tipping chart (see inside back-cover) and a reference section in the back of the book
- an introduction to some basics of Hungarian grammar

Certain sections will be particularly appreciated by travellers: the extensive "Eating Out" chapter which explains what's on the menu, in the soup and under the sauce, with translations, and the complete "Shopping Guide" which enables you to be almost as specific and selective as you would be at home. Trouble with the car? Turn to the mechanic's manual with its dual-language terms. Feeling ill? Our medical section provides the most rapid communication possible between you and the doctor.

To make the most of *Hungarian for Travellers,* we suggest that you start with the "Guide to Pronunciation". Then go on to "Some Basic Expressions". This not only gives you a minimum vocabulary, it also helps you get used to pronouncing the language.

We are particularly grateful to Mr. David Pulman and Mr. Norbert Urban for their help in the preparation of this book, and to Dr. T.J.A. Bennett who devised the phonetic transcription system. We also wish to extend special thanks to Vue Touristique I.P.V., Budapest, and to Prof. Joseph J. Hollos for their decisive roles in guiding this project to fruition.

We shall be very pleased to receive any comments, criticisms and suggestions that you think may help us in preparing future editions.

Have a good trip.

Throughout this book the symbols illustrated here indicate sections containing phrases your listener might like to say to *you.* If you don't understand him, just give him the book and let him point to the phrase in his language. The English translation is just beside.

A very basic grammar

Hungarian is a unique, intricate, subtle language belonging to the Finno-Ugric family.* It's completely unrelated to Slavonic, Germanic or any other Indo-European tongue.

Hungarian words are highly derivative, various ideas and nuances being expressed by a root-word modified in different ways. Instead of prepositions ("to", "from", "in", etc.), Hungarian uses a variety of suffixes (tags added to the ends of words) to achieve the same effect. Special endings are also added to verbs, pronouns and other parts of speech. The choice of suffix is partly governed by a complicated set of rules of vowel harmony. What this means is that the vowels in the root-word determine which alternative of the required suffix must be added.

Take a stab at the suffix

In some phrases in this book we have had no alternative but to leave the choice of suffix open, since it depends on the word you wish to insert in front of it. It's impossible for us to give here a watertight summary of the technicalities of vowel harmony. However, if you follow the rules of thumb given below you'll considerably shorten the odds on picking the correct suffix.

- If the basic word is dominated by "open" vowels (**e**, **é**, **i**, **í**, **ö**, **ő**, **ü**, **ű**), add that suffix which also contains an "open" vowel.
- If the basic word is dominated by "closed" vowels (**a**, **á**, **o**, **ó**, **u**, **ú**), add that suffix which also contains a "closed" vowel.

Don't worry about making a mistake, you'll be understood—and most likely complimented for trying hard!

* Its closest, yet still extremely distant, relative is Finnish.

Articles

1. **Definite article** (the):

The word for *the* is **a** before a word beginning with a consonant, and **az** before a vowel, in both singular and plural. It is indeclinable.

singular		plural	
a vonat	the train	**a vonatok**	the trains
az asztal	the table	**az asztalok**	the tables

2. **Indefinite article** (a/an):

The indefinite article is always **egy** (the same as the word for "one"). It is indeclinable.

egy vonat	a train	**egy asztal**	a table

Nouns

As in English, there is no grammatical gender. However, nouns take various endings depending on their case.

Here is a general model of the declension of nouns based on the word **könyv** (book), showing the endings to be added. Note, however, that endings are often subject to change according to the rules of vowel harmony.

case	singular	plural	usage
subject	**könyv**	**könyvek**	the book(s) (is/are ...)
dir. obj.	**könyveket**	**könyveket**	(I read) the book(s)
possess.	**könyvnek a**	**könyveknek a**	of the book(s)
ind. obj.	**könyvnek**	**könyveknek**	to the book(s)
place	**könyvben**	**könyvekben**	in the book(s)
"from"	**könyvről**	**könyvekről**	from the book(s)

Adjectives

1. The adjective precedes the noun, with no endings.

a piros autó the red car **a piros autók** the red cars

2. The comparative of an adjective is formed by adding the endings **-bb**, **-abb**, **-ebb** or **-obb** to its simple form.

3. In the superlative, the adjective takes the same endings but is also preceded by **leg**. Here are some useful examples.

simple	comparative	superlative
jó good	**jobb** better	**legjobb** best
magas tall	**magasabb** taller	**legmagasabb** tallest
szép beautiful	**szebb** more beautiful	**legszebb** most beautiful
nagy big	**nagyobb** bigger	**legnagyobb** biggest

Personal pronouns

subject		direct object (me, etc.)	indirect object (to me, etc.)
I	**én**	**engem**	**nekem**
you	**maga***	**magát***	**magának***
you	**te**	**téged**	**neked**
he/she/it	**ő**	**őt**	**neki**
we	**mi**	**minket**	**nekünk**
you	**maguk***	**magukat***	**maguknak***
you	**ti**	**titeket**	**nektek**
they	**ők**	**őket**	**nekik**

* Polite form for "you".

Demonstratives

this **ez** these **ezek** that **az** those **azok**

Possessives

To form the possessive case, take the definite article + the personal pronoun + the noun. The noun takes endings (again, governed by a complicated set of rules).

my book	**az én könyvem**	our book	**a mi könyvünk**
your book	**a maga könyve***	your book	**a maguk könyve***
your book	**a te könyved**	your book	**a ti könyvetek**
his/her book	**az ő könyve**	their book	**az ő könyvük**

Verbs

Because of the complexity of Hungarian verbs we have restricted ourselves to showing how to form the present and future tenses of verbs, including the special cases of the verbs "to be" and "to have".

1. Present tense of the verbs "to be" and "to have":

to be (**lenni**)			
I am	**én vagyok**	we are	**mi vagyunk**
you are	**maga van***	you are	**maguk vannak***
you are	**te vagy**	you are	**ti vagytok**
he/she/it is	**ő van**	they are	**ők vannak**

to have (**vanéki**)			
I have	**nekem van**	we have	**nekünk van**
you have	**magának van***	you have	**maguknak van***
you have	**neked van**	you have	**nektek van**
he/she/it has	**neki van**	they have	**nekik van**

* Polite form for "you", "your".

2. Present tense of other verbs:

The present tense may be formed in various ways. Here is a common pattern for transitive verbs (i. e. those which can take a direct object) based on the infinitive **olvasni** (to read).

I read	**én olvasom**	we read	**mi olvassuk**
you read	**maga olvassa***	you read	**maguk olvassák***
you read	**te olvasod**	you read	**ti olvassátok**
he/she reads	**ő olvassa**	they read	**ők olvassák**

Questions: **olvassa ő?** = does he/she read? etc.

3. Future

A simple method of forming the future tense is to use the personal pronoun + the word corresponding to "shall" or "will" (**fogok/fogsz**, etc.) + the infinitive. Here we take the verb **vásárolni** (to shop) as an example (I shall shop/go shopping, etc.).

I ...	**én fogok vásárolni**	we ...	**mi fogunk vásárolni**
you ...	**maga fog vásárolni***	you ...	**maguk fognak vásárolni***
you ...	**te fogsz vásárolni**	you ...	**ti fogtok vásárolni**
he/she ...	**ő fog vásárolni**	they ...	**ők fognak vásárolni**

Negatives

In a sentence, the word **nem** is usually placed after the subject. There is also a change of word order (inversion).

I am here	**én itt vagyok**
I am not here	**én nem vagyok itt**

* Polite form for "you".

Guide to pronunciation

This and the following chapter are intended to make you familiar with the phonetic transcription we devised and to help you get used to the sounds of Hungarian.

As a minimum vocabulary for your trip, we've selected a number of basic words and phrases under the title "Some Basic Expressions" (pages 16–21).

An outline of the spelling and sounds of Hungarian

You'll find the pronunciation of the Hungarian letters and sounds explained below, as well as the symbols we use for them in the transcription. Note that Hungarian has some diacritical signs—special markings over certain letters—which we don't use in English.

The imitated pronunciation should be read as if it were English except for any special rules set out below. It is based on Standard British pronunciation, though we have tried to take into account General American pronunciation as well. Of course, the sounds of any two languages are never exactly the same; but if you follow carefully the indications supplied here, you'll have no difficulty in reading our transcription in such a way as to make yourself understood.

Letters written in **bold** type should be stressed (pronounced louder).

Consonants

Letter	Approximate pronunciation	Symbol	Example	
b, d, f, h, m, n, v, x, z	as in English			
c	like **ts** in nets	ts	**arc**	orts

cs	like **ch** in **chap**	ch	**kocsi**	**kaw**chee
g	always as in **go**, never as in **gin**	g/gh	**gáz** **régi**	gaaz **ray**ghee
gy	like **di** in **medium**, said fairly quickly	d^y	**ágy**	**aa**d^y
j	like **y** in **yes**	$y/^y$	**jég**	yayg
k	always as in si**ck**, never as in **k**ill	k	**kör**	kurr
l	always as in **l**eap, never as in ba**ll**	l	**ital**	**ee**tol
ly	like **y** in **yes**	$y/^y$	**Károly**	**kaa**raw^y
ny	quite like **ni** in **onion**	n^y	**hány**	haan^y
p	always as in si**p**, never as in **p**ill	p	**posta**	**pawsh**to
r	pronounced with the tip of the tongue, like Scottish **r**	r	**ír**	$\overline{ee}$r
s	like **sh** in **shoot**	sh	**saláta**	**shol**laato
sz	like **s** in **so**	s/ss	**szó** **ész**	s$\overline{aw}$ ayss
t	always as in si**t**, never as in **t**ill	t	**túra**	**t**$\overline{oo}$ro
ty	quite like **tti** in **prettier**, said quickly	t^y	**atya**	ot^{y}o
zs	like **s** in **pleasure**	zh	**zsír**	zh$\overline{ee}$r

Vowels

a	quite like **o** in **not** (British pronunciation)	o	**hat**	hot
á	like **a** in **car**, but without any **r**-sound	aa	**rág**	raag
e	quite like **e** in **yes**, but with the mouth a little more open, i.e. a sound between **e** in **yes** and **a** in **hat**	æ	**te**	tæ
é	like **ay** in **say**, but a pure vowel, not a diphthong, i.e. neither the tongue nor the lips move during the pronunciation of it	ay	**mér**	mayr

i	like **ee** in **fee**t (short)	ee	**hideg**	**hee**dæg
í	like **ee** in s**ee** (long)	e̅e̅	**míg**	me̅e̅g
o	quite like **aw** in s**aw** (British pronunciation), but shorter	aw	**bot**	bawt
ó	like **aw** in s**aw**, but with the tongue higher in the mouth	a̅w̅	**fotó**	**faw**ta̅w̅
ö	like **ur** in f**ur**, but short, without any **r**-sound, and with rounded lips	ur	**örök**	**ur**rurk
ő	like **ur** in f**ur**, but without any **r**-sound, and with the lips tightly rounded	u̅r̅	**lő**	lu̅r̅
u	as in the British pronunciation of p**u**ll	oo	**kulcs**	koolch
ú	like **oo** in f**oo**d	o̅o̅	**kút**	ko̅o̅t
ü	a "rounded **ee**"; while pronouncing **ee** as in s**ee**, round your lips as if to pronounce **oo** as in s**oo**n; the resulting sound should be as in French **u**ne or German f**ü**nf	ew	**körül**	**kur**rewl
ű	the same sound as **ü**, but long and with the lips more tightly rounded	e̅w̅	**fűt**	fe̅w̅t

N.B. 1) There are no "silent" letters in Hungarian, so all letters must be pronounced. This means that double consonants are pronounced long, e.g. **tt** in ke**ttő** (**kæt**-tu̅r̅) sounds rather like **t-t** in a fast pronunciation of par**t-t**ime. (But a double consonant appearing at the end of a word is pronounced short). It also means that vowels standing next to each other are pronounced separately and do not combine to produce diphthongs.

2) When two or more consonants stand next to each other, the last one can influence the pronunciation of the others. If it is "voiceless", it will make a preceding "voiced" consonant into a "voiceless" one, and vice versa, e.g. *végtelen* is

pronounced as if it were written *véktelen.* The "voiceless" consonants are **c**, **f**, **k**, **p**, **s**, **sz**, **t**, **ty**, and the corresponding "voiced" ones are **dz**, **v**, **g**, **b**, **zs**, **z**, **d**, **gy**.

3) Every word, when pronounced alone, has a strong stress on its first syllable. When words are combined in sentences, the stress on the less important words weakens.

4) The "double" forms of **cs**, **gy**, **ly**, **ny**, **sz**, **ty**, **zs** are **ccs**, **ggy**, **lly**, **nny**, **ssz**, **tty**, **zzs**. If the "double" form is divided at the end of a line, then the single form is written twice, e.g. **cs-cs** instead of **c-cs**.

5) In Hungarian, the letter **j** can combine with a preceding vowel to produce diphthongs, e.g. *új* (pronounced $\overline{oo}$^{y}), *fej* (pronounced fæ^{y}), *sajt* (pronounced soyt). In all these cases, the **y** should be pronounced only fleetingly, as in boy.

Pronunciation of the Hungarian alphabet

A	o	**GY**	d^{y}e	**NY**	æn^{y}	**T**	te
Á	aa	**H**	haa	**O**	aw	**TY**	t^{y}e
B	be*	**I**	ee	**Ó**	$\overline{aw}$	**U**	oo
C	tse	**Í**	$\overline{ee}$	**Ö**	ur	**Ú**	$\overline{oo}$
CS	tche	**J**	ye	**Ő**	$\overline{ur}$	**Ü**	ew
D	de	**K**	kaa	**P**	pe	**Ű**	$\overline{ew}$
E	æ	**L**	æl	**Q**	kew	**V**	ve
É	e	**LY**	æl **eep**seelon	**R**	ær	**W**	dooplovvay
F	ayf	**M**	æm	**S**	æsh	**Z**	ze
G	ghe	**N**	æn	**SZ**	æs	**ZS**	zhe

* **e** doesn't appear in the transcriptions, but has more or less the same value as **a** in late.

Some basic expressions

Yes.	**Igen.**	**ee**gæn
No.	**Nem.**	næm
Please.	**Kérem.**	**kay**ræm
Yes, please.	**Igen, kérem.**	**ee**gæn **kay**ræm
Thank you.	**Köszönöm.**	**kur**surnurm
No, thank you.	**Nem, köszönöm.**	næm **kur**surnurm
Thank you very much.	**Köszönöm szépen.**	**kur**surnurm **say**pæn
You're welcome.	**Szívesen.**	**s$\overline{\text{ee}}$**væshæn
Sorry.	**Sajnálom.**	**shoy**naalawm

Greetings

Good morning.	**Jó reggelt.**	y$\overline{\text{aw}}$ **ræg**-gælt
Good afternoon.	**Jó napot.**	y$\overline{\text{aw}}$ **nop**pawt
Good evening.	**Jó estét.**	y$\overline{\text{aw}}$ **æsh**tayt
Good night.	**Jó éjszakát.**	y$\overline{\text{aw}}$ **ay**^{y}sokkaat
Goodbye.	**Viszontlátásra.**	**vee**sawntlaataashro
See you later.	**Viszlát.**	**vees**laat
This is Mr. ...	**Szeretném bemutatni... urat.**	**sæ**rætnaym **bæ**moototnee ... **oo**rot
This is Mrs. ...	**Szeretném bemutatni... urnőt.**	**sæ**rætnaym **bæ**moototnee ... **oor**n$\overline{\text{ur}}$t
This is Miss...	**Szeretném bemutatni... kisasszonyt.**	**sæ**rætnaym **bæ**moototnee ... **kee**shoss-sawn^{y}t
I'm pleased to meet you.	**Örülök, hogy megismerhetem.**	**ur**rewlurk hawd^{y} **mæ**geeshmærhætæm
How are you?	**Hogy van?**	hawd^{y} von
Very well, thank you. And you?	**Köszönöm, nagyon jól. És Ön?**	**kur**surnurm **nod**^{y}awn y$\overline{\text{aw}}$l. aysh urn

Questions

Where?	**Hol?**	hawl
Where is ...?	**Hol van ...?**	hawl von
Where are ...?	**Hol vannak ...?**	hawl **von**-nok
How?	**Hogy?**	hawd^{Y}
How much?	**Mennyi/Mennyit?**	mæn^{Y}ee/mæn^{Y}eet
How many?	**Hány?**	haan^{Y}
When?	**Mikor?**	meekawr
Why?	**Miért?**	meeayrt
Who?	**Ki?**	kee
Which?	**Melyik?**	mæ^{Y}eek
What?	**Mi?**	mee
What do you call this/that?	**Mi a neve ennek/annak?**	mee o **n**æ**v**æ æ**n**-næk/**on**-nok
What does this/that mean?	**Ez/Az mit jelent?**	æz/oz meet **y**æ**l**æ**nt**

Do you speak ...?

Do you speak English/French/German?	**Beszél angolul/franciául/németül?**	**b**æ**sayl ongawlool/front**-seeaaool/**nay**mætewl
Does anyone here speak English?	**Van itt valaki aki angolul beszél?**	von eet **vo**llokkee **okkee ongawlool b**æ**sayl**
I don't speak much Hungarian.	**Alig beszélek magyarul.**	olleeg **b**æ**sayl**æk **mod^{Y}o**-rrool
How do you say this in Hungarian?	**Hogy mondják ezt magyarul?**	hawd^{Y} **mawnd^{Y}**aak æst **mod^{Y}**orrool
I beg your pardon?	**Bocsánat de nem értem önt.**	**baw**chaanot dæ næm **ayr**-tæm urnt
Could you speak more slowly?	**Elmondaná lassabban?**	**æl**mawndonnaa **losh**-shob-bon
Could you repeat it?	**Megismételné?**	**mæ**gheeshmaytælnay

Please write it down.	**Kérem, írja ezt le.**	kayræm **ēē**ryo æst læ
Can you translate this for me?	**Lefordítaná ezt nekem?**	læfawrdēētonnaa æst nækæm
Please point to the phrase in the book.	**Kérem, mutassa meg ezt a kifejezést a könyvben.**	kayræm **moo**tosh-sho mæg æst o **kee**fæyæzaysht o **kurn**^{y}vbæn
Just a minute. I'll see if I can find it in this book.	**Egy pillanat. Megnézem, benne van-e a könyvben.**	æd^{y} **peel**-lonnot. **mæg**nayzæm **bæn**-næ von-æ o **kurn**^{y}vbæn
I understand.	**Értem.**	ayrtæm
I don't understand.	**Nem értem.**	næm **ayr**tæm
Do you understand?	**Ön érti?**	urn **ayr**tee

Can ...?

Can I have ...?	**Kaphatok ...?**	**kop**hottawk
Can we have ...?	**Kaphatunk ...?**	**kop**hottoonk
Can you show me ...?	**Megmutatná ...?**	**mæg**moototnaa
I can't.	**Nem tudok.**	næm **too**dawk
Can you tell me ...?	**Megmondaná ...?**	**mæg**mawndonnaa
Can you help me, please?	**Segítene nekem?**	**shæ**ghēētænæ **næ**kæm
Can you direct me to ...?	**Elvezetne a ...?**	**æl**væzætnæ o

Wanting

I'd like ...	**Szeretnék ...**	særætnayk
We'd like ...	**Szeretnénk ...**	særætnaynk
Please give me ...	**Kérem, adjon ...**	kayræm **od**^{y}awn*
Please give me this/that.	**Kérem, adjon ezt/azt.**	kayræm **od**^{y}awn æst/ost
Please bring me ...	**Kérem, hozzon ...**	kayræm **hawz**-zawn

* j after d is pronounced like gy (d^{y}).

Please bring me this/that.	**Hozzon kérem ezt/ azt.**	**hawz**-zawn **kay**ræm æst/ost
I'm hungry.	**Éhes vagyok.**	ayhæsh **vod**^{y}awk
I'm thirsty.	**Szomjas vagyok.**	**saw**myosh **vod**^{y}awk
I'm tired.	**Fáradt vagyok.**	**faa**rot **vod**^{y}awk
I'm lost.	**Eltévedtem.**	æltayvædtæm
I'm looking for ...	**A ...-t keresem.**	o...-t **kæ**ræshæm
It's important.	**Fontos.**	**fawn**tawsh
It's urgent.	**Sürgős.**	**shewr**g$\overline{ur}$sh
Hurry up!	**Siessen!**	**shee**æsh-shæn

It is/There is ...

It is ...	**Van ...**	von
Is it ...?	**Van ...?**	von
It isn't ...	**Nincs ...**	neench
There is/There are ...	**Van .../Vannak ...**	von.../**von**-nok
Is there/Are there ...?	**Van .../Vannak ...?**	von.../**von**-nok
There isn't any.	**Ez/Az nincs.**	æz/oz neench
There aren't any.	**Ezek/Azok nincsenek.**	æzæk/**oz**zawk **neen**chænæk

A few common words

big/small	**nagy/kicsi**	nod^{y}/**kee**chee
cheap/expensive	**olcsó/drága**	**awl**ch$\overline{aw}$/**draa**go
good/bad	**jó/rossz**	yaw/rawss
better/worse	**jobb/rosszabb**	yawb/**rawss**-sob
right/wrong	**helyes/helytelen**	**hæ**^{y}æsh/**hæ**^{y}tælæn
easy/difficult	**egyszerű/bonyolult**	æd^{y}sær$\overline{ew}$/**bawn**^{y}awloolt
light/heavy	**könnyű/nehéz**	**kurn**$^{y}\overline{ew}$/**næ**hayz
full/empty	**teli/üres**	tælee/**ew**ræsh

free/occupied	**szabad/foglalt**	sobbod/**faw**glolt
open/shut	**nyitva/zárva**	n^y^eetvo/zaarvo
old/young	**öreg/fiatal**	urræg/**fee**ottol
old/new	**régi/új**	rayghee/o͞o^y^
quick/slow	**gyors/lassú**	d^y^awrsh/**losh**-sho͞o
beautiful/ugly	**szép/csúnya**	sayp/**cho͞o**n^y^o
warm/cold	**meleg/hideg**	mælæg/**hee**dæg
never/always	**soha/mindig**	**shaw**ho/**meen**deeg
early/late	**korán/később**	**kaw**raan/**kay**shu͞rn
here/there	**itt/ott**	eet/awt
near/far	**közel/távol**	**kur**zæl/**taa**vawl
left/right	**bal/jobb**	bol/yawb
first/last	**első/utolsó**	**æl**shu͞r/ootawlshaw
now/then	**ekkor/akkor**	**æk**-kawr/**ok**-kawr
immediately/later	**azonnal/később**	ozzawn-nol/**kay**shu͞rb

Some prepositions ...

at	**-kor** (time) **-nál/-nél** (place)	-kawr -naal/-nayl
on	**-rá/-ra/-re/-on/** **-en/-ön**	-raa/-ro/-ræ/-awn -æn/-urn
in	**-ban/-ben**	-bon/-bæn
before (time)	**előtt**	**æ**lu͞rt
before (place)	**előtt**	**æ**lu͞rt
after	**után**	**oo**taan
behind	**mögött**	**mur**gurt
to	**felé/oda**	**fæ**lay/**aw**do
from	**-ból/-ből**	-ba͞wl/-bu͞rl
with	**-val/-vel**	-vol/-væl

* English prepositions are often rendered by suffixes in Hungarian. See p. 7.

without	**nélkül**	naylkewl
inside	**belül**	bælewl
outside	**kívül**	k$\overline{\text{ee}}$vewl
through	**keresztül**	kæræstewl
towards	**felé**	fælay
up	**fent**	fænt
down	**lent**	lænt
above	**felett**	fælæt
below	**alatt**	ollot
over	**fölött**	furlurt
under	**alatt**	ollot
until	**eddig/addig**	æd-deeg/od-deeg
for	**-ért**	-ayrt
between	**között**	kurzurt
during	**közben**	kurzbæn
since	**óta**	$\overline{\text{aw}}$to

... and a few more useful words

and	**és**	aysh
or	**vagy**	vod^{y}
but	**de**	dæ
not	**nem**	næm
nothing	**semmi**	sæm-mee
none	**egyik sem**	æd^{y}eek sæm
very	**nagyon**	nod^{y}awn
soon	**hamarosan**	hommorrawshon
perhaps	**talán**	tollaan
already	**már**	maar
again	**ismét**	eeshmayt
also	**is**	eesh

Arrival

You've arrived. Whether you come by train, plane, car or Danube steamer, you'll have to go through passport and customs formalities. (All except Austrian and Finnish nationals require a visa in addition to their passport.) If you didn't obtain one in advance through your travel agency or a Hungarian consulate, you can get one at road crossing points, river ports and at Budapest airport.

Customs officials and police on duty at crossing points speak some English and German.

Note: rail travellers *cannot* have a visa issued on the spot.

Passport control

Here's my passport.	**Tessék, az útlevelem.**	**tæsh**-shayk oz **o̅o̅t**lævælæm
I'll be staying...	**... maradok.**	... **mo**rroddawk
a few days	**Néhány napig**	**nay**haan^{y} **no**ppeeg
a week	**Egy hétig**	æd^{y} **hay**teeg
2 weeks	**2 hétig**	2 **hay**teeg
a month	**Egy hónapig**	æd^{y} **ha̅w̅**noppeeg
I don't know yet.	**Még nem tudom.**	mayg næm **too**dawm
I'm here on holiday.	**A szabadságomat töltöm itt.**	o **sob**bodshaagawmot **turl**turm eet
I'm here on business.	**Üzleti úton vagyok.**	**ewz**lætee **o̅o̅**tawn **vod**^{y}awk
I'm just passing through.	**Csak átutazóban vagyok.**	chok **aa**tootozza̅w̅bon **vod**^{y}awk

If the going gets hard, say:

I'm sorry, I don't understand.	**Sajnálom, de nem értem.**	**shoy**naalawm dæ næm **ayr**tæm
Does anyone here speak English?	**Beszél itt valaki angolul?**	**bæ**sayl eet **vol**lokkee **on**gawlool

CAR/BORDER FORMALITIES: see page 146

Customs

After collecting your baggage, leave by the green exit if you have nothing to declare or by the red exit if you have goods on which you must pay duty. Spot checks are frequently made in the green channel.

The chart shows what main items you may take into Hungary duty-free.*

 Cigarettes		 Cigars		 Tobacco	 Spirits		 Wine
250	or	50	or	250 g	1 l.	and	2 l.

Narcotics and obscene publications will be confiscated, with more severe penalties reserved.

I've nothing to declare.	**Nincs elvámolni valóm.**	neench ælvaamawlnee vollāwm
I've a ...	**Van egy ...**	von æd^{y}
carton of cigarettes bottle of whisky	**karton cigarettám üveg viszkim**	kortawn **tsee**gorræt-taam **ew**væg **vees**keem
This is a gift.	**Ez ajándék.**	æz oyaandayk
It's for my personal use.	**Ez a személyes használatomat szolgálja.**	æz o **sæ**may^{y}æsh **hos**-naalottawmot **sawl**gaalyo
This is not new.	**Ez nem új.**	æz næm o͞o^{y}

Kérem az útlevelét.	Your passport, please.
Önnek vízumra van szüksége. Legyen szíves jöjjön velem.	You need a visa. Come with me, please.
Kérem, nyissa ki ezt a táskát.	Please open this bag.
Ezért vámot kell fizetnie.	You'll have to pay duty on this.
Van még egyéb csomagja is?	Have you any more luggage?

* All allowances subject to change without notice.

Baggage – Porters

Porters are in short supply, though with perseverence you should be able to locate one. You'll generally find baggage trolleys. Against an extra tip, your taxi driver will help you.

Porter!	**Hordár!**	**haw**rdaar
Please take these bags.	**Kérem,vigye ezeket a bőröndöket.**	kayræm **veed**^{y}æ æzækæt o **bur**rurndurkæt
That's my ...	**Ez az én ...**	æz oz ayn
bag/luggage suitcase	**táskám/csomagom bőröndöm**	**taash**kaam/**chaw**moggawm **bur**rurndurm
There's one piece missing.	**Egy csomag hiányzik.**	æd^{y} **chaw**mog **hee**aan^{y}-zeek
Take these bags to the ...	**Kérem, vigye ezeket a csomagokat ...**	kayræm **veed**^{y}æ æzækæt o **chaw**moggawkot
bus taxi luggage lockers	**az autóbuszhoz a taxihoz a csomagmegőrzőbe**	oz **oo**tawbooss-hawz o **tox**eehawz o **chaw**mogmægurrzurbæ
Where are the baggage trolleys?	**Hol vannak a podgyász kézi-kocsik?**	hawl **von**-nok o **pawd**^{y}aass **kay**zeekawcheek

Changing money

You'll find currency exchange facilities at the airport, major railway stations and all entry points for road traffic. If you arrive after hours, your hotel will be able to change a certain amount of dollars, pounds sterling or some other foreign currencies for you. Keep all receipts.

See page 134 for details of money and currency exchange as well as banking hours.

Where's the nearest currency exchange?	**Hol tudok valutát beváltani?**	hawl **too**dawk **vol**lootaat **bæ**vaaltonnee
Can you change these traveller's cheques (checks)?	**Beváltják ezeket a traveller's csekkeket?**	**bæ**vaaltyaak æzækæt o **trov**væl-lærs **chæk**-kækæt

TIPPING: see page 1

I want to change some ...	**... akarok beváltani.**	... okkorrawk **bæ**vaal-tonnee
dollars	**Dollárt**	**dawl**-laart
pounds sterling	**Angol fontot**	ongawl **fawn**tawt
Can you change this into forints?	**Átváltaná ezt forintra?**	**aat**vaaltonnaa æst **faw**reentro

Directions—Finding a room

Tourist information offices are to be found at Budapest international airport, major railway stations and border crossing points. They are often able to book you a hotel room if you arrive without a reservation. Some staff members may speak English or German.

How do I get to this address?	**Hogy jutok el ide?**	hawd^y **yoo**tawk æl **ee**dæ
How do I get to this hotel?	**Hogy jutok el ehhez a szállodához?**	hawd^y **yoo**tawk æl **æh**-hæz o **saal**-lawdaahawz
Is there a bus into town?	**Van autóbuszjárat a városba?**	von **oo**otawboosyaarot o **vaa**rawshbo
Where can I get a taxi?	**Hol kapok taxit?**	hawl **kop**pawk **tox**eet
Where can I hire a car?	**Hol lehet autót bérelni?**	hawl **læ**hæt **oo**otawt **bay**rælnee
Have you a map of the town?	**Van térképe a városról?**	von **tayr**kaypæ o **vaa**rawshrawl
Could you book me a hotel room, please?	**Kérem, foglaljon részemre egy szobát.**	**kay**ræm **fawg**lolyawn **ray**ssæmræ æd^y **saw**baat
in the town centre	**a központban**	o **kurz**pawntbon
near the station	**az állomás mellett**	oz **aal**-lawmaash **mæl**-læt
a single room	**egy egyágyas szobát**	æd^y **æd^y**aad^{y}osh **saw**baat
a double room	**egy kétágyas szobát**	æd^y **kay**taad^{y}osh **saw**baat
not too expensive	**nem túl drágát**	næm **tool** **draa**gaat
Where is the hotel located?	**Hol található a szálloda?**	hawl **tol**laalhottaw o **saal**-lawdo

CHECKING IN: see page 30

Car rental

Car hire firms have offices at Budapest international airport and major railway stations. You can also hire a vehicle through a tourist office or your hotel. You must be at least twenty-one years of age and have held a full driving licence for more than one year. See the section beginning on page 142 for information on driving in Hungary.

You'll usually find someone at the agency who speaks English, but if not, use the following phrases to specify your requirements.

I'd like to hire a ... car.	**Egy ... kocsit szeretnék bérelni.**	æd^{y} ... **kaw**cheet **sæ**rætnayk **bay**rælnee
large/small	**nagyot/kicsit**	**nod**^{y}awt/**kee**cheet
I'd like it for ...	**... szeretném.**	... **sæ**rætnaym
a day/4 days a week/2 weeks	**Egy napra/4 napra** **Egy hétre/2 hétre**	æd^{y} **no**pro/4 **no**pro æd^{y} **hay**træ/2 **hay**træ
What's the charge per ... ?	**Mennyi a bérleti díj ... ?**	**mæn**^{y}ee o **bay**rlætee **dēē**^{y}
day/week	**naponként/hetenként**	**no**ppawnkaynt/ **hæ**tænkaynt
Does that include mileage?	**A bérleti díjban a kilométer járulék is benne van?**	o **bay**rlætee **dēē**^{y}bon o **kee**lawmaytær **yaa**roolayk eesh **bæn**-næ von
What's the charge per kilometre?	**Mennyi a járulék kilométerenként?**	**mæn**^{y}ee o **yaa**roolayk **kee**lawmaytærænkaynt
Is petrol (gas) included?	**Ebben benn van az üzemanyag költsége?**	**æb**-bæn bæn von oz **ew**zæmon^{y}og **kurlt**shaygæ
I want full insurance.	**Casco biztosítást kérek.**	**kosh**kaw **beez**tawshēē-taasht **kay**ræk
I'll be doing about 200 kilometres.	**Körülbelül 200 kilométert utazom a kocsival.**	**kur**rewbælewl 200 **kee**law-maytært **oo**tozzawm o **kaw**cheevol
What's the deposit?	**Mennyi a garanciális letét?**	**mæn**^{y}ee o **go**rrontseeaa-leesh **læ**tayt
I've a credit card.	**Rendelkezem hitelkártyával.**	**ræn**dælkæzæm **hee**tæl-kaart^{y}aavol

SIGHTSEEING: see page 75

Taxi

Metered vehicles both state-owned and private are available in Budapest and all larger towns. When they are free, the rooftop *Taxi* sign is lit. It's advisable to state your destination before entering the cab, as a driver may refuse trips which are too long or out of the way. For reasons of crime prevention (attacks on drivers) your taxidriver will want to phone in your name and passport number to his control centre if you are going beyond city limits. It's customary to give a tip in addition to the amount shown on the meter.

Where can I get a taxi?	**Hol kapok taxit?**	hawl **kop**pawk **tox**eet
Please get me a taxi.	**Kérem, szerezzen egy taxit.**	**kay**ræm **sæ**ræz-zæn æd^{y} toxeet
What's the fare to ...?	**... -ig mennyi a viteldíj?**	...-eeg **mæn**^{y}ee o **vee**tæl-dēē^{y}
Take me to ...	**Kérem, vigyen el ...**	**kay**ræm **veed**^{y}æn æl
this address	**erre a címre**	**ær**-ræ o **tsēēm**ræ
the airport	**a repülőtérre**	o **ræ**pewlūrtayr-ræ
the station	**a vasútállomásra**	o **vosh**ōōtaal-lawmaashro
the ... Hotel	**a ... szállóba**	o ... **saal**-lāwbo
the city centre	**a városközpontba**	o **vaa**rawshkurzpawntbo
Turn ... at the next corner.	**Forduljon ... a következő sarkon.**	**fawr**doolyawn... o **kur**-vætkæzūr **shor**kawn
left	**balra**	**bol**ro
right	**jobbra**	**yawb**ro
Stop here, please.	**Kérem, itt álljon meg.**	**kay**ræm eet **aal**yawn mæg
I'm in a hurry.	**Sietek.**	**shee**ætæk
Could you drive more slowly, please?	**Kérem, hajtson lassabban.**	**kay**ræm **hoyt**shawn **losh**-shob-bon
Would you help me carry my bags?	**Kérem, segítsen vinni a podgyászt.**	**kay**ræm **shæ**ghēētshæn **veen**nee o **pawd**^{y}aast
Would you please wait for me?	**Kérem, várjon.**	**kay**ræm **vaar**yawn

TIPPING: see page 1

Hotel—Other accommodation

Hotel rooms are often in short supply, both in the capital and in popular tourist areas such as around Lake Balaton. Whenever possible, make your bookings well in advance though your home travel agency, and take along written confirmation so as to avoid any misunderstandings on the spot. The busiest periods are the summer holiday season and any time when trade fairs, exhibitions or major international conferences are being held, particularly in Budapest. Travel agencies in your own country will probably be able to give you the precise dates of such events. Otherwise you may like to write to one of the foreign agencies of *Ibusz*, the Hungarian national tourist organization. They are located in the following cities in western Europe: Brussels, Cologne, Frankfurt, London, Paris, Rome, Stockholm and Vienna. There is also an *Ibusz* office in New York. Your home travel agency will be able to give your their addresses.

Students might ask their national student travel service for details of inexpensive accommodation available in Hungary. You should take along an international student identity card if you intend to make use of such facilities.

Should you arrive in the country without prearranged accommodation, there are several offices you can turn to for assistance in finding a room. Tourist information offices are maintained at virtually all entry points. Local travel agencies may also make reservations for you. If hotels are full, they may be able to put you up in private homes. A booking fee is charged for on-the-spot reservations.

Rates are up to 30 per cent lower outside the main summer tourist season. A room for two works out appreciably cheaper than two single rooms.

CAMPING: see page 90

Szálloda
(**saal**-lawdo)

Hotels large and small go under this name (though the foreign word "hotel" is also used quite widely). They are graded by stars, from 5-star de-luxe establishments to 1-star budget hotels.

Only two or three top-rank international hotels in the capital are air-conditioned. Very few have swimming pools or saunas. Hotels are clean and standards of service acceptable, depending on the category of hotel. Most 3-, 4- and 5-star hotels offer shopping arcades, tourist and airline offices and a variety of sightseeing programs.

Motel
(**maw**tæl)

These are relatively rare in Hungary. Most are to be found along the shores of Lake Balaton as well as at some principal road junctions.

Fizetővendég-szolgálat
(**fee**zætūrvæn-dayg**sawl**gaalot)

This is the term for private accommodation, a service operated by most travel agencies both in Budapest and throughout the country. In Budapest, rates overlap with those of modest hotels, but in the countryside they are usually very moderate. You may have the choice of room only or with breakfast included. Bathroom facilities, generally shared, are available.

Along major roads and in holiday centres you will also see numerous signs for private accommodation reading *Szoba kiadó* or, in German, *Fremdenzimmer*. Both are the equivalent of the English "Bed and Breakfast". Feel free to knock on the door yourself, phrase book in hand—there's no need to go through an agency for this type of accommodation.

Checking in—Reception

My name is ...	**... vagyok.**	... vod^{y}awk
I've a reservation.	**Már foglaltam szobát.**	maar **fawg**loltom **saw**baat
We've reserved two rooms, one single and a double.	**Két szobát foglaltunk, egy egyágyasat és egy kétágyasat.**	kayt **saw**baat **fawg**loltoonk æd^{y} **æd^{y}**aad^{y}oshot aysh æd^{y} **kay**taad^{y}oshot
Here's the confirmation.	**Itt a visszaigazolásuk.**	eet o **vess**-so-eegozzawlaashook
I'd like a ...	**Szeretnék ...**	**sær**ætnayk
single room	**egyágyas szobát**	**æd^{y}**aad^{y}osh **saw**baat
double room	**kétágyas szobát**	**kay**taad^{y}osh **saw**baat
room with a bath	**fürdőszobás szobát**	**fewr**dūrsawbaash **saw**baat
room with a shower	**egy szobát zuhannyal**	æd^{y} **saw**baat **zoo**han^{y}ol
room with a balcony	**erkélyes szobát**	**ær**kay^{y}æsh **saw**baat
room with a view	**szobát szép kilátással**	**saw**baat sayp **kee**laataash-shol
in the front	**az utcai oldalon**	oz **oot**tsoee **awl**dollawn
at the back	**a hátsó oldalon**	o **haat**shāw **awl**dollawn
facing the lake	**amelyik a tóra néz**	**om**mæ^{y}eek o **tāw**ro nayz
facing the courtyard	**az udvari oldalon**	oz **ood**vorree **awl**dollawn
It must be quiet.	**Egy csendes szobát kérek.**	æd^{y} **chæn**dæsh **saw**baat **kay**ræk
I'd like a room a bit higher up/lower down.	**A szobát egy kissé feljebb/lejjebb szeretném.**	o **saw**baat æd^{y} **keesh**-shay **fæl**yæb/**læ^{y}**-yæb **sær**ætnaym
Is there ...?	**Van ...?**	von
central heating	**központifűtés**	**kurz**pawnteefēwtaysh
a radio in the room	**rádió a szobában**	**raa**deeāw o **saw**baabon
a TV set in the room	**TV a szobában**	**tay**vay o **saw**baabon
room service	**felszolgálás a szobában**	**fæl**sawlgaalaash o **saw**baabon
hot water	**meleg víz**	**mæ**læg vēez
running water	**hideg víz**	**hee**dæg vēez
a private toilet	**külön W.C.**	**kew**lurn **vay**tsay

In the higher-category hotels, most of the staff at the reception desk speak some English or German.

How long?

We'll be staying ...	**... maradunk.**	... morroddoonk
overnight only	**Csak erre az éjszakára**	chock ær-ræ oz ay^{y}ssokkaaro
a few days	**Néhány napig**	nayhaan^y noppeeg
a week (at least)	**(Legalább) egy hétig**	(lægollaab) æd^y hayteeg
I don't know yet.	**Még nem tudom.**	mayg næm toodawm

How much?

What's the price ...?	**Mennyibe kerül ...?**	mæn^{y}eebæ kærewl
per night	**egy éjszakára**	æd^y ay^{y}ssokkaaro
per week	**egy hétre**	æd^y haytræ
for bed and breakfast	**a szoba reggelivel**	o sawbo ræg-gæleevæl
without meals	**étkezés nélkül**	aytkæzaysh naylkewl
for half board	**napi két étkezéssél**	noppee kayt aytkæzaysh-shayl
Does that include ...?	**Ez magában foglalja ...?**	æz moggaabon fawglolyo
service	**a kiszolgálási díjat**	o keessawlgaalaashee dēēyot
resort tax	**az üdülőhelyi illetéket**	oz ewdewlūrhæ^{y}ee eel-lætaykæt
Is there any reduction for children?	**Van kedvezmény a gyerekek után?**	von kædvæzmayn^y o d^{y}ærækæk ootaan

Decision

May I see the room?	**Megnézhetem a szobát?**	mægnayzhætæm o sawbaat
I asked for a room with a bath.	**Egy fürdőszobás szobát rendeltem.**	æd^y fewrdūrsawbaash sawbaat rændæltæm
Do you have anything ...?	**Volna egy ... szobájuk?**	vawlno æd^y ... sawbaayook
better/bigger	**jobb/nagyobb**	yawb/nod^{y}awb
cheaper/quieter	**olcsóbb/csendesebb**	awlchawb/chændæshæb
That's fine. I'll take it.	**Ez jó lesz. Ezt kiveszem.**	æz yāw læs. æst keevæsæm

NUMBERS: see page 175

Registration

Upon arrival at a hotel, motel or private boarding house, you'll have to fill in a registration form *(bejelentőlap)*. If it doesn't carry an English translation, ask:

What does this mean?	**Ez mit jelent?**	æz meet **yæ**lænt

If you don't understand what he's saying, show him this section:

Megkaphatom az útlevelét?	May I see your passport, please?
Legyen szíves, töltse ki ezt a bejelentőlapot.	Would you mind filling in this registration form?
Kérem, itt írja alá.	Please sign here.
Meddig marad?	How long will you be staying?

What's my room number?	**Mi a szoba számom?**	mee o **saw**bo **saa**mawm
Where can I park my car?	**Hol hagyhatom a kocsimat?**	hawl **hod**^{y}hottawm o **kaw**cheemot
I'd like to leave this in your safe.	**Ezt a széfjükben szeretném hagyni.**	æzt o **sayf**yewkbæn særætnaym **hod**^{y}nee
Will you have my luggage sent up?	**Felvitetné a csomagjaimat?**	**fæl**veetætnay o **chaw**-mod^{y}oeemot
Will you please wake me up at ...?	**Kérem ébresszen fel ... órakor.**	**kay**ræm **ay**bræs-sæn fæl... a͞w͞rokawr

The bill (check)

Bills are usually paid weekly or, of course, upon departure if you stay less than a week. A 10-15 per cent service charge is generally included in the bill, but you may like to ask:

Is service included?	**A felszolgálási díj benne van az árban?**	o **fæl**sawlgaalaashee d͞e͞e^{y} **bæn**-næ von oz **aar**bon

Tipping is practically a must in Hungary. See inside back cover.

TELLING THE TIME: see page 178

Service, please!

Now that you are safely installed, meet some members of the hotel staff:

bellboy	**kifutó**	**kee**foot**aw**
maid	**szobalány**	**saw**bollaan^{y}
manager	**szálloda igazgató**	**saal**-lawdo **ee**gozgott**aw**
porter	**hordár**	**hawr**daar
switchboard operator	**telefonközpontos**	tælæfawnkurzpawntawsh
waiter	**pincér**	**peen**tsayr
waitress	**pincérnő**	**peen**tsayrn**ur**

If you want to address members of the staff, you don't use the actual names shown above, but a general introductory phrase:

Excuse me ...	**Elnézést ...**	**æl**nayzaysht

General requirements

Please ask the maid to come up.	**Kérem, küldje fel a szobalányt.**	**kay**ræm **kewld**^{y}æ fæl o **saw**bollaan^{y}t
Who is it?	**Ki az?**	kee oz
Just a minute.	**Egy pillanat.**	æd^{y} **peel**-lonnot
Come in!	**Jöjjön be!**	**yur**^{y}-yurn bæ
Please bring us ...	**Kérem, hozzon nekünk ...**	**kay**ræm **hawz**-zawn **næ**kewnk
2 cups of coffee	**2 csésze kávét**	2 **chay**ssæ **kaa**vayt
a sandwich	**egy szendvicset**	æd^{y} **sænd**veechæt
Can we have breakfast in our room?	**Reggelizhetünk a szobában?**	**ræg**-gæleez-hætewnk o **saw**baabon
What's the voltage here?	**Milyen a feszültség?**	**mee**^{y}æn o **fæ**sewltshayg
Is there a bath on this floor?	**Van fürdőszoba ezen az emeleten?**	von **fewr**dursawbo æzæn oz æmælætæn
Can you get me a babysitter?	**Tudnának egy bébiszittert szerezni?**	**tood**naanok æd^{y} **bay**beesseet-tært **sæ**ræznee

May I have a/an/some ...?	**Kaphatok ...?**	kophottawk
ashtray	**egy hamutálcát**	æd^{y} hommooltaaltsaat
bath towel	**egy fürdőtörülközőt**	æd^{y} fewrdurturrewlkurzurt
extra blanket	**egy plusz takarót**	æd^{y} plooss tokkorrawt
envelopes	**egy borítékot**	æd^{y} bawreetaykawt
(more) hangers	**vállfákat**	vaalfaakot
hot-water bottle	**ágymelegítőt**	aad^{y}mælægheeturt
ice cubes	**jégkockákat**	yaygkawtskaakot
needle and thread	**tűt, cérnát**	tewt tsayrnaat
reading lamp	**egy olvasólámpát**	æd^{y} awlvoshawlaampaat
soap	**szappant**	sop-pont
writing paper	**levélpapírt**	lævaylpoppeert
Where's the ...?	**Hol van ...?**	hawl von
bathroom	**a fürdőszoba**	o fewrdursawbo
cocktail lounge	**a koktél bár**	o kawktayl baar
dining room	**az étterem**	oz ayt-tæræm
emergency exit	**a vészkijárat**	o vayskee^{y}aarot
hairdresser's	**a fodrász**	o fawdraass
telephone	**a telefon**	o tælæfawn
television room	**a TV szoba**	o tayvay sawbo
toilet	**a W.C.**	o vaytsay

Breakfast

The Hungarian breakfast is a very substantial affair and is considered one of the most important meals of the day. It may consist of rolls and butter, jam, salami, cheese and eggs. Some even like a dish of excellent goulash or some stew to start off the day. If this is too much for you, just specify what you would like from the following list.

I'd like breakfast, please.	**Reggelizni szeretnék.**	ræg-gæleeznee særætnayk
I'll have some ...	**Kérek ...**	kayræk
cocoa	**kakaót**	kokkoawt
coffee	**kávét**	kaavayt
with whipped cream	**tejszínhabbal**	tæ^{y}sseenhob-bol
with milk	**tejjel**	tæ^{y}-yæl
juice	**gyümölcslét**	d^{y}ewmurlchlayt
grapefruit	**grépfrutot**	graypfrootawt
orange	**narancslét**	norronchlayt

EATING OUT: see page 38

milk	**tejet**	tæ^{y}æt
hot	**melegen**	mælægæn
cold	**hidegen**	heedægæn
tea	**egy teát**	æd^{y} **tayaat**
with milk	**tejjel**	**tæ^{y}**-yæl
with lemon	**citrommal**	**tsee**trawm-mol
May I have a/some ...?	**Kaphatok ...?**	**kop**hottawk
boiled egg	**főtt tojást**	fūrt **taw^{y}**aasht
hard	**kemény tojást**	**kæ**mayn^{y} **taw^{y}**aasht
medium	**közepes tojást**	**kur**zæpæsh **taw^{y}**aasht
soft	**lágy tojást**	laad^{y} **taw^{y}**aasht
bread	**kenyeret**	**kæn^{y}**æræt
butter	**vajat**	**vo**yot
cheese	**egy adag sajtot**	æd^{y} **od**dog **shoy**tawt
crescent rolls	**kiflit**	**kee**fleet
fried eggs	**tükör tojást**	**tew**kurr **taw^{y}**aasht
ham and eggs	**sonkát tojással**	**shawn**kaat **taw^{y}**aash-shol
honey	**mézet**	**may**zæt
jam	**egy adag lekvárt**	æd^{y} **od**dog **læk**vaart
rolls	**péksüteményt**	**payk**shewtæmayn^{y}t
salami	**egy adag szalámit**	æd^{y} **od**dog **sol**laameet
scrambled eggs	**tojásrántottát**	**taw^{y}**aashraantawt-taat
toast	**tósztot**	**taw**stawt
yoghurt	**egy joghurtot**	æd^{y} **yaw**ghoortawt
Would you bring me some ...?	**Kérem, hozzon nekem ...?**	**kay**ræm **hawz**-zawn **næ**kæm
cream	**tejszínt**	**tæ^{y}**sseent
lemon	**citromot**	**tsee**trawmawt
pepper	**borsot**	**bawr**shawt
salt	**sót**	**shawt**
sugar	**cukrot**	**tsook**rawt
(a glass of) water	**(egy pohár) vizet**	(æd^{y} **paw**haar) **vee**zæt
hot water	**forróvizet**	**fawr**-rawveezæt

Difficulties

But perhaps there's something wrong...

The ... doesn't work.	**A ... nem működik.**	o ... næm **mew**kurdeek
heating	**fűtés**	**few**taysh
light	**világítás**	**vee**laagheetaash
radiator	**fűtőtest**	**few**turtæsht
radio	**rádió**	**raa**deeaw

shower	**zuhany**	**zoo**hon^{y}
tap	**csap**	chop
television	**TV**	**tay**vay
toilet	**W.C.**	**vay**tsay
ventilator	**ventillátor**	**væn**teel-laatawr
The washbasin is clogged.	**A mosdó el van dugulva.**	o **mawsh**dāw æl von **doo**goolvo
The window is jammed.	**Az ablak be van szorulva.**	oz **ob**lok bæ von **saw**roolvo
The blind is stuck.	**A roló fennakadt.**	o **raw**lāw **fæn**okkodt
These aren't my shoes.	**Ez nem az én cipőm.**	æz næm oz ayn **tsee**pūrm
This isn't my laundry.	**Ez nem az én fehérnemüm.**	æz næm oz ayn **fæ**hayrnæmewm
There's no hot water.	**Nincs melegvíz.**	neench **mæ**lægvēez
My room has not been made up.	**Nem rakták rendbe a szobámat.**	næm **rok**taak **rænd**bæ o **saw**baamot
I've left the key in my room.	**A szobában felejtettem a kulcsomat.**	o **saw**baabon **fæ**læ^{y}-tæt-tæm o **kool**chawmot
The bulb is burnt out.	**Kiégett a körte.**	**kee**aygæt o **kurr**tæ
The ... is broken.	**Eltörött ...**	**æl**turrurt
lamp	**a lámpa**	o **laam**po
plug	**a dugasz**	o **doo**goss
shutter	**a zsalu**	o **zhol**loo
socket	**a konnektor**	o **kaw**næktawr
switch	**a kapcsoló**	o **kop**chawlāw
venetian blind	**a redőny**	o **ræ**dūrn^{y}
window shade	**az ablakroló**	oz **ob**lokrawlāw
Can you get it repaired?	**Meg tudja javíttatni?**	mæg **too**dyo **yo**vvēetotnee

Telephone—Mail—Callers

Can you get me London 123 4567?	**Kérem, hívja fel a London 123 4567 számot!**	**kay**ræm **hēe**vyo fæl o **lawn**dawn 123 4567 **saa**mawt
Has anyone phoned for me?	**Keresett valaki?**	**kæ**ræshæt **vol**lokkee

POST OFFICE AND TELEPHONE: see pages 137–141

Is there any mail for me?	**Van a részemre posta?**	von o **rayssæmræ pawsh**to
Are there any messages for me?	**Érkezett a részemre valami üzenet?**	ayrkæzæt o **rayssæmræ** vollommee **ewzænæt**
Do you sell stamps?	**Postabélyegük van?**	**pawsh**tobbay^{y}ægewk von
Would you please post this for me?	**Kérem, feladná ezt nekem?**	kayræm **fælodnaa æst** nækæm

Checking out

May I have my bill?	**Kérem, a számlámat.**	kayræm o **saamlaamot**
I must leave at once.	**Rögtön indulnom kell.**	**rurg**turn **een**doolnawm kæl
We'll be checking out soon/around noon.	**Korán elutazunk./ Dél körül utazunk el.**	kawraan ælootozzoonk/ dayl **kurrewl ootozzoonk** æl
I'm leaving early tomorrow. Please have my bill ready.	**Holnap korán utazom el. Kérem, készítsék el a számlámat.**	**haw**lnop **kaw**raan **ootozzawm** æl. **kayræm** kaysse͞etshayk æl o **saam**laamot
Is everything included?	**Ebben minden szerepel?**	**æb**-bæn **meen**dæn **sæ**ræpæl
You've made a mistake in this bill, I think.	**Azt hiszem, hibásan állította össze a számlát.**	ost **hee**ssæm **hee**baashon **aal**-le͞etawt-to **urs**-sæ o **saam**laat
When's the next ... to Vienna?	**Mikor indul a követ-kező ... Bécsbe?**	**mee**kawr **een**dool o **kur**vætkæzūr ... **baych**bæ
bus/plane/train	**autóbusz/repülő/ vonat**	**oo**tāwbooss/**ræ**pewlūr/ **vaw**not
Would you get me a taxi?	**Hívna egy taxit?**	**he͞e**vno æd^{y} **tox**eet
Would you please have somebody bring down our luggage?	**Kérem, küldjön valakit, aki leviszi a csomagjainkat.**	kayræm **kewld^{y}urn** vollokkeet okkee **læ**veessee o **chaw**mogyo-eenkot
We're in a great hurry.	**Borzasztóan sietünk.**	**bawr**zostāwon **shee**ætewnk
Here's my forwarding address.	**Ez a következő címem.**	æz o **kur**vætkæzūr **tse͞e**mæm
It's been a very enjoyable stay.	**Nagyon jól éreztük itt magunkat.**	**nod^{y}**awn yāwl **ay**ræztewk eet **mog**goonkot

TAXI: see page 27

HOTEL SERVICE

Eating out

There are many different types of places in which to enjoy meals and drink, from simple snackbars to luxury restaurants:

Bisztró
(**beestrāw**)

A small restaurant, generally offering reasonably priced standard meals and drinks, including coffee and tea, at any time during opening hours. Usually frequented by people in a hurry.

Büfé
(**bew**fay)

Found at railway and bus stations, in shopping centres and department stores, buffets serve hot and cold sandwiches, cakes, desserts and all kind of drinks including coffee and tea. Some are open round the clock. Prices are reasonable.

Csárda
(**chaardo**)

A country inn, usually offering regional food and drink specialities in the medium price range. In the evening, gypsy bands often provide romantic music to go with the meal. Found mainly on major highways.

Cukrászda
(**tsook**raazdo)

A pastry shop serving sandwiches, cakes, desserts, ice cream, soft drinks, coffee, tea and alcoholic drinks. Larger establishments have light or pop music, either taped or live. Prices tend to be rather high.

Étkező
(**ayt**kæzūr)

A small inn, often with only a few tables, serving regional specialities, local wines and beer at modest prices.

Étterem
(**ayt**-tæræm)

The traditional restaurant, serving a wide range of dishes and drinks. These establishments are classified according to location, facilities and standard of service, with the category indicated on the menu (see page 40). Prices do not necessarily reflect quality of food, and the self-same dish may cost much more in a first-class restaurant than in a modest one. Gypsy bands often play at night. In a hotel *étterem,* price and quality depend on the category of the hotel.

Kifőzés
(**kee**fūrzaysh)
A small, low-priced inn, often a family concern, open mainly during the tourist season. First-class country food as well as local wine and beer are served. In the Lake Balaton area some of these establishments are famous for their gourmet creations.

Önkiszolgáló
(**urn**keessawlgaalāw)
A self-service snackbar-type establishment. Mostly located in town centres and near railway stations, they are inexpensive but not always too clean.

Snackbár
("snackbar")
A superior *önkiszolgáló* offering sandwiches, cakes and all kinds of drinks including espresso coffee and tea at slightly higher prices.

Vendéglő
(**væn**dayglūr)
A larger restaurant, usually with rustic décor, serving moderately priced meals and all kinds of drinks. Good gypsy music is often played at night.

Mainly for drinking

Borozó
(**baw**rawzāw)
A wine bar, offering a variety of wines and some snacks. Prices vary widely.

Borpince
(**bawr**peentsæ)
A wine cellar, usually run by a wine-producing cooperative or farm. Exceptionally high-quality wines and light food are available at moderate prices.

Drinkbár
("drinkbar")
A bar, frequented mostly by tourists, serving mainly spirits (liquor). Prices are high.

Eszpresszó
(**æs**præss-sāw)
A small coffee bar offering mainly espresso coffee but also some other non-alcoholic and alcoholic beverages at moderate prices. Light refreshments and ice-cream are also available.

Mulató
(**moo**lottāw)
A modest nightclub, with a minor floor show. The accent is on expensive imported spirits. Light snacks are available.

Söröző
(**sur**rurzūr)
A beer hall, with moderate prices. Some imported beers are available but at higher prices.

Tejbár/Tejivó
(**tæ**^{y}baar/**tæ**^{y}eevāw)
Milkbars go under either of these two names. In addition to milk and milk-based drinks, sandwiches, cakes and other snacks are available, all at very reasonable prices. Just the place for breakfast or a mid-morning snack.

Meals and menus

By law, all eating places must offer at least two complete set menus (*napi menü*—**no**ppee **mæ**new) at low to moderate prices. These menus typically comprise a soup, a main course and dessert or fruit. However, many people prefer to order à la carte. As a rule, drinks are listed on a separate card and they may be served by a different waiter. Some top restaurants also offer special dishes for those on certain diets as well as smaller portions for children. It is customary to tip the waiter 8–10 per cent of the bill, depending on quality of service.

You will generally see one or more of the following explanatory notices on the bill of fare:

I. osztályu étterem	First-class restaurant
II. osztályu étterem	Second-class restaurant
III. osztályu étterem	Third-class restaurant
Osztályon felüli étterem.	Top-class restaurant
Az árak köret nélkül értendők.	Prices do not include garnishes.
Az ételeket körettel szolgáljuk fel.	Meals are served with garnishes.
Az X—el jelölt ételek elfogytak.	Meals marked with X are no longer available.
... Ft. kötelező fogyasztás.	Minimum order: ... forints.

Meal times

Breakfast (*reggeli*—**ræg**-gælee): 7–10 a.m.

Lunch (*ebéd*—**æ**bayd): noon–2 or 3 p.m.

Dinner (*vacsora*—**vo**chawro): 7–10 or 11 p.m.

Restaurants in leading hotels will often serve à-la-carte meals in your room round the clock.

BREAKFAST: see page 34

Hungry

I'm hungry/I'm thirsty.	**Éhes vagyok/ Szomjas vagyok.**	ayhæsh vod^{y}awk/ sawmyosh vod^{y}awk
Can you recommend a good restaurant?	**Ajánlana egy jó éttermet?**	oyaanlonno æd^{y} yaw ayt-tærmæt
Are there any inexpensive restaurants around here?	**Találhatók a környéken olcsó éttermek?**	tollaalhottawk o kurr-n^{y}aykæn awlchaw ayt-tærmæk

To be sure of getting a table in a well-known restaurant it's advisable to reserve your table in advance by telephone.

I'd like to book a table for 4, please.	**4 fő részére szeretnék asztalt foglalni.**	4 fūr rayssayræ særæt-nayk ostolt fawglolnee
We'll come at 8.	**8 órakor jövünk.**	8 awrokkawr yurvewnk

Asking and ordering

Good evening. I'd like a table for 2.	**Jó estét kívánok. 2 fő részére kérek egy asztalt.**	yaw æshtayt keevaanawk. 2 fūr rayssayræ kayræk æd^{y} ostolt
I've reserved a table for 4.	**4 fő részére rendeltem asztalt.**	4 fūr rayssayræ rændæltæm ostolt
Could we have a table ...?	**Lenne szabad asztaluk ...?**	læn-næ sobbod ostollook
in the corner	**a sarokban**	o shorrawkbon
by the window	**az ablaknál**	oz obloknaal
outside	**kinnt**	keent
on the terrace	**a teraszon**	o tærossawn
Are these seats taken?	**Ezek a helyek foglaltak?**	æzæk o hæ^{y}æk fawgloltok
Waiter!/Waitress!	**Pincér!/Pincérnő!**	peentsayr/peentsayrnūr
I'd/We'd like something to drink/eat.	**Szeretnék/Szeretnénk valamit inni/enni.**	særætnayk/særætnaynk vollommeet een-nee/æn-nee
What are the set menus?	**Mi a mai menü?**	mee o moee mænew

NUMBERS: see page 175

May I have the menu and the drinks card?	**Kérem az étlapot és az itallapot.**	kay**ræm** oz **ayt**loppawt aysh oz **ee**tol-loppawt
Can you serve me straight away? I'm in a hurry.	**Azonnali kiszolgálást kérek. Sietek.**	ozzawn-nollee **kee**ssawlgaalaasht kayræk. **shee**æltæk
Could we have a plate for the child, please?	**Hozna egy tányért a gyereknek?**	**haw**zno æd^{y} **taan**^{y}ayrt o d^{y}æræknæk
Do you have any local dishes?	**Ajánlana valami helyi különlegességet?**	oyaanlonno **vo**llommee **hæ**^{y}ee **kew**lurnlægæsh-shaygæt
What's this?	**Ez mi?**	æz mee
Could we have a/an/some ..., please?	**Kaphatunk ...?**	**kop**hottoonk
another chair	**még egy széket**	mayg æd^{y} **say**kæt
ashtray	**egy hamutartót**	æd^{y} **hom**mootortawt
bottle of ...	**egy üveg ...-t***	æd^{y} **ew**væg ...-t
fork	**egy villát**	æd^{y} **veel**-laat
glass	**egy poharat**	æd^{y} **paw**horrot
glass of water	**egy pohár vizet**	æd^{y} **paw**haar **vee**zæt
knife	**egy kést**	æd^{y} kaysht
lighter	**egy öngyújtót**	æd^{y} **urn**d^{y}oo^{y}tawt
matches	**gyufát**	d^{y}oofaat
plate	**egy tányért**	æd^{y} **taan**^{y}ayrt
serviette	**egy szalvétát**	æd^{y} **sol**vaytaat
spoon	**egy kanalat**	æd^{y} **kon**nollot
toothpicks	**fogpiszkálót**	**fawg**peeskaalawt

Mit parancsol?	What would you like?
Szabad ezt ajánlanom?	May I recommend this?
Mit óhajt inni?	What would you like to drink?
Sajnos, nem szolgálhatunk ...val.	We don't have any ...
Parancsol ...-t?	Do you want ...?

* See Grammar section for word endings.

I'd like ...	**Kérnék ...**	**kayr**nayk
aperitif	**egy aperitívet**	æd^{y} opæreetēēvæt
appetizer	**elöételt**	æluraytælt
beer	**sört**	shurrt
bread	**kenyeret**	**kæn**^{y}æræt
butter	**vajat**	**voy**ot
cheese	**sajtot**	**shoy**tawt
chicken	**csirkét**	**cheer**kayt
chips (Br.)	**sült burgonyát**	shewlt **boor**gawn^{y}aat
coffee	**kávét**	**kaa**vayt
dessert	**édességet**	**ay**dæsh-shaygæt
fish	**halat**	**hol**lot
French fries	**sült burgonyát**	sewlt **boor**gawn^{y}aat
fruit	**gyümölcsöt**	**d^{y}ew**murlchurt
fruit juice	**gyümölcslét**	**d^{y}ew**murlchlayt
game	**vadas ételt**	**vod**dosh **ay**tælt
goulash	**gulyáslevest**	**goo**^{y}aashlævæsht
ice-cream	**fagylaltot**	**fod**^{y}loltawt
ketchup	**ketchupot**	**kæ**churpurt
lemonade	**limonádét**	**lee**mawnaadayt
lettuce	**fejes-salátát**	**fæ**^{y}aysh **shol**laataat
meat	**húst**	hōōsht
milk	**tejet**	**tæ**^{y}æt
mineral water	**ásványvizet**	**aash**vaan^{y}veezæt
mustard	**mustárt**	**moosh**taart
noodles	**metéltet**	**mæ**tayltæt
oil	**étolajat**	**ay**tawloyot
pepper	**borsot**	**bawr**shawt
potatoes	**burgonyát**	**boor**gawn^{y}aat
poultry	**szárnyast**	**saarn**^{y}osht
rice	**rizst**	reezht
rolls	**péksüteményt**	**payk**shewtæmayn^{y}t
saccharine	**szaharint**	**so**horreent
salad	**salátát**	**shol**laataat
salt	**sót**	shāwt
sandwich	**szendvicset**	**sænd**veechæt
soft drink	**üdítőitalt**	**ew**deetūr-eetolt
soup	**levest**	**læ**væsht
spaghetti	**spagettit**	**shpog**gæt-teet
sugar	**cukrot**	**tsoo**krawt
tea	**teát**	**tæ**aat
vegetables	**főzeléket**	**fūr**zælaykæt
vinegar	**ecetet**	**æ**tsætæt
water	**vizet**	**vee**zæt
wine	**bort**	bawrt

What's on the menu?

Our menu is presented according to courses. Under each heading you'll find an alphabetical list of dishes likely to be offered on a Hungarian menu, with their English equivalents. You can also show the book to the waiter. Should you want some soup, for example, show him the corresponding list and let him point to what's available. Use pages 41-44 for ordering in general.

In Hungary, a typical à-la-carte meal consists of soup, an entrée, the main course and then a dessert or cheese. Many enjoy an aperitif to start off with and accompany the meal with one or two matching wines. (If you prefer beer or mineral water, your choice will raise no eyebrows.) Invariably, the occasion is rounded off with a good, strong coffee and a fruit brandy.

Here, then, is our guide to good eating and drinking. Just turn to the section you want.

Appetizers

Restaurants offer a rich choice of both international and typically Hungarian appetizers, both hot and cold. For a light meal it's quite acceptable to take a soup, then an appetizer, and skip the rest.

I'd like a ...	**... is kérnék.**	... eesh **kayr**nayk
cold appetizer	**Hideg előételt**	**hee**dæg **æ**lu̅r̅aytælt
hot appetizer	**Meleg előételt**	**mæ**læg **æ**lu̅r̅aytælt
What would you recommend?	**Mit ajánlana?**	meet **oy**aanlonno

Cold appetizers

apró fánk	**opra̅w̅** faank	small chicken fritter
bécsi hering-saláta	**bay**chee **hæ**reeng-shollaato	herring salad Vienna style (with vinegar)
dinnye koktél	**deen**^{y}æ **kawk**tayl	melon cocktail
dinnye sonkával	**deen**^{y}æ **shawn**kaavol	melon with ham
francia saláta	**front**seeo **shol**laato	Russian salad
halmajonéz	**hol**moyawnayz	fish with mayonnaise
jérce koktél	**yayr**tsæ **kawk**tayl	chicken cocktail
kaszinó tojás	**kos**seena̅w̅ **taw**^{y}aash	eggs with mayonnaise
kaviár	**kov**veeaar	caviar
majonézes kukorica	**moy**awnayzæsh **koo**kawreetso	sweetcorn with mayonnaise
orosz hússaláta	**aw**rawss **ho̅o̅sh**-shollaato	Russian salad with meat
ráksaláta	**raak**shollaato	crab salad
töltött tojás kaviárral	**turl**turt **taw**^{y}aash **kov**veeaar-rol	eggs stuffed with caviar

alföldi saláta (**ol**furldee **shol**laato) — salad Alföldi style ("Puszta salad"): slices of sausage in a vinaigrette sauce (oil, vinegar, herbs)

almás cékla (**ol**maash **tsay**klo) — apple slices and diced beetroot in a vinaigrette sauce

fokhagymás majonézes fejes saláta (**fawk**hod^{y}maash **moy**awnayzæsh **fæ**^{y}æsh **shol**laato) — lettuce salad with garlic-flavoured mayonnaise

gombafejek máj-krémmel töltve (gawmboffæ^{y}æk maa^{y}kraymmæl turltvæ)
mushrooms stuffed with liver paté

halsaláta szegedi módra (holshollaato sægædee mawdro)
fish salad Szeged style: fish pieces, diced peppers, tomatoes and chives turned in oil and accompanied by lettuce and hard-boiled eggs

hideg fogas tartár-mártással (heedæg fawgosh tortaarmaartaash-shol)
kind of pike-perch with tartar sauce (mayonnaise with gherkins, chives, capers and olives)

paprika szeletek körözöttel töltve (popreeko sælætæk kurrurzurt-tæl turltvæ)
green peppers, sliced in four, filled with a mix of ewe's cheese, butter, mustard, paprika, caraway seeds and some beer

Hot appetizers

csirág csőben sütve	cheeraag chūrbæn shewtvæ	baked asparagus
libamáj rizottó	leebomaa^{y} reezawt-taw	goose-liver risotto
tálon sült tojás	taalawn shewlt taw^{y}aash	fried eggs, meat slices and vegetables
zöldbab csőben sütve	zurldbob chūrbæn shewtvæ	fried string beans

hortobágyi húsos palacsinta (hawrtawbaad^{y}ee hooshawsh pollo-cheento)
stuffed omelet Hortobágy style: filled with veal or pork meat and sour cream, then briefly gratinated

libamáj pástétom (leebommaa^{y} paashtaytawm)
goose-liver paté mixed with butter and béchamel (white) sauce, spices and brandy, served in a flaky-pastry shell

omlet debreceni módra (awmlæt dæbrætsænee mawdro)
omelet Debrecen stype: filled with *lecsó* (a mix of sliced green peppers, tomatoes, rice ans spices) and dry sausage slices

veseszeletek para-dicsommal (væshæsælætæk porroddeechawm-mol)
kidney slices with tomato

Bread and other bakery products

"The Hungarians will even eat bread with bread" goes an old saying—which may give you an idea of the varied and tasty range of bakery products you can look forward to in this country. Most milk bars, beer halls and better restaurants automatically place a selection of them on your table when you order.

fodros fehér kalács (fawdrawsh fæhayr kollaach)	spongy white milk-bread, available as rolls or in slices
mazsolás kalács (mozhawlaash kollaach)	spongy white milk-bread with raisins
óriás kifli (aw̄reeaash keeflee)	large, flaky, crescent-shaped roll
paprikás stangli (popreekaash shtonglee)	paprika-seasoned bread finger, reddish in colour
sajtos pogácsa (shoytawsh pawgaacho)	bread cone with cheese
tepertős pogácsa (tæpærtūrsh pawgaacho)	crispy bread cone, slightly salted and peppered, with bacon pieces
túrós karika (tōōraw̄sh korreeko)	dough ring with curds

Soups

Richly flavoured soups are part of the Hungarian way of life. They are generally quite thick. In some regions soup may be served for breakfast.

I'd like some soup.	**Levest kérek.**	lævæsht kayræk
almaleves hidegen/ melegen	olmollævæsh heedægæn/ mælægæn	cold/hot apple soup
bajai halászlé	boyo-ee hollaaslay	fish and potato soup
burgonyakrémleves	boorgawn^{y}okraymlævæsh	cream of potato soup
csontleves	chawntlævæsh	bone consommé

erőleves húsgombóccal	ærurlævæsh **hoosh**gawmbawtstsol	consommé with meat dumplings
gombaleves	**gawm**bollævæsh	mushroom soup
kalocsai halászlé	**ko**llawcho-ee **ho**llaaslay	fish soup in red wine
paradicsomleves	**po**rroddeechawmlævæsh	tomato soup
savanyútojás leves	**sho**vvon^{y}ootaw^{y}aash **læ**væsh	sour egg soup
spárgakrém leves	**shpaar**gokraym **læ**væsh	cream of asparagus soup
tejfeles bableves	**tæ**^{y}fælæsh **bob**lævæsh	bean soup with sour cream
vegyes gyümölcsleves hidegen	**væ**d^{y}æsh **d^{y}ew**murlchlævæsh **hee**dægæn	chilled fruit soup

Soup specialities

bakonyi betyárleves (**bo**kkawn^{y}ee **bæ**t^{y}aarlævæsh) "outlaw soup"—soup Bakony style: a mix of chicken, beef chunks, thin noodles, mushrooms and vegetables, richly spiced

gulyásleves (**goo**yaashlævæsh) Hungarian goulash: a mix of beef chunks, potatoes, onions, tomatoes and peppers, richly spiced with paprika, caraway seeds and garlic

Jókai bableves (**yaw**ko-ee **bob**lævæsh) bean soup Jókai style (Jókai was a famous Hungarian writer): a mix of smoked pig's knuckles, butter beans and carrots, seasoned with pepper, garlic, paprika and parsley

kunsági pandúrleves (**koon**shaaghee **pon**doorlævæsh) chicken or pigeon soup Kunság style: seasoned with paprika, grated nutmeg, ginger and garlic

magyaros burgonyaleves (**mo**d^{y}orrawsh **boor**gawn^{y}ollævæsh) Hungarian potato soup: diced potatoes and onions with paprika

magyaros csirkeaprólék leves (**mo**d^{y}orrawsh **cheer**kæoprawlayk **læ**væsh) Hungarian chicken giblet soup with mushrooms, diced potatoes, pepper rings and tomatoes

palócleves (**po**llawtslævæsh) a mix of mutton, French beans, potatoes and sour cream, seasoned with paprika, garlic and caraway seeds

szegedi halászlé (**sæ**gædee **ho**llaaslay) a mix of various kinds of fish (usually carp, pike and wels), tomato and pepper rings, with hot paprika seasoning

Fish

I'd like some fish.	**Halat szeretnék.**	hollot særætnayk
What fish do you recommend?	**Milyen halat ajánl?**	mee^{y}æn hollott oyaanl

csuka	chooko	pike
fogas	fawgosh	a local fish of the pike-perch family
harcsa	horcho	wels
kecsege	kæchægæ	sterlet
nyelvhal	n^{y}ælvhol	sole
pisztráng	peestraang	trout
ponty	pawnt^{y}	carp
tőkehal	t$\overline{\text{ur}}$kæhol	cod
tonhal	tawnhol	tunny (Am. tuna)

Fish specialities

csuka tejfölben sütve (chooko tæ^{y}furlbæn shewtvæ)	pike fried and served with sour cream
fogas fehér bormártásban (fawgosh fæhayr bawrmaartaashbon)	*fogas* in a white-wine sauce
fogasszeletek Gundel módra (fawgoshsælætæk goondæl m$\overline{\text{aw}}$dro)	slices of *fogas* Gundel style (Gundel was a famous Hungarian restaurateur): breaded fillet of pike
halfatányéros (holfottaan^{y}ayrawsh)	assorted fish, some breaded or fried, served on a wooden plate, accompanied by tartar sauce
harcsaszelet fűszermártásban (horchossælæt (f$\overline{\text{ew}}$sæmaartaashbon)	fillet of wels in a spicy sauce doused with white wine
kecsege tejszínes paprikás mártásban (kæchægæ tæ^{y}s$\overline{\text{ee}}$næsh popreekaash maartaashbon)	sterlet in a cream and paprika sauce

paprikás ponty (**po**preekaash pawnt^{y})	carp served in a paprika sauce
pisztráng tejszín mártásban (**pee**straang **tæ**^{y}sseen **maar**taashbon)	trout baked in cream
rostélyos töltött ponty (**rawsh**tay^{y}awsh **turl**turt pawnt^{y})	fried carp, stuffed with a mix of bread, fish liver or roe, egg and herbs

Other specialities from Hungary's lakes and rivers include:

békacomb gombával és rákkal (**bay**kotsawmb **gawm**-baavol aysh **raak**-kol)	frog's legs with freshwater crab-meat and mushrooms
békacomb paprikásan (**bay**kotsawmb **po**pree-kaashon)	frog's legs in a paprika sauce
rákpörkölt (**raak**purrkurlt)	broiled crab

Sauces

The sauces that accompany Hungarian dishes are distinctively flavoured to enhance the pleasures of the palate. (Contrary to widespread belief, spicy-hot preparations are not typical of the national cuisine.)

almamártás	**ol**mommaartaash	apple sauce
bakonyi gombamártás	**bok**kawn^{y}ee **gawm**bommaartaash	mushroom sauce
ecetes torma	**æ**tsætæsh **tawr**mo	horse-radish sauce
fehérhagyma mártás	**fæ**hayrhod^{y}mo **maar**taash	onion sauce
fokhagymás mártás	**fawk**hod^{y}maash **maar**tash	garlic sauce
kapormártás	**kop**pawrmaartaash	dill sauce
meggymártás	**mæd**^{y}maartaash	morello sauce
paprikás mártás	**po**preekaash **maar**taash	paprika sauce
tárkonyos mártás	**taar**kawn^{y}awsh **maar**taash	tarragon sauce
vadasmártás	**vod**doshmaartaash	brown sauce

Meat

I'd like some ...	**... kérek.**	... **kay**ræk
beef	**Marhahúst**	**mor**hohōōsht
lamb	**Bárányhúst**	**baa**raan^y hōōsht
pork	**Disznóhúst**	**dees**nawhōōsht
veal	**Borjúhúst**	**bawr**yōōhōōsht

borda	**bawr**do	chop
comb	tsawmb	leg
fasírozott	**fo**shēērawzawt	meatballs
filé	**fee**lay	fillet
kolbászfélék	**kawl**baasfaylayk	sausages
lapocka	**lop**pawtsko	shoulder
máj	maa^y	liver
nyelv	n^y ælv	tongue
sonka	**shawn**ko	ham
szalonna	**sol**lawn-no	bacon

boiled	**főve**	**fūr**væ
braised	**dinsztelve**	**deens**tælvæ
breaded	**rántva**	**raan**tvo
fried	**sütve**	**shewt**væ
grilled	**roston sütve**	**raw**shtawn **shewt**væ
roasted	**sülve**	**shewl**væ
stewed (quickly)	**főzve**	**fūrz**væ
stewed (slowly)	**pörköltnek**	**purr**kurltnæk
underdone (rare)	**félig nyersen**	**fay**leeg **n^y ær**shæn
medium	**közepesen kisütve**	**kur**zæpæshæn **kee**shewtvæ
well-done (fried)	**jól megsütve**	yāwl **mæg**shewtvæ
well-done (boiled)	**jól megfőzve**	yāwl **mæg**fūrzvæ

Veal

borjúpaprikás (**bawr**yōōpopreekaash) veal fricassée with onions, pepper rings, tomatoes and a seasoning of paprika and garlic

borjúpörkölt (**bawr**yōōpurkurlt) a stew composed of veal chunks, onions, tomatoes, pepper rings, seasoned with paprika and garlic

lecsós borjúmáj rántva (**læ**chāwsh **bawr**yōōmaa^y **raan**tvo) breaded veal liver, garnished with a mix of pepper slices, tomatoes, rice, spiced with paprika and garlic

Beef

alföldi marharos-télyos (**ol**furldee **mor**horrawsh-tay^{y}awsh)	steak Alföldi style: with a rich sauce and stewed vegetables
cigányrostélyos (**tsee**gaan^{y}-rawshtay^{y}awsh)	steak gypsy style: with a brown sauce and braised vegetables
csikós tokány (**chee**ka͞wsh **taw**kaan^{y})	strips or chunks of beef braised in a mix of bacon strips or bits, onion rings and sour cream and tomato concentrate
erdélyi tokány (**æ**rday^{y}ee **taw**kaan^{y})	a dish originating in Transylvania: virtually the same as *csikós tokány*, but without the sour cream
hortobágyi rostélyos (**haw**rtawbaad^{y}ee **rawsh**tay^{y}awsh)	steak Hortobágy style: braised in a mix of stock and bacon bits and accompanied by a large semolina dumpling

Pork

erdélyi rakott-káposzta (**æ**rday^{y}ee **ro**kkawtkaapawsto)	a Transylvanian dish consisting of layers of cabbage interspersed with rice and minced, spiced pork, covered with sour cream and baked in the oven
debreceni fatányéros (**dæ**brætsænee **fo**ttaan^{y}ayrawsh)	a Debrecen speciality, prepared only for parties of three or more, usually containing pork chops and choice fillets as well as some veal; garnished with lettuce
rablóhús nyárson (**ro**bla͞who͞osh **n^{y}aar**shawn)	alternating pieces of pork, onions, mushrooms, bacon and veal roasted and served on a skewer
tejfölös-gombás sertésborda (**tæ^{y}**furlursh **gawm**-baash **shær**tayshbawrdo)	pork chop with mushrooms and sour cream
töltött malac újfalusi módra (**turl**turt **mo**llots **o͞o^{y}**follooshee **ma͞w**dro)	stuffed suckling-pig Újfalu style: with a mix of spiced minced meat, liver, egg and bread

Game and fowl

I'd like some game.	**Vadasat szeretnék.**	voddoshot særaætnayk
csirke	**cheer**kæ	chicken
fácán	**faa**tsaan	pheasant
fogoly	**faw**gaw^{y}	partridge
galamb	**gol**lomb	pigeon
kacsa	**ko**cho	duck
kappan	**kop**-pon	capon
liba	**lee**bo	goose
nyúl	n^{y}ōōl	rabbit
őz	ūrz	venison
pulyka	**poo**^{y}ko	turkey
vaddisznó	**vod**-deesnāw	wild boar
vadkacsa	**vod**kocho	wild duck
vadliba	**vod**leebo	wild goose

csabai szarvascomb (**chob**boee **sor**voshtsawmb) — venison stuffed with spicy Csabai sausage served in a paprika sauce

fácán gesztenyével töltött gombával (**faa**tsaan gætæn^{y}-ayvæl **turl**turt **gawm**baavol) — pheasant with a mushroom and chestnut filling

fogoly szalonnában sütve (**faw**gaw^{y} **sol**lawn-naabon **shewt**væ) — partridge in a bacon envelope, served in a sauce of stock, tomato concentrate and seasoning

nyúlszeletek pirított szárnyasmájjal (n^{y}ōōlsælætæk **pee**rēētawt **saar**n^{y}oshmaa^{y}-yol) — rabbit with roasted chicken liver

pulykacomb tejfeles gombamártással (**poo**^{y}kotsawmb **tæ**^{y}fælæsh **gawm**-bommaartaash-shol) — turkey cutlet in a mushroom sauce

vaddisznó borókamártással (**vod**-deesnāw **baw**rāwkommaartaash-shol) — wild boar served in a juniper sauce

Vegetables—Salads

Vegetables and salads are served along with the main course in set menus. Otherwise, you may order them separately from the bill of fare.

burgonya	**boor**gawn^{y}o	potatoes
fehérrépa	fæhayr-raypo	turnips
gomba	**gawm**bo	mushrooms
hagyma	**hod^{y}**mo	onions
káposzta	**kaa**pawsto	cabbage
kelbimbó	**kæl**beemb$\overline{aw}$	Brussels sprouts
kelkáposzta	**kæl**kaapawsto	cauliflower
kukorica	**koo**kawreetso	type of sweetcorn
lencse	**læn**chæ	lentils
paprika	**pop**reeko	pepper
paradicsom	**po**rroddeechawm	tomatoes
saláta	**shol**laato	lettuce
sárgarépa	**shaar**gorraypo	carrots
spárga	**shpaar**go	asparagus
spenót	**shpæ**n$\overline{aw}$t	spinach
sültkrumpli	**shewlt**kroomplee	chips (French fries)
uborka	**oo**bawrko	cucumber
vegyesfőzelék	**væd^{y}**æshf$\overline{ur}$zælayk	mixed vegetables
vegyesköret	**væd^{y}**æshkur-ræt	mixed vegetables (served along with the dish)
zeller	**zæl**-lær	celery
zöldbab	**zurld**bob	French beans
zöldborsó	**zurld**bawrsh$\overline{aw}$	peas

Some herbs and spices used in Hungarian cooking:

édeskömény	**ay**dæshkurmayn^{y}	caraway seeds
édespaprika	**ay**dæshpopreeko	mild paprika
fokhagyma	**fawk**hod^{y}mo	garlic
fűszerpaprika	**f$\overline{ew}$**særpopreeko	chillies
kakukkfű	**kok**kookf$\overline{ew}$	thyme
komló	**kawm**l$\overline{aw}$	hops
majoránna	**mo**yawraan-no	marjoram
pirospaprika	**pee**rawshpopreeko	strong paprika
rozmaring	**rawz**morreeng	rosemary
sáfrány	**shaa**fraan^{y}	crocus leaf
szegfűszeg	**sæg**f$\overline{ew}$sæg	cloves
szekfűbors	**sæk**f$\overline{ew}$bawrsh	allspice
szerecsendió	**sæ**ræchændeea$\overline{w}$	nutmeg

Desserts

The Hungarians have a decidedly sweet tooth and much to offer in the way of desserts.

I'd like a dessert, please.	**Egy adag deszertet kérek.**	æd^{y} oddog dæsærtæt kayræk
Something light, please.	**Valami könnyűt legyen szíves.**	vollommee kurn^{y}ewt læd^{y}æn seevæsh
Nothing more, thank you.	**Köszönöm, többet nem kérek.**	kursurnurm turb-bæt næm kayræk

almás palacsinta	olmaash pollocheento	apple pancake
aranygaluska	orron^{y}gollooshko	sweet dumpling
csokoládéfánk	chawkawlaadayfaank	chocolate doughnut
csúsztatott palacsinta	choostottawt pollo-cheento	multi-layer pancake
dobostorta	dawbawshtawrto	caramel-topped chocolate cream cake
gesztenyepüré tejszínhabbal	gæstæn^{y}æpewray tæ^{y}sseenhob-bol	chestnut purée with whipped cream
Gundel palacsinta	goondæl pollocheento	pancake with nut-cream and raisin filling, flambéd
kapros túrós rétes	koprawsh toorawsh raytæsh	curds strudel with dill
kapucineres felfújt	koppootseenæræsh fælfoo^{y}t	mocha soufflé
kecskeméti barack-puding	kæchkæmaytee borrotsk-"pudding"	apricot pudding with vanilla cream
képviselőfánk	kaypveeshælurfaank	cream puff
máglyarakás	maag^{y}orrokkaash	apple and jam pudding
mákosrétes	maakawshraytæsh	poppy-seed strudel
mandula felfújt	mondoolo fælfoo^{y}t	almond soufflé
rakott palacsinta	rokkawt pollocheento	multi-layer pancakes with various fillings
somlói galuska	shawmlawee gollooshko	sweet dumplings made with vanilla, nuts and chocolate, in an orange-and-rum sauce
sült derelye	shewlt dæræ^{y}æ	fried jam turn-over
szilvás rétes	seelvaash raytæsh	plum strudel
töltött alma	turlturt olmo	apple stuffed with vanilla, raisins and cream

Ice-cream

Ice-cream and parfaits are often available as desserts. In addition, pastry shops and milkbars serve a variety of imaginative ice-based creations, frequently including fruit, cream or fancy cakes. As a dessert, ice-cream is sometimes served with a fresh-fruit salad. Alternatively, it may be flambéd with rum. There will generally be a choice of flavours.

Have you any ice-cream?	**Van fagylaltjuk?**	von **fod**ʸloltʸook
banán	**bon**naan	banana
citrom	**tsee**trawm	lemon
csokoládé	**chaw**kawlaaday	chocolate
dió	**dee**aw̄	walnut
eper	**æ**pær	strawberry
kávé	**kaa**vay	coffee
málna	**maal**no	raspberry
meggy	**maed**ʸ	sour cherry
mogyoró	**mawd**ʸawraw̄	hazelnut
narancs	**nor**ronch	orange
pisztás	**pees**taash	pistachio
vanília	**von**nēēleeo	vanilla
Could I have it flambéd?	**Kaphatok lángoló fagylaltot?**	**kop**hottawk **laan**gawlaw̄ **fod**ʸloltawt

Cheese

Though Hungary produces more than a hundred types of cheese, on the whole they range little in taste. Most are rather bland, but there are some spiced or smoked varieties. Imitation camembert, cheddar, Dutch edam and other foreign cheeses are also available in better restaurants.

Processed cheeses, conveniently packaged in tubes or the familiar individual triangular portions, may be flavoured with pepper, paprika or a variety of vegetable aromas.

I'd like some cheese.	**Sajtot szeretnék.**	**shoy**tawt **sæ**rætnayk
Do you have a cheese-board?	**Milyen sajt van?**	**mee**ʸæn shoyt von

Fruit

Do you have fresh fruit?	**Van friss gyümölcsük?**	von freesh **d^{y}ew**murlchewk
What sort of fruit do you have?	**Milyen gyümölcsük van?**	**mee**^{y}æn **d^{y}ew**murlchewk von
I'd like a fresh-fruit cocktail.	**Friss gyümölcs-koktélt kérek.**	freesh **d^{y}ew**murlchkawk-taylt **kay**ræk

alma	**ol**mo	apple
áfonya	**aa**fawn^{y}a	blueberries
ananász	**on**nonnaas	pineapple
banán	**bon**naan	banana
citrom	**tsee**trawm	lemon
császárkörte	**chaa**ssaarkurrtæ	type of pear
cseresznye	**chæ**ræsn^{y}æ	cherries
datolya	**do**ttaw^{y}o	dates
dió	**dee**$\overline{aw}$	walnuts
egres	**æ**græsh	gooseberries
eper	**æ**pær	strawberries
fekete cseresznye	**fæ**kætæ **chæ**ræsn^{y}æ	heart cherries
fekete ribizli	**fæ**kætæ **ree**beezlee	blackcurrants
füge	**few**gæ	figs
gesztenye	**gæ**stæn^{y}æ	chestnuts
görögdinnye	**gu**rrurgdeen^{y}æ	water melon
jonatán alma	**yaw**nottaan **ol**mo	Jonathan apple
körte	**kurr**tæ	pear
málna	**maal**no	raspberries
mandarin	**mon**doreen	tangerine
mandula	**mon**doolo	almonds
meggy	**mæ**d^{y}	sour cherries
mogyoró	**maw**d^{y}awr$\overline{aw}$	hazelnuts
narancs	**no**rronch	orange
őszibarack	$\overline{ur}$seeborrotsk	peach
ribizli	**ree**beezlee	redcurrants
ringló	**reen**gl$\overline{aw}$	greengage
sárgabarack	**shaar**gobborrotsk	apricot
sárgadinnye	**shaar**goddeen^{y}æ	honeydew melon
starking alma	**shtor**keeng **ol**mo	starking apple
szeder	**sæ**dær	mulberries
szilva	**seel**vo	plum
szőlő	**s**$\overline{ur}$l$\overline{ur}$	grapes

The bill (check)

I'd like the bill, please.	**Kérem a számlát.**	kayræm o saamlaat
We'd like to pay separately.	**Külön-külön kívánunk fizetni.**	kewlurn kewlurn keevaanoonk feezætnee
What is this amount for?	**Ez mire vonatkozik?**	æz meeræ vawnotkawzeek
You've made a mistake in this bill, I think.	**Azt hiszem, ez a számla hibás.**	ost heessæm æz o saamlo heebash
Is everything included?	**Minden szerepel a számlában?**	meendæn særæpæl o saamlaabon

A FELSZOLGÁLÁSI DÍJ AZ ÁRAKBAN BENNFOGLALTATIK
SERVICE INCLUDED

How much do I owe you?	**Mennyi a számla összege?**	mænʸee o saamlo urssægæ
Do you accept traveller's cheques?	**Fizethetek traveller's csekkel?**	feezæt-hætæk trovvæl-lærs chæk-kæl
Can I pay with this credit card?*	**Fizethetek ezzel a hitelkártyával?**	feezæt-hætæk æz-zæl o heetælkaartʸaavol
Thank you, this is for you.	**Köszönöm. Ez a magáé.**	kursurnurm. æz o moggaa-ay
Keep the change.	**A többi a magáé.**	o turb-bee o moggaa-ay
That was an excellent/ delicious meal.	**Az étel kiváló/ finom volt.**	oz aytæl keevaalaw/ feenawm vawlt
We've enjoyed ourselves very much, thank you.	**Jól szórakoztunk.**	yawl sawrokkawztoonk

* In Hungary, credit cards are generally accepted in all establishments frequented by foreign tourists.

Complaints

But perhaps you'll have something to complain about:

That's not what I ordered.	**Nem ezt rendeltem.**	næm æst **ræn**dæltæm
I asked for...	**Én...-t rendeltem.**	ayn ...-t **ræn**dæltæm
I asked for a small portion (for the child).	**Egy kisadagot rendeltem (a gyereknek).**	æd^{y} **keesh**oddoggawt **ræn**dæltæm (o d^{y}æræknæk)
There must be some mistake.	**Itt valami félre-értés lesz.**	eet **vo**llommee **fayl**ræayr-taysh læs
May I change this?	**Hozna valami mást helyette?**	**haw**zno **vo**llommee maasht hæ^{y}æt-tæ
The meat is...	**A húst...**	o hooosht
overdone	**agyonsütötték**	**o**d^{y}awnshewturt-tayk
underdone	**csak félig sütötték meg**	chok **fay**leeg **shew**turt-tayk mæg
This is too...	**Ez nagyon...**	æz **no**d^{y}awn
bitter	**keserű**	**kæ**shærew
salty	**sós**	shawsh
sour	**savanyú**	**sho**vvon^{y}oo
sweet	**édes**	**ay**dæsh
The food is cold.	**Ez az étel hideg.**	æz oz **ay**tæl **hee**dæg
It's not fresh.	**Ez nem friss.**	æz næm freesh
What's taking you so long?	**Mi tart ilyen sokáig?**	mee tort **ee**^{y}æn **shaw**kaa-eeg
Have you forgotten our drinks?	**Az innivalókat elfelejtette?**	oz **een**-neevollawkot **æl**fælæ^{y}tæt-tæ
The wine is too cold.	**A bor túl hideg.**	a bawr tool **hee**dæg
The wine tastes of cork.	**Ez a bor dugóízű.**	æz o bawr **doo**gaweezew
The beer isn't chilled.	**A sör nincs behűtve.**	o shurr neench **bæ**hewtvæ
This beer is flat.	**Ez a sör állott.**	æz o shurr **aal**-lawt
This isn't clean.	**Ez nem tiszta.**	æz næm **tees**to
There's a draught here.	**Huzat van.**	**hoo**zot von
Would you ask the headwaiter to come over?	**Kérem, hívja ide a főpincért!**	**kay**ræm **hee**vyo **ee**dæ o **fur**peenchayrt

Drinks

Give me the drinks card, please.	**Legyen szíves az itallapot idehozni!**	læd^yæn **see**væsh oz **ee**tolloppawt **ee**dæhawznee

Beer

Both local beer (which is rather strong) and foreign brands are usually available. It may be sold by the bottle or on draught. A 3-decilitre glass is called a *pohár*, a half-litre mug a *korsó*.

I'd like a bottle of ... beer.	**Egy üveg ... sört kérnék.**	æd^y **ew**væg shurrt **kayr**nayk
German	**német**	**nay**mæt
Hungarian	**magyar**	**mod**^yor
Pilsen	**pilzeni**	**peel**zænee
dark/light	**barna/világos**	**bor**no/**vee**laagawsh
A *pohár/korsó* of beer, please.	**Egy pohár/korsó sört kérek.**	æd^y **paw**haar/**kawr**shaw shurrt **kay**ræk

EGÉSZSÉGÉRE!
(ægayssaygayræ)
CHEERS!

Wine

For its size, Hungary produces an impressive range of good wines.

What kind of wine do you have?	**Milyen boruk van?**	**mee**^yæn **baw**rook von
I'd like a... of wine.	**Egy... bort kérek.**	æd^y ... bawrt **kay**ræk
glass/bottle	**pohár/üveg**	**paw**haar/**ew**væg
A bottle of white/red wine, please.	**Egy üveg fehér/vörös bort kérek.**	æd^y **ew**væg **fæ**hayr/**vur**rursh bawrt **kay**ræk

FLUID MEASURES: see page 130

Type of wine	Examples	Accompanies
sweet white wine	Balatonfüredi szemelt rizling, Csopaki olasz rizling, Akali zöldszilváni, Tokaji aszu	desserts and pastry, but also thick soups
light dry white wine	Badacsonyi kéknyelű, Badacsonyi szürkebarát, Badacsonyi zöldszilváni, Egri Leányka, Tokaji furmint, Tokaji szamorodni	fish meals, liver, lighter meat dishes, goulash and other stews, steaks, cold meats, fruit
light-bodied red wine	Vaskúti kadarka, Villányi burgundi, Villányi kadarka, Egri pinot noir	fish soups, veal, pork, lamb, ham, beef, fowl, game, cheese
full-bodied red wine	Egri bikavér, Villányi medoc noir, Tihanyi merlot	game, duck, cheese
sparkling wine (sweet)	Törley réserve, Pannonia	desserts and fruit
sparkling wine (dry)	Pompadur, Pannonia	fowl, game
sparkling wine (extra dry)	Pannonia dry	light cheese

Tokay wine

This world-famous wine comes from the area near the city of Tokaj, considered by many the country's most outstanding wine-growing region. Its excellence is attributed to the properties of the local soil, the mineral content of the water, the traditional production methods employed and, some local people insist, the peculiar quality of the sunshine there.

Tokay wines come in three different categories: *Tokaji furmint* (dry), *Tokaji szamorodni* (medium-sweet) and *Tokaji aszu* (full-bodied, very sweet). Tokay vintages are graded according to excellence on a scale of from 3 to 5 *puttonyos* or points.

Other alcoholic drinks

Cocktails and highballs are unfamiliar to most Hungarians, and you are unlikely to find any available in ordinary restaurants and drinking places. Imported spirits can be found in some better bars and restaurants.

Do you have any...?	**Van...?**	von
cognac	**konyakjuk**	**kawn**^{y}okyook
gin	**dzsinjük**	**dzheen**yewk
liqueur	**likörjük**	**lee**kurr^{y}ewk
rum	**rumjuk**	**room**yook
vermouth	**vermutjuk**	**vær**mootyook
whisky	**viszkijük**	**vees**kee^{y}ewk
vodka	**vodkájuk**	**vawd**kaa^{y}ook
A (double) whisky, please.	**Egy (dupla) viszkit, kérek.**	æd^{y} (**doo**plo) **vees**keet **kay**ræk
neat (straight)	**tisztán**	**tees**taan
on the rocks	**jéggel kérem**	**yayg**-gæl **kay**ræm
with a little water	**kevés vízzel**	**kæ**vaysh **v$\overline{ee}$z**-zæl
Give me a gin and tonic, please.	**Egy adag dzsint kérek tonikkal.**	æd^{y} **od**dog dzheent **kay**ræk **taw**neek-kol
Just a dash of soda, please.	**Csak egy csöpp szódával kérem.**	chok æd^{y} churp **s$\overline{aw}$**daavol **kay**ræm
2 rum-and-cokes, please.	**2 rumot kérek kólával.**	2 **room**awt **kay**ræk **k$\overline{aw}$**laavol

For a change, you might like to try one of Hungary's excellent fruit brandies:

I'd like a glass of... brandy.	**Kérek egy pohár... pálinkát.**	**kay**ræk æd^{y} **paw**haar... **paa**leenkaat
apple	**alma**	**ol**mo
apricot	**barack**	**bor**rotsk
cherry	**cseresznye**	**chæ**ræsnæ
pear	**körte**	**kur**tæ
plum	**szilva**	**seel**vo

A potent concoction you are unlikely to want to order but may be offered is a "Puszta cocktail"—a mixture of three kinds of fruit brandies and vermouth, served with lemon and iced. Treat it with respect!

Soft drinks

Some international soft-drink brands are widely available, along with a variety of fruit juices. Bottled mineral water, usually sparkling, is on sale everywhere.

I'd like some...	**... kérek.**	... **kay**ræk
apple juice	**Almalevet**	**ol**mollævæt
apricot juice	**Baracklét**	**bo**rrotsklayt
cola drink	**Kólát**	**k$\overline{\text{aw}}$**laat
fruit juice	**Gyümölcslevet**	**d^{Y}ew**murlchlævæt
grapefruit juice	**Grépfruit-lét**	"grapefruit" layt
lemonade	**Limonádét**	**lee**mawnaadayt
lemon juice	**Citromlét**	**tsee**trawmlayt
mineral water	**Ásvány vizet**	**aash**vaan^{Y} **vee**zæt
orange juice	**Narancslét**	**no**rronchlayt
soda water	**Szóda vizet**	**s$\overline{\text{aw}}$**do **vee**zæt
tomato juice	**Paradicsomlét**	**po**rroddeechawmlayt

Coffee and tea

As you come to notice the Hungarians drinking coffee at all hours of the day, you'll be able to believe that the nation's per-capita consumption is one of the world's highest. Coffee is drunk strong (espresso style), black, usually sweet and very hot—though you obviously need not follow the local custom if you prefer your coffee otherwise. At most places, even white breakfast coffee is based on espresso.

Tea in Hungary is generally found rather weak and tasteless by British and American visitors.

I'd like a small/ large coffee.	**Egy szimpla/dupla kávét kérek.**	æd^{Y} **seem**plo/**doo**plo **kaa**vayt **kay**ræk
A white coffee, please.	**Egy tejeskávét kérek.**	æd^{Y} **tæ^{Y}**æshkaavayt **kay**ræk
A cup of tea, please.	**Egy csésze teát kérek.**	æd^{Y} **chay**ssæ **tæ**aat **kay**ræk
Please bring me some ...	**... kérem.**	... **kay**ræm
cream/milk	**Krémmel/Tejjel**	**kraym**-mæl/**tæ^{Y}**yæl
lemon/sugar	**Citrommal/Cukorral**	**tsee**trawm-mol/**tsoo**kawr-rol

Eating light—Snacks

For a quick sit-down meal, go to a *bisztro, büfé, cukrászda, önkiszolgáló, tejivó* or *tejbár* (see pages 38–39).

I'll have one of those, please.	**Egy ilyet kérek.**	æd^{y} **ee^{y}**æt **kay**ræk
biscuits	**apró sütemény**	opraw̄ **shew**tæmayn^{y}
bread	**kenyér**	**kæn^{y}**ayr
cakes	**tea sütemény**	**tæ**o **shew**tæmayn^{y}
cheese	**sajt**	shoyt
chicken	**csirke**	**cheer**kæ
half a roasted chicken	**fél gril csirke**	fayl "grill" **cheer**kæ
chips	**sült krumpli**	shewlt **kroom**plee
chocolate	**tábla csokoládé**	taablo **chaw**kawlaaday
frankfurters	**pár virsli**	paar **veersh**lee
French fries	**sült krumpli**	shewlt **kroom**plee
fried doughnut	**lángos**	**laan**gawsh
fried eggs	**tükörtojás**	**tew**kurrtaw^{y}aash
fried fish	**sült hal**	shewlt hol
fried potato slices	**roseibni**	**raw**shæeebnee
fried sausages	**sült kolbász**	shewlt **kawl**baass
ham and eggs	**sonkát tojással**	**shawn**kaat **taw^{y}**aash-shol
ham sandwich	**sonkás szendvics**	**shawn**kaash **sænd**veech
ice-cream	**fagylalt**	**fod^{y}**lolt
ketchup	**ketchup**	**kæ**churp
meat sandwich	**húsos szendvics**	**hoo**shaws **sænd**veech
mustard	**mustár**	**mosh**taar
salami sandwich	**szalámis szendvics**	**sol**laameesh **sænd**veech
sandwich	**szendvics**	**sænd**veech
scrambled eggs	**rántotta**	**raan**tawt-to
sweetcorn	**kukorica**	**koo**kawreetso

DRINKS: see page 60

Travelling around

Plane

Budapest Ferihegy is the country's only commercial airport. There are, therefore, no scheduled domestic flights. Airport staff mostly speak some English or German, but here are a few useful expressions, just in case:

Is there a flight to Vienna?	**Van Bécsbe járatuk?**	von **baych**bæ **yaa**rottook
When is the next plane to London?	**Mikor indul a következő gép Londonba?**	**mee**kawr **een**dool o **kur**vætkæzu͞r gayp **lawn**dawnbo
Is it nonstop?	**Leszállás nélkül?**	**læ**ssaal-laash **nayl**kewl
Can I make a connection to New York?	**Át tudok szállni egy Nju-jork-i gépre?**	aat **too**dawk **saal**nee æd^{y} n^{y}oo-yawrk-ee **gay**præ
I'd like a ticket to Rome.	**Rómába kérek egy jegyet.**	**ra͞w**maabo **kay**ræk æd^{y} yæd^{y}æt
What's the fare ...?	**Mennyibe kerül egy jegy ...?**	**mæn**^{y}eebæ **kæ**rewl æd^{y} yæd^{y}
single (one-way)	**egy irányban**	æd^{y} **ee**raan^{y}bon
return (roundtrip)	**oda-vissza**	**aw**do **vees**-so
economy class	**turista osztályon**	**too**reeshto **aw**staa^{y}awn
first class	**első osztályon**	**æl**shu͞r **aw**staa^{y}awn
When is the departure time?	**Mikor indul a járat?**	**mee**kawr **een**dool o **yaa**rot
What time do I have to check in?	**Mikor kell bejelentkeznem?**	**mee**kawr kæl **bæ**^{y}ælæntkæznæm
What's the flight number?	**Mi a járat száma?**	mee o **yaa**rot **saa**mo
What time do we arrive?	**Mikor érkezünk meg?**	**mee**kawr **een**dool o **yaa**rot

ÉRKEZÉS	**INDULÁS**
ARRIVAL	DEPARTURE

TELLING THE TIME: see page 178

Train

The Hungarian State Railways maintain quite a dense rail network, partly electrified, with both first- and second-class seating. First-class compartments, marked I, are comfortable. Second-class compartments, marked II, are adequate but not always as clean as they might be; they are also likely to be rather crowded and noisy. Service is punctual. International connections are generally good.

Rail travel within Hungary is quite inexpensive and is an excellent way to get to see the country. Hungary is linked to the Inter Rail agreement which allows young people up to the age of 25 to travel throughout some thirty countries of Europe for one month at a low-cost flat-rate charge. Travel agents in all Western European countries have details.

For trips within Hungary, tickets can be purchased from railway stations and travel agencies. A variety of options exist—regular, excursion, trade-fair and student tickets.

The three main railway stations in Budapest are: *Nyugati* (West), *Déli* (South) and *Keleti* (East). At all of them, some staff speak a little English or German.

Type of trains

Nemzetközi gyorsvonat (næmzætkurzee d^{y}awrshvawnot)	International express with first- and second-class seating; advance reservation (at an extra charge) is highly advisable.
Sebesvonat (shæbæshvawnot)	Express train, stopping at major centres only.
Gyorsvonat (d^{y}awrshvawnot)	A domestic express train which stops more frequently.
Személyvonat (sæmay^{y}vawnot)	Slow train, stopping at all stations.
Helyiérdekű (hæ^{y}eeayrdækew̄)	Suburban train, painted green, often integrated into the municipal public transport system.
Motorvonat (mawtawrvawnot)	Rail coach, diesel, comprising three or four cars, used for shorter distances.

To the railway station

Where's the railway station?	**Hol a vasútállomás?**	hawl o **vosh**ōōtaal-lawmaash
Taxi, please!	**Halló, taxi!**	**hol**-lāw **toxee**
Take me to the ... Station.	**Vigyen kérem a ... pályaudvarra.**	veed^{y}æn **kay**ræm o ... paa^{y}o-oodvor-ro
East	**keleti**	kælætee
South	**déli**	daylee
West	**nyugati**	n^{y}oogottee
Which bus goes to the ... Station?	**Melyik busz megy a ... pályaudvarra?**	mæ^{y}eek booss mæd^{y} o ... paa^{y}o-oodvor-ro

FELVILÁGOSITÁS	INFORMATION
VALUTABEVÁLTÁS	CURRENCY EXCHANGE

Where's the ...?

Where is the ...?	**Hol van ...?**	hawl von
currency exchange office	**a valutabeváltó hely**	o vollootobbævaaltāw hæ^{y}
information office	**az információs iroda**	oz **een**fawrmaatseeāwsh eerawdo
letter box	**a postaláda**	o **pawsh**tollaado
lost-property (lost-and-found) office	**az elhagyott tárgyak irodája**	oz ælhod^{y}awt **taard^{y}ok** eerawdaa^{y}o
luggage lockers	**a csomagmegőrző**	o **chaw**mogmægūrzūr
newsstand	**az újságos kioszk**	oz ōō^{y}shaagawsh **kee**awsk
platform 5	**az 5-ödik peron**	oz 5 **urdeek** pærawn
restaurant	**az étterem**	oz **ayt**-tæræm
snack bar	**a gyorsbüfé**	o **d^{y}awrsh**bewfay
ticket office	**a jegypénztár**	o **yæd^{y}**paynztaar
travel agency	**az utazási iroda**	oz **oo**tozzaashee **ee**rawdo
waiting room	**a váróterem**	o **vaa**rāwtæræm
Where are the toilets?	**Hol vannak az illemhelyek?**	hawl **von**-nok oz **eel**-læmhæ^{y}æk

TAXI: see page 27

TRAVELLING AROUND

Inquiries

When is the ... train to Siófok?	**Mikor megy ... vonat Siófokra?**	meekawr mæd^{y} ... vawnot sheeāwfawkro
first	**az első**	oz ælshūr
last	**a következő**	o kurvætkæzūr
next	**az utolsó**	oz ootawlshāw
What time does the train for Pécs leave?	**Mikor indul a vonat Pécsre?**	meekawr eendool o vawnot paychræ
What's the fare to Szeged?	**Mibe kerül egy jegy Szegedig?**	meebæ kærewl æd^{y} yæd^{y} sægædeeg
Is it an express train?	**Ez gyorsvonat?**	æz d^{y}awrshvawnot
What time does the train arrive at Győr?	**Mikor érkezik meg a vonat Győrből?**	meekawr ayrkæzeek mæg o vawnot d^{y}ūrrbūrl
Does the train stop at Héviz?	**Megáll a vonat Hévizen?**	mægaal o vawnot hayveezæn
Is there a dining car on the train?	**Van ezen a vonaton étkezőkocsi?**	von æzæn o vawnottawn aytkæzūrkawchee
What platform does the train for Vienna leave from?	**A bécsi gyorsvonat melyik vágányról indul?**	a baychee d^{y}awrsh-vawnot mæ^{y}eek vaagaan^{y}rāwl eendool

Vonat indul ...-ra/-re ... órakor.	There's a train to ... at ...
Ez egy gyorsvonat.	It's an express train.
... nál/nél át kell szállnia.	You have to change at ...
... nál/nél szálljon át és utazzon tovább egy helyi vonattal.	Change at ... and get a local train.
A 6. peron ...	Platform 6 is ...
ott/lent	over there/downstairs
balra/jobbra	on the left/right
Az ön vonata a ...-odik/-edik vágányról indul.	Your train leaves from platform ...
... perces késéssel indul.	There's a delay of ... minutes.

NUMBERS: see page 175

Tickets

I'd like a ticket to Keszthely.	**Kérek egy jegyet Keszthelyre.**	kayræk æd^{y} yæd^{y}æt kæsthæ^{y}ræ
single (one-way)	**egy útra**	æd^{y} $\overline{oo}$tro
return (roundtrip)	**oda-vissza**	awdo **vees**-so
first class	**első osztályra**	ælsh$\bar{u}$r **awstaa^{y}ro**
second class	**második osztályra**	maashawdeek **awstaa^{y}ro**
I'd like to make a seat reservation.	**Szeretnék helyjegyet váltani.**	særætnayk **hæ^{y}yæd^{y}æt** vaaltonnee
I'd like a timetable, please.	**Kérek egy menetrendet.**	kayræk æd^{y} **mænætræn**-dæt

Első vagy második osztályra?	First or second class?
Egy útra vagy oda-vissza?	Single (one way) or return (roundtrip)?
10 éves korig a gyerekek félárú jeggyel utaznak.	It's half fare up to age 10.

Baggage—Porters

Porter!	**Hordár!**	hawrdaar
Take my luggage to the ... train.	**Kérem, vigye a csomagjaimat a ...-i vonathoz.**	kayræm **veed^{y}æ** o **chaw**-mog^{y}o-eemot o ...-ee vawnot-hawz
Can I have this luggage registered?	**Ezeket a podgyászokat szeretném feladni.**	æzækæt o **pawd^{y}assawkot** særætnaym **fælodnee**
Where can I find a baggage trolley?	**Hol találhatok podgyász kézikocsit?**	hawl **tollalhottawk** **pawd^{y}ass kazeekawcheet**

BEJÁRAT	ENTRANCE
KIJÁRAT	EXIT
A VÁGÁNYOKHOZ	TO THE PLATFORMS

BAGGAGE and PORTERS: see also page 24

All aboard

Does the train for Budapest leave from this platform?	**A Budapestre menő vonat erről a peronról indul?**	o boodoppæshtræ **mænūr vawnot ær-rūrl** o **pærawn-rāwl eendool**
Is this the train for Debrecen?	**Ez a debreceni vonat?**	æz o **dæbrætsænee vawnot**
Is this seat taken?	**Ez a hely foglalt?**	æz o hæ^y **fawglolt**
I think that's my seat.	**Azt hiszem, ez az én helyem.**	ost **heessæm** æz oz ayn **hæ^{y}æm**
Would you mind looking after my luggage for a moment?	**Vigyázna kérem egy percre a podgyászomra?**	**veed^{y}aazno kayræm** æd^y **pærtsræ** o **pawd-d^{y}aassawmro**
Do you mind if I open/close the window?	**Kinyithatnám/ Becsukhatnám az ablakot?**	**keen^{y}eet-hotnaam/ bæchook-hotnaam oz oblokkawt**
Would you let me know before we get to Szeged?	**Szólna, mielőtt Szegedre érkezünk?**	**sāwlno meeælūrt sægædræ ayrkæzewnk**
What station is this?	**Ez milyen állomás?**	æz **mee^{y}æn aal-lawmaash**
How long does the train stop here?	**Meddig áll itt a vonat?**	**mæd-deeg aal eet o vawnot**
When do we get to the border?	**Mikor, érkezünk a határra?**	**meekawr ayrkæzewnk o hottaar-ro**

TILOS A DOHÁNYZÁS NO SMOKING	DOHÁNYZÓ SMOKING ALLOWED

Eating

Long-distance expresses, both domestic and international, have dining cars which serve meals at normal hours. On some trains, alcoholic drinks and light refreshments are also served at a buffet, or an attendant may come round with baskets of supplies.

Where's the dining car?	**Merre van az étkezőkocsi?**	**mær-ræ von oz aytkæzūr-kawchee**

MEAL TIMES: see page 40

Sleeping

Are there any free compartments in the sleeping car?	**Van még szabad hely a hálókocsiban?**	von mayg **sobbod** hæ^{y} o **haalawkawcheebon**
Are there any couchettes available?	**Van még szabad kusettjük?**	von mayg **sobbod kooshæt^{y}ewk**
Where's my berth?	**Melyik az én ágyam?**	mæ^{y}eek oz ayn **aad^{y}om**
Compartments 10 and 11, please.	**A 10-es és 11-es fülkéket kérem.**	o 10-æsh 11-æsh **fewl**-kaykæt **kayræm**
I'd like an upper/lower berth.	**Felső/Alsó ágyat kérek.**	**fælshür/olshaw aad^{y}ot kayræk**
Would you make up our berths, please?	**Kérem, vesse meg az ágyamat.**	**kayræm væsh**-shæ mæg oz **aad^{y}ommot**
Would you call me at 7 o'clock?	**Kérem, keltsen fel 7 órakor.**	**kayræm kæltshæn fæl** 7 **aw**rokkawr
Would you please bring me tea/coffee in the morning?	**Kérem, reggel hozzon teát/kávét.**	**kayræm ræg**-gæl **hawz**-zawn **tæaat/kaavayt**

Lost property

We hope you'll never need this section during your journey, but just in case:

Where's the lost-property (lost-and-found) office?	**Hol van a talált tárgyak irodája?**	hawl von o **tollaalt taard^{y}ok eerawdaayo**
I've lost my ...	**Elvesztettem ...**	**ælvæstæt-tæm**
handbag	**a kézitáskámat**	o **kayzeetaashkaamot**
passport	**az útlevelemet**	oz **oo**tlævælæmæt
ring	**a gyűrűmet**	o **d^{y}ewrewmæt**
ticket	**a jegyemet**	o **yæd^{y}æmæt**
wallet	**az irattárcámat**	oz **eerot-taartsaamot**
watch	**az órámat**	oz **aw**raamot
I lost it in ...	**... -ban/-ben hagytam el.***	...-bon/-bæn **hod^{y}tom** æl
It's very valuable.	**Nagyon értékes.**	**nod^{y}awn ayrtaykæsh**

* See Grammar section for word endings.

Intercity coach (bus) services

Hungary has an extensive intercity coach network reaching into all parts of the country. Vehicles are comfortable and service is reasonably rapid, making bus travel the preferred means of transport of many. Prices are on a par with those for first-class rail travel. Most coaches are operated by the Volán and Mavaut companies. They are generally painted yellow.

Where can I get a coach to Esztergom?	**Hol érem el az Esztergomba induló autóbuszt?**	hawl **ay**ræm æl oz **æs**-tærgawmbo **een**doolaw̄ ootaw̄boost
Which coach must I take for Tiszafüred?	**Melyik busszal jutok el Tiszafüredre?**	mæ^{y}eek **boos**-sol **yoo**tawk æl **tee**ssoffewrædræ
Where's the coach station?	**Hol van az autóbusz állomás?**	hawl von oz **oo**taw̄booss **aa**lawmaash
When is the ... coach to Győr?	**Mikor indul ... busz Győrbe?**	**mee**kawr **een**dool ... booss d^{y}ūrrbæ
first	**az első**	oz **æ**lshūr
last	**az utolsó**	oz **oo**tawlshaw̄
next	**a következő**	o **kur**vætkæzūr
Do I have to change coaches?	**Át kell közben szállnom?**	aat kæl **kurz**bæn **saal**-nawm
I'd like a timetable, please.	**Kérek egy menetrendet.**	**kay**ræk æd^{y} **mæ**nætræn-dæt

Urban public transport

The nation's larger towns have well-organized public transport services consisting of bus, tram (streetcar) and/or suburban train networks. Buses are blue, trams yellow, and suburban trains green. In addition, Budapest has an underground (subway) system.

Though the first underground (subway) on the continent of Europe was built in Budapest, large-scale construction was only taken up about 1950. There are now four lines in operation.

Modern, clean rolling stock serves the most important points throughout the capital. Stations are marked with a large M sign and a route number.

City buses, trams, suburban trains and the underground operate variously between 4 a.m. and midnight. On the underground, frequency of service is regulated to conform to passenger demand.

Smoking is prohibited on all urban public transport vehicles.

Tickets for buses, trams and the underground are on sale at termini, major news-stands, tobacconists' shops and post offices—but not on board the vehicles themselves. Tickets for suburban trains must be purchased at the railway station.

Rates for suburban trains vary according to the distance travelled. Buses, trams and the underground each charge a—slightly different—flat rate for a ticket which is valid only on the one vehicle (no transfers). You must punch your ticket in the automatic machine on board (or, for the underground, at the station entrance).

Season tickets, valid on all four forms of urban public transport, are available for one-month periods only. However, if you are likely to be making extensive use of public transport facilities you might still find that their convenience outweighs the extra cost, even for a stay of only a few days—particularly in Budapest.

Inspectors make spot-checks on tickets, and you can expect quite a hefty fine if yours is not in order.

Where can I buy a ticket for the ...?	**Hol vehetek... jegyet?**	hawl væhætæk ... yæd^{y}æt
bus	**az autóbuszra**	oz oootāwboosro
tram	**a villamosra**	o **veel**-lommawshro
suburban train	**a H. É. V.-re**	o **hayv**-ræ
underground (subway)	**a metróra**	o mætrāwro

A ... ticket, please.	**Egy ... jegyet kérek.**	æd^y ... yæd^yæt **kay**ræk
bus/tram/ underground	**autóbusz/villamos/ metró**	**oo**tawbooss/**veel**-lommawsh/**mæ**traw̄
I'd like a season ticket, please.	**Szeretnék egy bérletet váltani.**	særatnayk æd^y **bayr**læ-tæt **vaal**tonnee
Where's the nearest underground station?	**Hol van a legköze-lebbi metró megálló?**	hawl von o **læg**kurzælæb-bee **mæ**traw̄ **mæ**gaal-law̄

Boats

For a change of pace and viewpoint, you might like to take one of the passenger boats which ply the Danube and Tisza rivers all year round. Or, during the summer months, you can go for a relaxing cruise on Lake Balaton. From May to September there is a daily hydrofoil service on the Danube between Budapest and Vienna which takes about five hours. Also during the summer season, a number of river excursion boats operate on the Danube leaving from Budapest Central Docks *(Vigadó-tér).*

A ... ticket to Vienna, please.	**... jegyet kérek Bécsbe.**	... yæd^yæt **kay**ræk **baych**bæ
boat/hydrofoil	**Hajó/Szárnyashajó**	**hoy**aw̄/**saar**n^yoshhoyaw̄

Other modes of transport

car	**autó**	**oo**taw̄
bicycle	**kerékpár**	**kæ**raykpaar
moped (motorbike)	**moped**	**maw**pæd
motorcycle	**motorkerékpár**	**maw**tawrkæraykpaar
pedalo	**vizibicikli**	**vee**zeebeetseeklee
rowing boat	**evezős csónak**	**æ**væzūrsh **chaw̄**nok
sailing boat	**vitorlás**	**vee**tawrlaash
scooter	**robogó**	**raw**bawgaw̄

Or perhaps you prefer:

hitch-hiking	**autóstoppal utazni**	**oo**taw̄shtawp-pol **oo**toznee
horse-riding	**lovagolni**	**law**voggawlnee
walking	**gyalogolni**	**d^y**ollawgawlnee

Around and about—Sightseeing

In this section we are more concerned with cultural attractions. For entertainment, see page 81.

If you want to buy a guide book, ask:

Can you recommend a good guide book on Budapest?	**Ajánlana Budapestről egy jó utikalauzt?**	oyaanlonno **boo**doppæsht-rūrl æd^{y} yaw **ooteekollo**-oozt
Is there a tourist office here?	**Van itt utazási iroda?**	von eet **oo**tozzaashee **ee**rawdo
Where's the tourist office?	**Hol van az utazási iroda?**	hawl von oz **oo**tozzaashee **ee**rawdo
What are the main points of interest?	**Melyek a fő nevezetességek?**	mæ^{y}æk o fūr **næ**væ-zætæsh-shaygæk
We're here for ...	**... vagyunk itt.**	... **vod**^{y}oonk eet
only a few hours	**Csak egy pár óráig**	chok æd^{y} paar **aw**raaeeg
a day	**Egy napig**	æd^{y} **noppeeg**
3 days	**3 napig**	3 **noppeeg**
a week	**Egy hétig**	æd^{y} **hayteeg**
Can you recommend a sightseeing tour?	**Ajánlana egy városnéző kőrútat?**	oyaanlonno æd^{y} **vaarawsh**-nayzūr **kur**rōotot
Where does the bus start from?	**Honnan indul az autóbusz?**	**hawn**-non **een**dool oz **ooo**tawbooss
Will it pick us up at the hotel?	**A busz a szállodánál vesz fel bennünket?**	o booss o **saal**-lawdaa-naal væs fæl **bæn**-newnkæt
Where do the cruises start from?	**Honnan indul a kiránduló hajó?**	**hawn**-non **een**dool o **kee**raandoolaw **hoy**aw
What bus/underground do we take?	**Melyik buszra/földalattira szálljunk fel?**	mæ^{y}eek **boos**ro/**furld**-ollot-teero **saal**yoonk fæl
How much does the tour cost?	**Mennyibe kerül a városnéző kőrút?**	**mæn**^{y}eebæ **kæ**rewl o **vaa**rawshnayzūr **kur**rōot
What time does the tour start?	**Mikor kezdődik a városnéző kőrút?**	**mee**kawr **kæz**dūrdeek o **vaa**rawshnayzūr **kur**rōot

TELLING THE TIME: see page 178

At what time do we get back?	**Mikor érkezünk vissza?**	**mee**kawr **ayr**kæzewnk **vees**-so
Is lunch included in the tour price?	**Az ebéd benne van az árban?**	oz æbayd **bæn**-næ von oz **aar**bon
Is there an English-speaking guide?	**Van angolul beszélő idegenvezetőjük?**	von **on**gawlool **bæ**saylūr **ee**dægænvæzætūryewk
We'd like to hire a car for the day.	**Gépkocsit szeretnénk kölcsönözni egy napra.**	**gayp**kawcheet **sæ**rætnaynk **kurl**churnurznee æd^y **no**pro
I'd like to hire a chauffeur-driven car.	**Szeretnék bérelni egy kocsit sofőrrel.**	**sæ**rætnayk **bay**rælnee æd^y **kaw**cheet **shaw**fūr-ræl
Can you get me an English-speaking chauffeur?	**Kaphatnék egy angolul beszélő sofőrt?**	**kop**hotnayk æd^y **on**gawlool **bæ**saylūr **shaw**fūrt
I'd like to hire an English-speaking private guide.	**Szeretnék külön, angolul beszélő idegenvezetőt kapni.**	**sæ**rætnayk **kew**lurn **on**-gawlool **bæ**saylūr **ee**-dægænvæzætūrt **kop**nee
for half a day	**fél napra**	fayl **no**pro
for a full day	**egy napra**	æd^y **no**pro
What will that cost me?	**Mennyibe kerül?**	**mæn**^{y}eebæ **kæ**rewl
Is that price all-inclusive?	**Az árban minden benne van?**	oz **aar**bon **meen**dæn **bæn**-næ von
Can I pay with ...?	**Fizethetek ...?**	**fee**zæt-hætæk
this credit card	**hitelkártyával**	**hee**tælkaart^{y}aavol
traveller's cheques	**traveller's csekkel**	**trov**væl-lærs **chæk**-kæl
Where is/are the ...?	**Hol van ...?**	hawl von
airport	**a repülőtér**	o **ræ**pewlūrtayr
art gallery	**a képzőművészeti galéria**	o **kayp**zūrmēwvayssætee gollayreeo
botanical gardens	**a botanikus kert**	o **baw**tonneekoosh kært
building	**az épület**	oz **ay**pewlæt
business district	**az üzleti negyed**	oz **ewz**lætee **næd**^{y}æd
castle	**a vár**	o vaar
cathedral	**a székesegyház**	o **say**kæshæd^{y}haaz
caves	**a barlang**	o **bor**long
cemetery	**a temető**	o **tæ**mætūr
chapel	**a kápolna**	o **kaa**pawlno
church	**a templom**	o **tæm**plawm
city centre	**a városközpont**	o **vaa**rawshkurzpawnt

SIGHTSEEING

concert hall	**a hangversenyterem**	o **hong**værshæn^{y}tæræm
conference centre	**a konferencia központ**	o **kawn**færæntseeo **kurz**pawnt
docks	**a móló**	o **maw**law
downtown area	**a városközpont**	o **vaa**rawshkurzpawnt
exhibition	**a kiállítás**	o **kee**aal-leetaash
fortress	**az erődítmény**	oz ærurdeetmayn ^{y}
fountain	**a forrás**	o **fawr**-raash
garden	**a kert**	o kært
lake	**a tó**	o taw
law courts	**a bíróság**	o **bee**rawshaag
library	**a könyvtár**	o **kurn**^{y}vtaar
market	**a piac**	o **pee**ots
memorial	**az emlékoszlop**	oz æmlaykawslawp
monument	**az emlékmű**	oz æmlaykmew
museum	**a múzeum**	o **moo**zæoom
observatory	**a csillagvizsgáló**	o **cheel**-logveezhgaalaw
old town	**a régi város**	o **ray**ghee **vaa**rawsh
opera house	**az opera**	oz **aw**pæro
palace	**a palota**	o **pol**lawto
park	**a park**	o pork
parliament building	**a Parlament épülete**	o **por**lommænt **ay**pewlætæ
planetarium	**a planetárium**	o **plon**nætaareeoom
port	**a kikötő**	o **kee**kurtur
post office	**a postahivatal**	o **pawsh**toheevottol
ruins	**a romok**	o **raw**mawk
shopping centre	**a bevásárló központ**	o **bæ**vaashaarlaw **kurz**pawnt
stadium	**a stadion**	o **shtod**deeawn
statue	**a szobor**	o **saw**bawr
synagogue	**a zsinagóga**	o **zhee**noggawgo
theatre	**a színház**	o **seen**haaz
tomb	**a síremlék**	o **sheer**æmlayk
tower	**a torony**	o **taw**rawn^{y}
TV studios	**a TV studio**	o tayvay **shtoo**deeaw
university	**az egyetem**	oz æd^{y}ætæm
zoo	**az állatkert**	oz **aal**-lotkært

SZABAD BELÉPÉS	ADMISSION FREE
TILOS A FÉNYKÉPEZÉS	NO CAMERAS ALLOWED

Admission

Is ... open on Sundays?	**A ... vasárnaponként nyitva van?**	o ... voshaarnoppawnkaynt n^{y}eetvo von
When does it open/close?	**Mikor nyit/zár?**	meekawr n^{y}eet/zaar
How much is the entrance fee?	**Mennyibe kerül a belépőjegy?**	mæn^{y}eebæ kærewl o bælaypuryæd^{y}
Is there any reduction for ...?	**... részére kedvezményes a belépőjegy?**	... rayssayræ kædvæzmayn^{y}æsh o bælaypuryæd^{y}
children	**Gyerekek**	d^{y}ærækæk
families	**Családok**	chollaadawk
the handicapped	**Nyomorékok**	n^{y}awmawraykawk
pensioners	**Nyugdíjasok**	n^{y}oogdeeyoshawk
students	**Diákok**	deeaakawk
Where can I get a ticket?	**Hol lehet jegyet kapni?**	hawl læhæt yæd^{y}æt kopnee
Can I buy a catalogue?	**Kaphatok egy katalógust?**	kophottawk æd^{y} kottollawgoosht
Have you any guide books in English?	**Van angolnyelvű útikalauzuk?**	von ongawln^{y}ælvew ooteekollo-oozook
Is it all right to take pictures?	**Szabad fényképezni?**	sobbod fayn^{y}kaypæznee

Who—What—When?

What's that building?	**Az az épület mi?**	oz oz aypewlæt mee
Who was the ...?	**Ki volt ...?**	kee vawlt
architect	**az építész**	oz aypeetayss
artist	**a művész**	o mewvayss
painter	**a festő**	o fæshtur
sculptor	**a szobrász**	o sawbraass
Who built it?	**Ki építette?**	kee aypeetæt-tæ
When was it built?	**Mikor épült?**	meekawr aypewlt
Who painted this picture?	**Ki festette ezt a képet?**	kee fæshtæt-tæ æst o kaypæt
When did he live?	**Mikor élt?**	meekawr aylt
Where's the house in which ... lived?	**Hol az a ház, amelyben ... élt?**	hawl oz o haaz ommæ^{y}bæn ... aylt

Just the adjective you've been looking for ...

It's ...	**Ez ...**	æz
awful	**borzasztó**	**baw**rzostaw
beautiful	**gyönyörű**	**d^yurn**^yurrew
fantastic	**csodálatos**	**chaw**daalottawsh
gloomy	**borongós**	**baw**rawngawsh
horrible	**rettenetes**	**ræt**-tænætæsh
impressive	**benyomást keltő**	**bæn**^yawmaasht **kæl**tur
interesting	**érdekes**	**ayr**dækæsh
magnificent	**pompás**	**pawm**paash
monumental	**óriási**	**aw**reeaashee
overwhelming	**lenyűgöző**	**læn**^yewgurzur
sinister	**rosszhangulatú**	**raw**shongoolottoo
strange	**különös**	**kew**lurnursh
superb	**kiváló**	**kee**vaalaw
surprising	**meglepő**	**mæg**læpur
ugly	**csúnya**	**choo**n^yo

What's your special interest?

I'm interested in ...	**Bennünket ... érdekel/ érdekelnek.***	**bæn**-newnkæt ... **ayr**-dækæl/**ayr**dækælnæk
antiques	**a régiségek**	o **ray**gheeshaygæk
archaeology	**az archeológia**	oz **or**hæawlawgheeo
botany	**a növénytan**	o **nur**vayn^yton
coins	**az érmék**	oz **ayr**mayk
fine arts	**a szépművészet**	o **sayp**mewvayssæt
furniture	**a bútorok**	o **boo**tawrawk
geography	**a földrajz**	o **furld**royz
geology	**a földtan**	o **furld**ton
handicrafts	**a mesterségek**	o **mæsh**tærshaygæk
history	**a történelem**	o **turr**taynælæm
horticulture	**a kertészet**	o **kær**tayssæt
Hungarian literature	**a magyar irodalom**	o **mod^y**or **ee**rawdollawm
languages	**a nyelvek**	o **n^yæl**væk
medicine	**az orvostudomány**	oz **awr**vawshtoodawmaan^y
music	**a zene**	o **zæ**næ
natural history	**a természettudományok**	o **tær**mayssæt-toodawmaan^yawk
ornithology	**a madártan**	o **mod**daarton

* Use *érdekelnek* with words in the following list which end in **k**.

painting	**a művészetek**	o m$\overline{ew}$vayssætæk
philately	**a bélyeggyüjtés**	o bay^{y}ægd^{y}ew^{y}taysh
pottery	**a fazekasság**	o fozzækosh-shaag
prehistory	**a történelem előtti kor**	o turrtaynælæm æl$\overline{ur}$t-tee kawr
science	**a tudományok**	o toodawmaan^{y}awk
sculpture	**a szobrászat**	o sawbraassot
zoology	**az állatvilág**	oz aal-lotveelaag
Where's the ... department?	**Hol van a/az ...-i részleg?**	hawl von o/oz ...-ee rayslæg

Religious services

Over 80 per cent of all Hungarians are Roman Catholics. Minorities include, notably, Protestants and members of the Eastern Orthodox church, and Jews.

Most churches are open to the public. If you visit a church for sightseeing purposes while a service is progress, stay in the rear part of the building so as not to disturb the worshippers. Mass may be said in either Hungarian or Latin.

If you are interested in taking photographs, don't forget to ask permission first.

Is there a ... near here?	**Van a közelben ...?**	von o kurzælbæn
Catholic church	**katolikus templom**	kottawleekoosh tæmplawm
mosque	**mecset**	mæchæt
Protestant church	**protestáns templom**	prawtæshtaansh tæmplawm
synagogue	**zsinagóga**	zheenogg$\overline{aw}$go
At what time is ...?	**Mikor van ...?**	meekawr von
mass	**a mise**	o meeshæ
the service	**a szertartás**	o særtortaash
Where can I find a ... who speaks English?	**Hol találok egy angolul beszélő ...?**	hawl tollaalawk æd^{y} ongawlool bæsayl$\overline{ur}$
minister	**plébánost**	playbaanawsht
priest	**papot**	poppawt
rabbi	**rabit**	robbeet

Relaxing

Cinema (movies)—Theatre

A visit to a Hungarian cinema will no doubt be quite an experience, as most foreign films are dubbed into the language of the country. You can expect a newsreel, perhaps a children's cartoon film and a feature film in addition to the main attraction. You'll find out what's showing from local newspapers and a special weekly movie magazine.

Cinemas are open every day of the week. Screening starts as early as 9 a.m., and some cinemas have late-night shows at about midnight.

Since showings are not continuous, you can purchase your ticket up to three days in advance for a specific time. Prices are very reasonable.

Theatre programmes and concerts generally start at 7 p.m. Theatres often close on Mondays.

Tickets can be purchased on the spot, but for a special event you would be wise to make your booking in advance, possibly through a ticket office in the centre of town or a tourist office. Theatre and concert tickets are also very advantageous, even for the National Opera House.

During summer, open-air performances are staged on Margaret Island *Margitsziget* in Budapest. At the same time of year Szeged, in the south of the country, is the scene of a music and opera festival, *Szegedi Ünnepi Játékok.*

Do you have an entertainment guide for …?	**Van …-i programjuk?**	von …-ee **praw**gromyook
What's on at the cinema tonight?	**Mi megy ma este a moziban?**	mee mæd^{Y} mo **æsh**tæ o **maw**zeebon
What's on at the … Theatre?	**Mit játszanak a … színházban?**	meet **yaat**sonnok o … **s̄ee̅n**haazbon

What sort of play is it?	**Ez milyen darab?**	æz **mee**^{y}æn **do**rrob
Who is it by?	**Ki a szerző?**	kee o **sær**zu̅r̅
Where is ...'s new film showing?	**... új filmjét hol játszák?**	... o̅o̅^{y} **feelm**yayt hawl **yaat**saak
Can you recommend a ...?	**Ajánlana egy ...?**	oyaanlonno æd^{y}
cartoon film	**rajzfilmet**	**royz**feelmæt
comedy	**bohózatot**	**baw**ha̅w̅zottawt
documentary film	**dokumentum filmet**	**daw**koomæntoom **feel**mæt
good film	**jó filmet**	ya̅w̅ **feel**mæt
musical	**zenés színdarabot**	**zæ**naysh **s̅e̅e̅n**dorrobbawt
play	**darabot**	**do**rrobbawt
revue	**revüt**	**ræ**vewt
something light	**valami könnyűt**	**vol**lommee **kurn**^{y}e̅w̅t
thriller (film)	**bűnügyi filmet**	**be̅w̅**newd^{y}ee **feel**mæt
thriller (play)	**bűnügyi darabot**	**be̅w̅**newd^{y}ee **do**rrobbawt
Western	**vadnyugati filmet**	**vod**n^{y}oogottee **feel**mæt
At which theatre is that new play by ... being performed?	**... új darabját hol adják?**	... o̅o̅^{y} **do**rrobyaat hawl **od**yaak
Who's in it?	**Ki játszik benne?**	kee **yaat**seek **bæn**-næ
Who's playing the lead?	**Ki játsza a főszerepet?**	kee **yaat**so o **fu̅r̅**særæpæt
What time does the show begin?	**Mikor kezdődik a darab?**	**mee**kawr **kæzdu̅r̅**deek o **do**rrob
What time does it end?	**Mikor van vége?**	**mee**kawr von **vay**gæ
Are there any tickets left for tonight?	**Van még jegyük ma estére?**	von mayg **yæd**^{y}ewk mo **æsh**tayræ
How much are the tickets?	**Mibe kerülnek a jegyek?**	**mee**bæ **kæ**rewlnæk o **yæd**^{y}æk
I'd like to book 2 seats for next (Friday) evening.	**(Péntek) estére szeretnék 2 jegyet rendelni.**	(**payn**tæk) **æsh**tayræ **sæ**rætnayk 2 **yæd**^{y}æt **rænd**ælnee
Can I have a ticket for the matinée on (Tuesday)?	**Kaphatok egy jegyet a (keddi) matinéra?**	**kop**hottawk æd^{y} **yæd**^{y}æt o (**kæd**-dee) **mot**teenayro
I'd like a seat in the stalls (orchestra)/ circle (mezzanine).	**A földszintre/ Az erkélyre kérek egy jegyet.**	o **furld**seentræ/ oz **ær**kay^{y}ræ **kay**ræk æd^{y} **yæd**^{y}æt

How much are the seats in the front row?	**Mibe kerül a jegy az első sorban?**	**mee**bæ **kæ**rewl o yæd^{Y} oz **æl**shūr **shawr**bon
I want 2 seats in the stalls (orchestra).	**A földszintre kérek 2 jegyet.**	o **furld**seentræ **kay**ræk 2 **yæd**^{Y}æt
Somewhere in the middle.	**Valahova középre.**	**vol**lohawvo **kur**zaypræ
May I have a programme, please?	**Kaphatok egy műsort?**	**kop**hottawk æd^{Y} **mēw**-shawrt
Where's the cloak-room?	**Hol a ruhatár?**	hawl o **roo**hawtaar

Sajnálom, minden jegyünk elkelt.	I'm sorry, we're sold out.
Csak az erkélyre van még néhány jegyünk.	There are only a few seats left in the circle (mezzanine).
Szabad a jegyét?	May I see your ticket?
Ez az Ön helye.	This is your seat.

Concert—Opera—Ballet

Where's the opera house?	**Hol az operaház?**	hawl oz **aw**pærohaaz
Where's the concert hall?	**Hol a hangver-senyterem?**	hawl o **hong**værshæn^{Y}-tæræm
What's on at the opera tonight?	**Mi megy ma az operában?**	mee mæd^{Y} mo oz **aw**pæ-raabon
Who's singing?	**Ki énekel?**	kee **ay**nækæl
Who's dancing?	**Ki táncol?**	kee **taan**tsawl
What time does the programme start?	**Mikor kezdődik a program?**	**mee**kawr **kæz**dūrdeek o **prawg**rom
What's the name of the orchestra?	**Melyik zenekar játszik?**	**mæ**^{Y}eek **zæ**nækor **yaat**seek
What are they play-ing?	**Mit játszanak?**	meet **yaat**sonnok
Who's the conductor?	**Ki vezényel?**	kee **væ**zayn^{Y}æl

Nightclub

Budapest has a number of nightclubs, several of them located in the larger hotels. Similar establishments can be found in lesser quantity in other major towns and, during the summer tourist season, along Lake Balaton.

They generally offer floor shows which, though entertaining, are rather more decorous than those found in some other capital cities—there's no striptease, for example. Music can be very good, and may include live jazz. Prices are predictably high.

Apart from light snacks, no meals are served.

Nightclub hours are from about 10 p.m. to 4 or 5 in the morning, six days a week. The closing day varies. Advance reservations are advisable for the select nightclubs in some five-star hotels, but elsewhere you should have no trouble finding a table.

Can you recommend a good nightclub?	**Ajánlana egy jó éjszakai mulatót?**	oyaanlonno æd^{y} yaw ay^{y}sokko-ee **moo**lottawt
Is there a floor show?	**Műsor van?**	**mew**shawr von
What time does the floor show start?	**Mikor kezdődik a műsor?**	**mee**kawr **kæz**durdeek o **mew**shawr
Is evening dress necessary?	**Alkalmi öltözet szükséges?**	**ol**kolmee **url**turzæt **sewk**shaygæsh

And once inside …

A table for 2, please.	**Egy asztalt kérek 2 fő részére.**	æd^{y} **os**tolt **kay**ræk 2 fur **ray**ssayræ
I've booked a table for 4.	**4 fő részére foglaltam asztalt.**	4 fur **ray**ssayræ **fawg**loltom **os**tolt
My name is …	**… vagyok.**	… **vod**^{y}awk
I phoned you earlier.	**Az előbb telefonáltam Önöknek.**	oz **æ**lurb **tæ**læfaw-naaltom **ur**nurknæk
We haven't a reservation.	**Nincs foglalásunk.**	neench **fawg**lollaashoonk

I'd like the drinks card, please.	**Az itallapot kérem.**	oz **ee**tol-loppawt **kay**ræm
We'd like a bottle of ...	**Egy üveg ... kérünk.**	æd^{y} **ew**vaeg ... **kay**rewnk
champagne	**pezsgőt**	**pæ**zhgūrt
red wine	**vörösbort**	**vur**rurshbawrt
white wine	**fehérbort**	**fæ**hayrbawrt

Dancing

Would you like to dance?	**Van kedve táncolni?**	von **kæ**dvæ **taan**tsawlnee
Where can we go dancing?	**Hol lehet táncolni?**	hawl **læ**hæt **taan**tsawlnee
Is there a disco-theque in town?	**Van a városban diszkó?**	von o **vaa**rawshbon **dees**kāw
Is there an entry fee?	**Belépőjegy van?**	**bæ**laypūryæd^{y} von
There's a dance at the ... Hotel.	**A ... Hotelban lehet táncolni.**	o ... **haw**tælbon **læ**hæt **taan**tsawlnee
May I have this dance?	**Szabad felkérnem egy táncra?**	**sob**bod **fæl**kayrnæm æd^{y} **taan**tsro

Do you happen to play ...?

Chess is a big favourite in Hungary. There is hardly a week without a major tournament being held somewhere.

Do you play chess?	**Sakkozik?**	**shok**-kawzeek

bishop	**futó**	**foo**tāw
castle (rook)	**bástya**	**baa**sht^{y}o
king	**király**	**kee**raa^{y}
knight	**huszár**	**hoo**ssaar
pawn	**gyalog**	**d^{y}o**llawg
queen	**vezér**	**væ**zayr
Check!	**Sakk!**	shok
Checkmate!	**Matt!**	mot

Do you play draughts (checkers)?	**Játszik francia sakkot?**	**yaatseek frontseeo shok**-kawt
Do you play cards?	**Kártyázik?**	**kaart^{y}aazeek**
bridge	**bridzs**	breedzh
canasta	**kanaszta**	**konnosto**
gin rummy	**römi**	**rurmee**
poker	**póker**	**p$\overline{aw}$**kær

hearts	**kőr**	**k$\overline{ur}$**r
diamonds	**káró**	**kaar$\overline{aw}$**
clubs	**treff**	træf
spades	**pikk**	peek
ace	**ász**	aass
king	**király**	**keeraa^{y}**
queen	**felső**	**fælsh$\overline{ur}$**
jack (knave)	**alsó**	**olsh$\overline{aw}$**
joker	**dzsóker**	**dzh$\overline{aw}$**kaer

Sports

The Hungarians are a sport-loving nation, and facilities for both watching and playing sports are widely available.

Soccer *(labdarugás)* is without a doubt the top spectator sport. Most towns have at least one team, and except in the height of summer you'll certainly be able to see a match whatever part of the country you happen to be in.

Basketball *(kosárlabda)* comes second in terms of popularity. It is played all year round, all over the country, in various leagues. The country boasts some 40,000 regular players.

Water polo *(vizilabda)* is another big favourite. The national team has won many international prizes. Main centres are the National Sports Pool *(Nemzeti Sportuszoda)* on Margaret Island and the Komjáti Swimming Pool *(Komjáti Uszoda)*, both in Budapest.

Horse racing *(lóverseny)* is widely organized during the season, with several meetings a week. The Budapest racecourse (track) is called *Budapesti ügető*. Bets can be placed at state-run offices (see page 88).

Sailing *(vitorlázás)* is popular on Lake Balaton and Lake Velence. Regattas and races take place on both lakes between May and October.

Table tennis *(asztalitenisz)* claims around 100,000 regular club players throughout the country, and you should not have too much difficulty in gaining access to a club's facilities during your visit.

Fencing *(vívás)* has a good number of adherents in the country. Its practitioners have made their mark in the field of international competition.

The daily sports paper *Népsport* contains details of what's on in the sporting world—including chess—throughout the country. Any local sports fan with some knowledge of English will be delighted to translate for you and help you find what you want.

Is there a football game on anywhere this Saturday?	**Most szombaton lesz valahol futballmeccs?**	mawsht **sawm**bottawn læs vollohawl **foot**bol mæch
I'd like to see a basketball match.	**Szeretnék megtekinteni egy kosárlabdamérkőzést.**	**sær**ætnayk **mæg**tækeentænee æd^{Y} **kaw**shaarlobdomayrkūrzaysht
Who's playing?	**Ki játszik?**	kee **yaat**seek
What's the admission charge?	**Mibe kerül a belépőjegy?**	**mee**bæ kærewl o **bæ**laypūr-yaed^{Y}
Can you get me 2 tickets?	**Szerezne nekem 2 jegyet?**	**sær**æznæ **næ**kæm 2 **yæd**^{Y}æt
Where's the Budapest race-course?	**Hol találom a budapesti ügetőpályát?**	hawl **tol**lawlawm o **boo**doppæshtee **ew**gætūrpaa^{Y}aat
Where are the tennis courts?	**Hol találok teniszpályát?**	hawl **tol**laalawk **tæ**neespaa^{Y}aat
Can I hire rackets?	**Bérelhetek ütőket?**	**bay**rælhætæk **ew**tūrkæt

Where can I play table tennis?	**Hol lehet ping-pongozni?**	hawl **læhæt peeng**-pawngawznee
What's the charge per ...?	**Mennyi a bérleti díj ...?**	**mæn^{y}ee** o **bayr**lætee d**e̅e̅**^{y}
day game hour	**naponta** **játszmánként** **óránként**	**no**ppawnto **yaats**maankaynt **a̅w̅**raankaynt
Is there a swimming pool near here?	**Van a környéken uszoda?**	von o **kurrn^{y}**aykæn **oo**ssawdo
Is it outdoors or indoors?	**Nyitott, vagy fedett?**	**n^{y}ee**tawt vod^{y} **fæ**dæt
Can one swim in the lake/river?	**Szabad úszni a tóban/folyóban?**	**so**bbod **o̅o̅**snee o **ta̅w̅**bon/ **faw^{y}**a̅w̅bon
Is there any good fishing around here?	**Hol lehet a környéken jól horgászni?**	hawl **læ**hæt o **kurrn^{y}**aykæn **ya̅w̅l hawr**gaasnoo
Do I need a licence?	**Kell hozzá engedély?**	kæl **hawz**-zaa **æn**gæday^{y}
Where can I get one?	**Hol lehet a horgászengedélyt beszerezni?**	hawl **læ**hæt o **hawr**gaass-ængæday^{y}t **bæ**ssæræznee

Betting

Betting on horses and soccer matches is legal and widespread. There is also a state lottery *(lottó)* every week.

The government betting authority, *Sportfogadási és Lottó Igazgatóság* maintains offices in most towns through which you can place your bets on horse races and soccer matches. They also sell lottery tickets. Forms for betting on soccer matches, as well as lottery tickets, can also be obtained from tobacconists', larger news-stands and street vendors. Winnings are paid out in local currency, after deduction of a profits tax.

Where's the nearest betting shop?	**Hol a legközelebbi fogadó iroda?**	hawl o **læg**kurzælæb-bee **faw**godda̅w̅ **ee**rawdo

On the beach

Landlocked Hungary may not have a sea coastline, but bathing, boating and sailing facilities are numerous along lake shores and river banks. The approximately 230-square-mile (600-square-kilometre) Lake Balaton is a special favourite, and its shallow waters are generally quite safe, provided normal precautions are taken. Note that power boats are not allowed on Balaton, so you'll have to go elsewhere for water-skiing (the Danube, Tisza and other rivers).

Is it safe for swimming?	**Itt biztonságos az úszás?**	eet **beez**tawnshaagawsh oz $\overline{\text{oo}}$ssaash
Is there a lifeguard?	**Mentőszolgálat van?**	**mæn**t$\overline{\text{ur}}$saawlgaalot von
Is it safe for children?	**Gyerekek részére biztonságos?**	**d^{y}**ærækæk **rayssayræ beez**tawnshaagawsh
The lake is very calm.	**A tó nagyon nyugodt.**	o t$\overline{\text{aw}}$ **nod^{y}**awn **n^{y}oo**gawdt
Are there any dangerous currents?	**Nincsenek veszélyes örvények?**	**neen**chænæk **væ**ssay^{y}æsh **urr**vayn^{y}æk

MAGÁN STRAND
PRIVATE BEACH

TILOS A FÜRDÉS
NO BATHING

What's the temperature of the water?	**Mennyi a víz hőmérséklete?**	**mæn**^{y}ee o **v$\overline{\text{ee}}$z h$\overline{\text{ur}}$**-mayrshayklætæ
I'd like to hire a/an/some...	**Szeretnék bérelni egy ....**	**sæ**rætnayk **bay**rælnee **æd^{y}**
air mattress	**gumimatracot**	**goo**meemotrotsawt
deck chair	**nyugágyat**	**n^{y}oo**gaad^{y}ot
kayak	**kajakot**	**koy**okkawt
rowing boat	**evezős csónakot**	**æ**væz$\overline{\text{ur}}$sh **ch$\overline{\text{aw}}$**nokkawt
sailing boat	**vitorláshajót**	**vee**tawrlaashhoy$\overline{\text{aw}}$t
skin-diving equipment	**búvárfelszerelést**	**b$\overline{\text{oo}}$**vaarfælsærælaysht
water skis	**vizisít**	**vee**zeesh$\overline{\text{ee}}$t
What's the charge per hour?	**Mibe kerül óránként?**	**mee**bæ **kæ**rewl **$\overline{\text{aw}}$**raankaynt

Camping—Countryside

Camping facilities are available at about 200 sites, the majority of which are clustered around Lake Balaton, South-West of Budapest. They are graded in three categories according to the amenities and services they offer. First- and second-class sites have shops, restaurants, showers, toilets and electrical outlets for campers. Tents and cabins can be rented at first-class sites.

If you wish to have the freedom of camping but a little more comfort, you can rent a holiday home sleeping from two to six people. Here you'll be able to enjoy various extra services including laundry, catering, shopping and some sports facilities. Some units have their own little gardens.

Most camping sites and holiday-home centres operate from May to October.

Foreign visitors generally find rates very advantageous, and members of internationally affiliated camping and caravaning clubs often enjoy reductions. Bills can be paid in local currency.

Lists of camping sites and holiday homes detailing facilities and rates can be obtained from local and foreign branches of Ibusz (see page 28 for addresses abroad), most hotels, the Hungarian Motoring Association *(Magyar Autóklub)* or the Hungarian Camping and Caravaning Club *(Magyar Kemping és Karaván Klub).*

Is there a camping site near here?	**Van a közelben kemping?**	von o **kurzælbæn kæmpeeng**
Have you room for a tent/caravan (trailer)?	**Van helyük egy sátor/lakókocsi részére?**	von **hæ^{y}ewk** æd^{y} **shaa-tawr/lokk$\overline{aw}$kawchee ray-ssayræ**
Where can we rent a holiday home?	**Hol bérelhetnénk egy nyaralót?**	hawl **bayrælhætnaynk** æd^{y} **n^{y}orroll$\overline{aw}$t**

CAMPING: see also page 106

May we light a fire?	**Szabad tüzet gyújtani?**	sobbod tewzæt d^{y}ōō^y-tonnee
Is this drinking water?	**Ivóvíz van?**	eevāwvēēz von
Are there any shops on the site?	**Vannak üzletek a kemping területén?**	von-nok ewzlætæk o kæmpeeng tærewlætayn
Are there any ...?	**Vannak ...?**	von-nok
baths	**fürdőszobák**	fewrdūrssawbaak
kitchens	**konyhák**	kawn^{y}haak
laundry facilities	**mosódák**	mawshāwdaak
showers	**zuhanyozók**	zoohon^{y}awzāwk
toilets	**vécék**	vaytsayk
What's the charge ...?	**Mennyibe kerül ...?**	mæn^{y}eebæ kærewl
per day	**naponta**	noppawnto
per person	**személyenként**	sæmay^{y}ænkaynt
for a car	**gépkocsinként**	gaypkawcheenkaynt
for a tent	**sátranként**	shaatronkaynt
for a caravan	**lakókocsinként**	lokkāwkawcheenkaynt
Do you known anyone who can put us up for the night?	**Ismer valakit, akinél éjszakára megszállhatunk?**	eeshmær vollokkeet okkeenayl ay^{y}ssokkaaro mægsaalhottoonk

TÁBOROZNI TILOS

NO CAMPING

TILOS LAKÓKOCSIVAL PARKIROZNI

NO CARAVANS (TRAILERS)

Landmarks

barn	**a csűr**	o chēwr
beach	**a part**	o port
bridge	**a híd**	o hēēd
brook	**a patak**	o pottok
building	**az épület**	oz aypewlæt
canal	**a csatorna**	o chottawrno
castle	**a vár**	o vaar
church	**a templom**	o tæmplawm
cliff	**a szikla**	o seeklo
cottage	**a tanya**	o ton^{y}o
crossroads	**a keresztút**	o kæræstōōt
farm	**a gazdaság**	o gozdoshaag
ferry	**a komp**	o kawmp
field	**a szántóföld**	o saantāwfurld

forest	**az erdő**	oz ærdur
fortress	**az erődítmény**	oz ærurdeetmayn^{y}
hamlet	**a kunyhó**	o **koon**^{y}haw
highway	**az országút**	oz **awr**saagoot
hill	**a domb**	o dawmb
house	**a ház**	o haaz
hut	**a menedékház**	o **mæ**nædayk-haaz
inn	**a vendéglő**	o **væn**dayglur
lake	**a tó**	o taw
marsh	**a mocsaras**	o **maw**chorrosh
moorland	**a legelő**	o **læ**gælur
mountain	**a hegy**	o hæd^{y}
path	**az ösvény**	oz **ursh**vayn^{y}
peak	**a csúcs**	o chooch
pond	**a tavacska**	o **tov**vochko
pool	**a víztároló**	o **veez**taarawlaw
railway line	**a vasúti pálya**	o **vosh**ootee **paa**^{y}o
river	**a folyó**	o **faw**^{y}aw
road	**az út**	oz oot
ruin	**a rom**	o rawm
spring	**a forrás**	o **fawr**-raash
stream	**a folyam**	o **faw**^{y}om
swamp	**a mocsár**	o **maw**chaar
tower	**a torony**	o **taw**rawn^{y}
track	**a földút**	o **furld**oot
tree	**a fa**	o fo
valley	**a völgy**	o vurld^{y}
village	**a falu**	o **fol**loo
vineyard	**a szölő**	o **sur**lur
water	**a víz**	o veez
waterfall	**a vízesés**	o **veez**æshaysh
well	**a kút**	o koot
wood	**a liget**	o **lee**gæt
What's the name of that river?	**Mi a folyó neve?**	mee o **faw**^{y}aw **næ**væ
How high is that mountain?	**Milyen magas az a hegy?**	**mee**^{y}æn **mog**gosh oz o hæd^{y}

... and if you're tired of walking, you can always try hitch-hiking *(autóstoppal utazni)*:

Can you give me a lift to ...?	**Elvinne ...-ba/-be/-ra/-re?***	**æl**veen-næ ...-bo/-bæ/-ro/-ræ

* See Grammar section for word endings.

Making friends

Introductions

A few phrases to get you started:

How do you do?	**Jónapot kívánok.**	yawnoppawt **kee**vaanawk
How are you?	**Hogy van?**	hawd^{Y} von
Fine, thank you. And you?	**Jól, köszönöm. És Ön?**	yawl **kur**surnurm. aysh urn
I'd like you to meet a friend of mine.	**Szeretném bemutatni az egyik barátomat.**	særætnaym **bæ**moototnee oz æd^{Y}eek **bor**raatawmot
May I introduce ...?	**Bemutathatom ...?**	**bæ**mootot-hotawm
John, this is ...	**John, ez ...**	dzhawn æz
My name is ...	**A nevem ...**	o nævæm
Glad to know you.	**Örülök, hogy megismerhetem.**	**ur**rewlurk hawd^{Y} **mæ**geeshmærhætæm
... sends his/her best regards.	**... szívélyesen üdvözli.**	... **see**vayl^{Y}æssæn **ewd**vurzlee
It's nice to see you (again).	**Örülök hogy (újra) találkozunk.**	**ur**rewlurk hawd^{Y}(oo^{Y}ro) **tol**laalkawzoonk

Follow-up

How long have you been here?	**Mióta van itt?**	**mee**awto von eet
We've been here a week.	**Egy hete vagyunk itt.**	æd^{Y} **hæ**tæ **vod**^{Y}oonk eet
Is this your first visit?	**Most vannak itt először?**	mawsht **von**-nok eet **æ**lurssurr
No, we came here last year.	**Nem, már tavaly is itt voltunk.**	næm maar **tov**voy eesh eet **vawl**toonk
Are you enjoying your stay?	**Jól érzik magukat?**	yawl **ayr**zeek **mog**gookot
Yes, I like ... very much.	**Igen ... nagyon tetszik.**	**ee**gæn ... **nod**^{Y}awn **tæt**seek
I like the countryside a lot.	**Nagyon szeretem a vidéket.**	**nod**^{Y}awn **sæ**rætæm o **vee**daykæt

This is a very interesting town.	**Ez nagyon érdekes város.**	æz **nod^{y}awn ayr**dækæsh **vaa**rawsh
Are you on your own?	**Egyedül van?**	æd^{y}ædewl von
I'm with ...	**... vagyok.**	... **vod^{y}**awk
my husband	**A férjemmel**	o **fay**ryæm-mæl
my wife	**A feleségemmel**	o **fæ**læshaygæm-mæl
my family	**A családommal**	o **chol**laadawm-mol
my children	**A gyerekeimmel**	o **d^{y}**æ**r**ækæeem-mæl
my parents	**A szüleimmel**	o **sew**læeem-mæl
some friends	**Néhány barátommal**	**nay**haan^{y} **bor**raatawm-mol
Where do you come from?	**Honnan jön?**	**hawn**-non yurn
Where are you staying?	**Hol lakik?**	hawl **lok**keek
I'm a student.	**Diák vagyok.**	**dee**aak **vod^{y}**awk
What are you studying?	**Mit tanul?**	meet **ton**nool
I'm here on business.	**Hivatalosan vagyok itt.**	**hee**vottollawshon **vod^{y}**awk eet
What kind of business are you in?	**Mi a foglalkozása?**	mee o **fawg**lolkawzaasho
I hope we'll meet again.	**Remélem, hamarosan.**	**ræ**maylæm **hommo**rawshon

The weather

The Hungarians love to talk about it—in fact, they like to blame most things that go wrong on the weather!

What a lovely day!	**Gyönyörű napunk van!**	**d^{y}**urn^{y}urrēw **nop**poonk von
What awful weather!	**Micsoda pocsék idő van!**	**mee**chawdo **paw**chayk **ee**dūr von
Isn't it cold/hot today!	**Nincs hideg/meleg?**	neench **hee**dæg/**mæ**læg
Do you think it will ... tomorrow?	**Mit gondol, holnap ...?**	meet **gawn**dawl **hawl**nop
clear up	**kiderül**	**kee**dærewl
rain	**esik**	**æ**sheek
snow	**havazik**	**hov**vozzeek
be sunny	**süt a nap**	shewt o nop

Invitations

My wife/My husband and I would like you to join us for dinner.	**Feleségemmel/Férjemmel együtt szeretnénk ha velünk vacsoráznának.**	fælæshaygæm-mæl/**fayr**-yæm-mæl **æd^{y}**ewt **sæ**rætnaynk ho **væ**lewnk **vo**chawraaznaanok
Can you come to dinner tonight?	**Eljönne ma este vacsorára?**	ælyurn-næ mo **æsh**tæ vochawraaro
Can you come over for a drink this evening?	**Átjönne ma este egy italra?**	**aat**yurn-næ mo **æsh**tæ **æd^{y} ee**tolro
There's a party. Are you coming?	**Összejövetelünk van. Eljön?**	**urs**-sæ^{y}urvætælewnk von. **æl**yurn
That's very kind of you.	**Nagyon kedves Öntől.**	**nod^{y}**awn **kæd**væsh **urn**-turl
Great! I'd love to come.	**Nagyszerű. Szívesen eljönnék.**	**nod^{y}**særew. **see**væshæn **æl**yurn-nayk
What time shall we come?	**Mikor jöjjünk?**	**mee**kawr **yur^{y}**-yewnk
May I bring a friend/girl friend?	**Egy barátomat/barátnőmet is elhozhatom?**	**æd^{y} bor**raatawmot/**bor**raatnurmæt eesh **æl**hawz-hottawm
I'm afraid we've got to go now.	**Azt hiszem, most már mennünk kell.**	ost **hees**sæm mawsht maar **mæn**-newnk kæl
Next time, you must come to visit us.	**Legközelebb feltétlenül látogassanak meg.**	**læg**kurzælæb **fæl**-taytlænewl **laa**taw-gosh-shonnok mæg
Thanks for the evening.	**Köszönet az estéért.**	**kur**surnæt oz **æsh**tayayrt
I/We enjoyed it very much.	**Nagyon élveztem/élveztünk.**	**nod^{y}**awn **ayl**væztæm/**ayl**væztewnk

Dating

May I get you a drink?	**Meghívhatom egy italra?**	**mæg**heevhottawm **æd^{y} ee**tolro
Would you like a cigarette?	**Parancsol egy cigarettát?**	**por**ronchawl **æd^{y} tsee**-gorræt-taat
Excuse me, could you give me a light?	**Bocsánat, van tüze?**	**baw**chaanot von **tew**zæ

Are you waiting for someone?	**Vár valakire?**	vaar vollokkeeræ
Leave me alone, please!	**Kérem, hagyjon békén!**	kayræm hod^{y}awn baykayn
Are you free this evening?	**Ráérne ma este?**	raaayrnæ mo æshtæ
I'm sorry, I already have an engagement this evening.	**Sajnálom, de ma estére már van programom.**	shoynaalawm dæ mo æshtayræ maar von prawgrommawm
Would you like to go out with me tomorrow night?	**Eljönne velem holnap este?**	ælyurn-næ vælæm hawlnop æshtæ
Would you like to go dancing?	**Lenne kedve táncolni?**	læn-næ kædvæ taan-tsawlnee
I know a good discotheque.	**Tudok egy jó diszkót.**	toodawk æd^{y} yaw dees-kawt
Do you know a good discotheque?	**Ismer egy jó diszkót?**	eeshmær æd^{y} yaw dees-kawt
Shall we go to the cinema?	**Menjünk moziba?**	mæn^{y}ewnk mawzeebo
Would you like to go for a drive?	**Van kedve autózni egyet?**	von kædvæ ootawznee æd^{y}æt
Where shall we meet?	**Hol találkozzunk?**	hawl tollaalkawz-zoonk
I'll pick you up at your hotel.	**A szállodájánál majd felveszem.**	o saal-lawdaa^{y}aanaal moyd fælvæsæm
I'll call for you at 8.	**8 órakor magáért jövök.**	8 awrok-kawr moggaa-ayrt yurvurk
May I take you home?	**Hazakisérhetem?**	hozzokkeeshayrhætæm
Can I see you again tomorrow?	**Holnap újra láthatom?**	hawlnop oo^{y}ro laat-hottawm
Thank you, it's been a very enjoyable evening.	**Köszönöm. Nagyon szép este volt.**	kursurnurm. nod^{y}awn sayp æshtæ vawlt
What's your telephone number?	**Mi a telefonszáma?**	mee o tælæfawnsaamo
What time is your last bus/train?	**Mikor indul az utolsó autóbusza/ villamosa?**	meekawr eendool oz oo-tawlshaw ootawboosso/ veel-lommawsho

Shopping guide

This shopping guide is designed to help you find what you want with ease, accuracy and speed. It features:

1. a list of all major shops, stores and services (p. 98)
2. some general expressions required when shopping to allow you to be selective and specific (p. 100)
3. full details of the shops and services most likely to concern you. Here you'll find advice, alphabetical lists of items and conversion charts, as listed under the headings below.

Shops—Stores—Services

Most shops are open from 10 a.m. to 6 p.m. (department stores from 9 a.m. to 7 p.m.), Monday–Friday, and from 9 a.m. to 2 p.m., Saturday, without a break. Some tobacconists' and most pastry shops also stay open on Sunday. Grocers' and dairy shops may start as early as 6 a.m.

Price tags in Hungarian shops show the price you actually pay. No tax is added, and discounts are not negotiable.

Intertourist shops, found in most main centres, are likely to have a wider range of goods on sale than you'll see elsewhere. Payment must be made in hard currency. Imported items such as whisky, perfumes, cigarettes and appliances will often be less expensive in these shops than at home.

Where's the nearest ...?	**Hol van a legközelebbi ...?**	hawl von o **læg**kurzælæb-bæ
antique shop	**régiség-kereskedés**	**ray**gheeshayg-kæræshkædaysh
art gallery	**képzőművészeti galéria**	**kayp**zūrmēwvaysætee **gol**layreeo
baker	**pék**	payk
barber	**borbély**	**bawr**bay^y
beauty salon	**kozmetikai szalon**	**kawz**mæteeko-ee **sol**lawn
bookshop	**könyvesbolt**	**kurn**^yvæshbawlt
butcher	**hentes**	**hæn**tæsh
camera shop	**fotószaküzlet**	**faw**tāwsokkewzlæt
candy store	**édességbolt**	aydæsh-shaygbawlt
chemist	**gyógyszertár**	**d^yāwd^y**sært aar
confectioner	**cukrászda**	**tsook**raasdo
dairy shop	**tejbolt**	**tæ^y**bawlt
delicatessen	**csemegebolt**	**chæ**mægæbawlt
department store	**áruház**	aaroohaaz
drugstore	**illatszerbolt**	**eel**-lotsærbawlt
dry-cleaner	**vegytisztító**	**væd^y**teestēetāw
fishmonger	**halkereskedés**	**hol**kæræshkædaysh
florist	**virágüzlet**	**vee**raaghewzlæt
furrier	**szőrme üzlet**	**sūr**mæ **ewz**læt
greengrocer	**zöldségesbolt**	**zurld**shaygæshbawlt
grocer	**élelmiszerbolt**	aylælmeessærbawlt
hairdresser (ladies')	**női-fodrászat**	**nūr**-ee-**fawd**raassot
hairdresser (men's)	**férfi-fodrászat**	**fayr**fee-**fawd**raassot

hardware store	**vasüzlet**	**vo**shewzlæt
Intertourist shop	**Intertourist bolt**	"intertourist" bawlt
jeweller	**ékszerész**	**ayk**særayss
laundry	**mosoda**	**maw**shawdo
liquor store	**szeszes italok**	**sæ**sæsh **ee**tollawk
market	**piac**	**pee**ots
newstand	**újságárus**	**oo^{y}**shaagaaroosh
off-licence	**szeszes italok**	**sæ**sæsh **ee**tollawk
optician	**látszerész**	**laat**særayss
pastry shop	**cukrászda**	**tsook**raasdo
pharmacy	**gyógyszertár**	**d^{y}awd^{y}**særtaar
photo shop	**fotószaküzlet**	**faw**tawsokkewzlæt
shoemaker (repairs)	**cipőjavító**	**tsee**pur-yoveetaw
shoe shop	**cipőbolt**	**tsee**purbawlt
souvenir shop	**szuvenírbolt**	**soo**væneerbawlt
sports shop	**sportszerkeres-kedés**	**shpawrt**særkæræshkæ-daysh
stationer	**papírüzlet**	**pop**peerewzlæt
supermarket	**szupermarket**	**soo**pærmaarkæt
sweet shop	**édességbolt**	**ay**dæsh-shaygbawlt
tailor	**szabó**	**sob**baw
tobacconist	**dohánybolt**	**daw**haan^{y}bawlt
toy shop	**játéküzlet**	**yaa**taykewzlæt
travel agency	**utazási iroda**	**oo**tozzaashee **ee**rawdo
vegetable store	**zöldségbolt**	**zurld**shaygbawlt
watchmaker	**órás**	**aw**raash
wine merchant	**bor szaküzlet**	bawr **sok**kewzlæt

...and some other useful addresses:

bank	**bank**	bonk
currency exchange office	**valuta beváltó hely**	**vol**looto **bæ**vaaltaw hæ^{y}
dentist	**fogorvos**	**fawg**awrvawsh
doctor	**orvos**	**awr**vawsh
filling station	**töltőállomás**	**turl**turaal-lawmaash
hospital	**kórház**	**kawr**haaz
library	**könyvtár**	**kurn^{y}**vtaar
lost property (lost-and found) office	**talált tárgyak hivatala**	**tol**laalt **taard^{y}**ok **hee**votollo
police station	**rendőrség**	**ræn**durrshayg
post office	**posta**	**pawsh**to
telegraph office	**távirda**	**taa**veerdo
tourist office	**turista ügynökség**	**too**reeshto **ewd^{y}**nurk-shayg

Where?

Where's there a good ...?	**Hol van egy jó ...?**	hawl von ædʸ yaw̄
Where can I find a ...?	**Hol találok egy ...?**	hawl **tollaalawk** ædʸ
Where can I buy ...?	**Hol kapok ...?**	hawl **koppawk**
Can you recommend an inexpensive ...?	**Ajánlana egy olcsó ...?**	**oy**aanlonno ædʸ **awlchaw̄**
Where's the main shopping area?	**Hol a bevásárlóközpont?**	hawl o **bæ**vaashaarlaw̄-**kurz**pawnt
Is it far from here?	**Messze van innen?**	**mæs**-sæ von **een**-næn
How do I get there?	**Hogy jutok el oda?**	hawdʸ **yootawk** æl **aw**do
Where's the courtesy desk?	**Hol a vevőszolgálat?**	hawl o **væ**vūrsawlgaalot

Service

Can you help me?	**Segítene?**	**shæ**gēētænæ
I'm just looking round.	**Csak nézelődök.**	chok **nay**zælūrdurk
I want ...	**Szükségem van egy ...**	**sewk**shaygæm von ædʸ
Can you show me some ...?	**Mutatna néhány ...?**	**moo**totno **nay**haanʸ
Do you have any ...?	**Kapható ...?**	**kop**hottaw̄

That one

Can you show me ...?	**Láthatnám ...?**	**laat**hotnaam
that one	**azt**	ost
those	**azokat**	**oz**zawkot
the one in the window	**azt ott a kirakatban.**	ost awt o **kee**rokkotbon
It's over there.	**Ott van.**	awt von

KIÁRUSÍTÁS SALE	**VÉGKIÁRUSÍTÁS** CLEARANCE

Defining the article

I'd like a ... one.	**...-ra/-re van szükségem.***	... -ro/-ræ von **sewk**-shaygæm
It must be ...	**...-ra/-re gondolok.***	... -ro/-ræ **gawn**dawlawk

big	**nagy**	nod^{y}
cheap	**olcsó**	**awl**ch$\overline{aw}$
dark	**sötét**	**shur**tayt
good	**jó**	y$\overline{aw}$
heavy	**nehéz**	**næ**hayz
large	**nagy**	nod^{y}
light (colour)	**világos**	**vee**laagawsh
light (weight)	**könnyű**	**kurn**$^{y}\overline{ew}$
oval	**ovális**	**aw**vaaleesh
rectangular	**négyzetes**	**nayd**^{y}zætæsh
round	**kerek**	**kæ**ræk
small	**kicsi**	**kee**chee
soft	**puha**	**poo**ho
square	**négyszögű**	**nayd**^{y}surg$\overline{ew}$

I don't want anything too expensive.	**Nem valami drága holmira gondolok.**	næm **vol**lommee **draa**go **hawl**meero **gawn**dawlawk

Preference

Haven't you anything ...?	**Nincs valami ...?**	neench **vol**lommee
better/cheaper	**jobb/olcsóbb**	yawb/**awl**ch$\overline{aw}$b
larger/smaller	**nagyobb/kisebb**	**nod**^{y}awb/**kee**shæb
Can you show me some more?	**Mutatna még másfélét is?**	**moo**totno mayg **maash**-faylayt eesh

How much?

How much is this?	**Mibe kerül?**	**mee**bæ **kæ**rewl
Please write it down.	**Kérem, írja le.**	**kay**ræm **$\overline{ee}$**ryo læ
I don't want to spend more than ...	**Nem akarok többet mint ...-t költeni.**	næm **ok**korrawk **turb**-bæt meent ...-t **kurl**tænee

* See Grammar section for word endings.

Decision

I'll take it.	**Ezt megveszem.**	æst **mæg**væsæm
No, I don't like it.	**Nem, nem tetszik.**	næm næm **tæt**seek

Ordering

Can you order it for me?	**Megrendelné a részemre?**	**mæg**grændælnay o **ray**-sæmræ
How long will it take?	**Meddig kell várni?**	**mæd**-deeg kæl **vaar**nee
I'd like it as soon as possible.	**A lehető leggyorsabban szeretném megkapni.**	o **læ**hætūr **lægd**^{y}awr-shob-bon **sæ**rætnaym **mæg**kopnee

Delivery

Please deliver it to the ... Hotel.	**Kérem, szállítsa le a ... szállodába!**	**kay**ræm **saal**-lēētsho læ o ... **saal**-lawdaabo
Please send it to this address.	**Kérem, küldje el erre a címre!**	**kay**ræm **kewld**^{y}æ æl **ær**-ræ o **tsēē**mræ
Will I have any difficulty with the customs?	**Nem lesz problémám a vámnál?**	næm læs **prawb**laymaam o **vaam**naal

Paying

How much is it?	**Mibe kerül?**	**mee**bæ **kæ**rewl
Can I pay with traveller's cheques?	**Fizethetek traveller's csekkel?**	**fee**zæt-hætæk **tro**vvæl-lærs **chæk**-kæl
Do you accept credit cards?	**Hitelkártyát elfogadnak?**	**hee**tælkaart^{y}at **æl**-fawgodnok
Do you accept ...?	**Elfogadnak ...?**	**æl**fawgodnok
U.S. dollars	**amerikai dollárt**	**om**mæreeko-ee **dawl**-laart
Canadian dollars	**kanadai dollárt**	**kon**noddo-ee **dawl**-laart
pounds sterling	**angol fontot**	**on**gawl **fawn**tawt
Can I please have a receipt?	**Kaphatok egy elismervényt?**	**kop**hottawk **æd**^{y} **æ**leesh-mærvayn^{y}t
Haven't you made a mistake in the bill?	**Nem állította tévesen össze a számlát?**	næm **aal**-lēētawt-to **tay**væ-shæn **urs**-sæ o **saam**laat
Will you please wrap it?	**Becsomagolva kéri?**	**bæ**chawmoggawlvo **kay**ree

CHANGING MONEY: see page 135

Anything else?

No thanks, that's all.	**Nem, köszönöm. Ez minden.**	næm **kur**surnurm. æz **meen**dæn
Yes, please show me ...	**Igen, kérem mutassa meg nekem a ...**	**ee**gæn **kay**ræm **moo**tosh-sho mæg **næ**kæm o
Could I have a carrier bag, please?	**Kérnék egy szatyrot.**	**kayr**nayk æd^y **sot^y**rawt
Thank you.	**Köszönöm.**	**kur**surnurm
Goodbye.	**Viszontlátásra.**	**vee**ssawntlaataashro

Segíthetek ...?	Can I help you?
Mit parancsol?	What are you looking for?
Milyen ... parancsol?	What ... would you like?
színt/fazont minőséget/mennyiséget	colour/shape quality/quantity
Sajnálom, ilyent nem tartunk.	I'm sorry, we haven't any.
Elfogyott.	We're out of stock.
Megrendeljük az Ön részére?	Shall we order it for you?
Összesen ... forintba kerül kérem.	That's ... forints, please.
A pénztár ott van.	You pay over there.
Hitelkártyát/Traveller's csekket nem fogadunk el.	We don't accept credit cards/ traveller's cheques.

Dissatisfied

Can you please exchange this?	**Kicserélné ezt?**	**kee**chæraylnay æst
I want to return this.	**Ezt vissza akarom váltani.**	æst **vees**-so **ok**korrawm **vaal**tonnee
I'd like a refund.	**Kérem a vételár visszatérítését.**	**kay**ræm o **vay**tælaar **vees**-sottayrēētayshayt
Here's the receipt.	**Itt az elismervény.**	eet oz **æ**leeshmærvayn^y

Bookshop—Stationer's—Newsstand

In Hungary, books and stationery items are usually sold in separate shops. Newspapers and magazines are sold at newsstands and at post offices. Western dailies and newsmagazines are available at major hotels and some kiosks in the capital.

Where's the nearest ...?	**Hol a legközelebbi ...?**	hawl o **læg**kurzælæb-bee
bookshop	**könyvesbolt**	**kurn**^{y}væshbawlt
newsstand	**újságáruda**	oo^{y}shaagaaroodo
stationer's	**papír és írószer-kereskedés**	**pop**peer aysh **ee**rawssær-kæræshkædaysh
Where can I buy an English-language newspaper?	**Hol kapok angol-nyelvű újságot?**	hawl **kop**pawk **on**gawl-n^{y}ælvew oo^{y}shaagawt
I'd like a/an/some ...	**Kérnék ...**	**kayr**nayk
address book	**egy címregisztert**	aed^{y} **tseem**rægheestært
ballpoint pen	**egy golyóstollat**	æd^{y} **gaw**^{y}awshtawl-lot
book	**egy könyvet**	æd^{y} **kurn**^{y}væt
box of paints	**egy doboz festéket**	æd^{y} **daw**bawz **fæsh**taykæt
carbon paper	**másolópapírt**	**maa**shawlawpoppeert
cellophane tape	**ragasztó szalagot**	**rog**gostaw **sol**loggawt
crayons	**krétát**	**kray**taat
dictionary	**egy szótárt**	æd^{y} **saw**taart
English-Hungarian	**angol-magyar**	**on**gawl-**mod**^{y}or
pocket dictionary	**zsebszótárt**	**zhæb**sawtaart
drawing paper	**rajzpapírt**	**royz**poppeert
drawing pins	**rajzszeget**	**royz**sægæt
envelopes	**néhány borítékot**	**nay**haan^{y} **baw**reetaykawt
eraser	**radírt**	**rod**deert
exercise book	**egy füzetet**	æd^{y} **few**zætæt
fountain pen	**egy töltőtollat**	æd^{y} **turl**turtawl-lot
glue	**ragasztót**	**rog**gostawt
grammar book	**egy tankönyvet**	æd^{y} **ton**kurn^{y}væt
guide book	**egy útikalauzt**	æd^{y} **oo**teekollo-oozt
ink	**tintát**	**teen**taat
black/blue/red	**fekete/kék/piros**	**fæ**kætæ/kayk/**pee**rawsh
magazine	**egy képes folyóiratot**	æd^{y} **kay**pæsh **faw**^{y}aweerottawt
map	**egy térképet**	æd^{y} **tayr**kaypæt
of the town	**egy várostérképet**	æd^{y} **vaa**rawshtayrkaypæt
road map	**egy térképet**	æd^{y} **tayr**kaypæt

newspaper	**egy ... újságot**	æd^{y} ... ōō^{y}shaagawt
American	**amerikai**	ommæreeko-ee
English	**angol**	ongawl
notebook	**egy jegyzetfüzetet**	æd^{y} yæd^{y}zætfewzætæt
note paper	**jegyzetpapírt**	yæd^{y}zætpoppēērt
paperback	**egy zsebkönyvet**	æd^{y} zhæbkurn^{y}væt
paper napkins	**csomagolópapírt**	chawmoggāw̄lawpoppēērt
paste	**ragasztót**	roggostāw̄t
pen	**egy tollat**	æd^{y} tawl-lot
pencil	**egy ceruzát**	æd^{y} tsæroozaat
pencil sharpener	**egy ceruza-hegyezőt**	æd^{y} tsæroozohæd^{y}æzūrt
picture book	**egy képeskönyvet**	æd^{y} kaypæshkurn^{y}væt
playing cards	**kártyát**	kaart^{y}aat
postcards	**levelező-lapokat**	lævælæzūr-loppawkot
rubber	**radírt**	roddēērt
ruler	**egy vonalzót**	æd^{y} vawnolzāw̄t
sketchpad	**egy vázlatfüzetet**	æd^{y} vaazlotfewzætæt
string	**zsineget**	zheenægæt
thumbtacks	**rajzszeget**	royzsægæt
tissue paper	**selyempapírt**	shæ^{y}æmpoppēērt
typewriter ribbon	**írógépszalagot**	ēērāw̄gaypsolloggawt
typing paper	**gépíró-papírt**	gaypēērāw̄-poppēērt
wrapping paper	**papír szalvétákat**	poppēēr solvaytaakot
writing pad	**egy jegyzettömböt**	æd^{y} yæd^{y}zæt-turmburt
Where's the guide-book section?	**Hol találom az útikalauzrészleget?**	hawl tollaalawm oz ooteekollo-oozrayslægæt
Where do you keep the English books?	**Hol tartják az angolnyelvű könyveket?**	hawl tort^{y}aak oz ongawl-n^{y}ælvēw̄ kurn^{y}vækæt
Have you any of ...'s books in English?	**Angol nyelven megvan ... valamelyik műve?**	ongawl n^{y}ælvæn mæg-von ... vollommæ^{y}eek mēw̄væ

Here are some Hungarian authors whose books are available in English translation. In accordance with Hungarian usage, we have given the writer's surname first.

Arany János
Jókai Mór
József Attila
Mikszáth Kálman
Petőfi Sándor
Rejtő Jenő*

*In English translation, Rejto's works are published under the name P. Howard.

Camping

Here we're concerned with items of equipment you may need.

I'd like a/an/ some ...	**Szeretnék ...**	særætnayk
bottle opener	**egy üvegnyítót**	æd^{y} ewvaegn^{y}eetawt
bucket	**egy vödröt**	æd^{y} vurdrurt
camp bed	**egy tábori ágyat**	æd^{y} taabawree aad^{y}ot
can opener	**egy konzervnyitót**	æd^{y} kawnzærn^{y}eetawt
candles	**gyertyákat**	d^{y}ært^{y}aakot
chair	**egy széket**	æd^{y} saykæt
folding chair	**egy összecsukható széket**	æd^{y} urs-sæchook-hottaw saykæt
clothes-pegs	**ruhaakasztó csipeszeket**	rooho-okkostaw cheepæsækæt
corkscrew	**egy dugóhúzót**	æd^{y} doogawhoozawt
crockery	**edényeket**	ædayn^{y}ækæt
cutlery	**evőeszközöket**	ævuræskurzurkæt
deck chair	**egy nyugágyat**	æd^{y} n^{y}oogaad^{y}ot
first-aid kit	**egy elsősegély-dobozt**	æd^{y} ælshurshægay^{y}-dawbawzt
fishing tackle	**egy horgász-felszerelést**	æd^{y} hawrgaasfælsæræ-laysht
flashlight	**egy zseblámpát**	æd^{y} zhæblaampaat
frying pan	**egy tepsit**	æd^{y} tæpsheet
groundsheet	**egy pokrócot**	æd^{y} pawkrawtsawt
hammer	**egy kalapácsot**	æd^{y} kolloppaachawt
hammock	**egy függőágyat**	æd^{y} fewg-guraad^{y}ot
ice-bag	**egy hűtőtáskát**	æd^{y} hewturtaashkaat
kerosene	**petróleumot**	pætrawlæoomawt
kettle	**egy fazekat**	æd^{y} fozzækot
lamp	**lámpát**	laampaat
lantern	**egy lámpást**	æd^{y} laampaasht
matches	**gyufát**	d^{y}oofaat
mattress	**egy matracot**	æd^{y} motrotsawt
air mattress	**egy gumimatracot**	æd^{y} goomeemotrotsawt
methylated spirits	**főzőspirituszt**	furzurshpeereetoost
nails	**szeget**	sægæt
pail	**egy vödröt**	æd^{y} vurdrurt
paraffin	**petróleumot**	pætrawlæoomawt
penknife	**egy zsebkést**	æd^{y} zhæbkaysht
picnic case	**egy kiránduló táskát**	æd^{y} keeraandoolaw taashkaat
plastic bags	**nájlonszatyrot**	næ^{y}lawnsot^{y}rawt

CAMPING: see also page 90

pot	**egy fazekat**	æd^y **fozzækot**
pressure cooker	**egy kuktát**	æd^y **kooktaat**
rope	**kötelet**	**kurtælæt**
rucksack	**egy hátizsákot**	æd^y **haateezhaakawt**
saucepan	**egy nyeles serpenyőt**	æd^y **n^yælæsh shær-pæn^yūrt**
scissors	**egy ollót**	æd^y **awl-lāwt**
screwdriver	**egy dugóhúzót**	æd^y **doogāwhōōzāwt**
sheath knife	**egy tőrt**	æd^y **tūrrt**
sleeping bag	**egy hálózsákot**	æd^y **haalāwzhaakawt**
stewpan	**egy serpenyőt**	æd^y **shærpæn^yūrt**
stove	**egy kályhát**	æd^y **kaa^yhaat**
string	**zsineget**	**zheenægæt**
table	**egy asztalt**	æd^y **ostolt**
folding table	**egy összecsukható asztalt**	æd^y **urs-sæchook-hottāw ostolt**
tent	**egy sátrat**	æd^y **shaatrot**
tent pegs	**sátorcölöpöket**	**shaatawrtsurlurpurkæt**
tent pole	**egy sátorrudat**	æd^y **shaatawr-roodot**
tin opener	**egy konzervnyitót**	æd^y **kawnzærvn^yeetāwt**
tongs	**egy fogót/egy csipeszt**	æd^y **fawgāwt/æd^y chee-pæst**
tool kit	**egy szerszámosládát**	æd^y **særsaamawshlaadaat**
torch	**egy zseblámpát**	æd^y **zhæblaampaat**
vacuum flask (bottle)	**egy hőpalackot**	æd^y **hūrpollotskawt**
water carrier	**egy vizhordót**	æd^y **veezhawrdāwt**
wood alcohol	**faszeszt**	**fossæst**

Crockery

cups	**csészék**	**chayssayk**
mugs	**bögrék**	**burgrayk**
plates	**tányérok**	**taan^yayrawk**
saucers	**csészealjak**	**chayssæolyok**

Cutlery

forks	**villák**	**veel-laak**
knives	**kések**	**kayshæk**
spoons	**kanalak**	**konnollok**
teaspoons	**teáskanalak**	**tæaashkonnollok**
(made of) plastic	**műanyag ...**	**mēwon^yog**
(made of) stainless steel	**rozsdamentes acél ...**	**rawzhdommæntæsh otsayl**

Chemist's—Drugstore

In Hungarian, the name for a chemist's shop, or drugstore, is *patika* (**po**tteeko) or *gyógyszertár* (**d$^{y}\overline{aw}$d^{y}**særtaar). Their range of wares is restricted to pharmaceutical and related products—they do not sell the wide range of goods found in most British or American pharmacies.

Outside normal hours, pharmacies open on a rota basis—in larger centres there will always be at least one on night and weekend duty. An illuminated sign in each pharmacy window tells you where you can get service after hours.

For cosmetics and toiletries, go to an *illatszerbolt* (**eel**lotsærbawlt), and for photo supplies, to a *fotószaküzlet* (**faw**t$\overline{aw}$sokewzlæt).

This section is divided into two parts:

1 Medicine, first aid, etc.
2 Toilet articles, cosmetics, etc.

General

Where's the nearest (all-night) chemist's?	**Hol a legközelebbi (éjjel-nappali) patika?**	hawl o **læg**kurzælæb-bee (**ay**^{y}-yæl-**nop**-pawlee) **po**tteeko
What time does the chemist's open/ close?	**Mikor nyit/zár a patika?**	**mee**kawr n^{y}eet/zaar o **po**tteeko

1 Medicines—First aid

I want something for...	**Kérek valami gyógyszert ... ellen.**	**kay**ræk **vo**llommee d$^{y}\overline{aw}$d^{y}sært ... **æl**-læn
a cold	**megfázás**	**mæg**faazaash
a cough	**köhögés**	**kur**hurgaysh
a hangover	**másnaposság**	**maash**noppawsh-shaag
hay fever	**szénanátha**	**say**nonnaat-ho
insect bites	**rovarcsípés**	**raw**vorch$\overline{ee}$paysh
sunburn	**napszúrás**	**nop**s$\overline{oo}$raash
travel sickness	**utazási rosszullét**	**oo**tozzaashee **raws**-sool-layt
an upset stomach	**gyomorrontás**	**d^{y}aw**mawr-rawntaash

DOCTOR: see page 162

Can I get it without a prescription?	**Ezt recept nélkül is megkaphatom?**	æst **ræt**sæpt **nayl**kewl eesh **mæg**kop-hottawm
Shall I wait?	**Várjak?**	**vaar**yok
I'd like a/an/some ...	**Kérnék ...**	**kayr**nayk
adhesive plaster	**sebtapaszt**	**shæb**toppost
antiseptic ointment	**fertőtlenítő kenőcsöt**	**fær**turtlæneetur **kæ**nurchurt
aspirins	**aszpirint**	**os**peereent
bandage	**kötszert**	**kurt**sært
calcium tablets	**mésztablettát**	**mays**toblæt-taat
clinical thermometer	**egy hőmérőt**	æd^{y} **hur**mayrurt
contraceptives	**fogamzásgátlót**	**faw**gomzaashgaatlawt
corn pads	**tyúkszemírtót**	**t^{y}ook**sæmeertawt
cotton wool	**vattát**	**vot**-taat
cough drops	**köhögés elleni cseppeket**	**kur**hurgaysh **æl**-lænee **chæp**-pækæt
disinfectant	**fertőtlenítőt**	**fær**turtlæneeturt
ear drops	**fülcseppeket**	**fewl**chæp-pækæt
ear plugs	**füldugót**	**fewl**doogawt
eye drops	**szemcseppeket**	**sæm**chæp-pækæt
first-aid kit	**egy elsősegélycsomagot**	æd^{y} **æl**shurshægay^{y}-**chaw**moggawt
gauze	**gézt**	gayzt
insect repellent	**rovarírtót**	**raw**vorreertawt
iodine	**jódot**	**yaw**dawt
laxative	**hashajtót**	**hosh**hoytawt
nose drops	**orrcseppeket**	**awr**chæp-pækæt
painkiller	**fájdalomcsillapítót**	**faa^{y}**dollawmcheel-loppeetawt
sanitary towels	**egészségügyi vattát**	ægayss-shayghews^{y}ee **vot**-taat
sleeping pills	**altatót**	**ol**tottawt
stomach pills	**gyomorfájás elleni tablettákat**	**d^{y}aw**mawrfaa^{y}aash **æl**-lænee **tob**læt-taakot
tampons	**tampont**	**tom**pawnt
throat lozenges	**toroköblítő tablettát**	**taw**rawkurbleetur **tob**-læt-taat
tranquillizers	**nyugtatót**	**n^{y}oog**tottawt
vitamin pills	**vitamin tablettákat**	**vee**tommeen **tob**læt-taakot

MÉREG!
POISON!

CSAK KÜLSŐLEG!
DO NOT SWALLOW!

2 Toilet articles—Cosmetics

I'd like a/an/ some ...	**Kérnék ...**	**kayr**nayk
acne cream	**egy pattanás elleni krémet**	æd^y **pot**-tonnaash **æl**-lænee **kray**mæt
after-shave lotion	**egy borotva kölnit**	æd^y **baw**rawtvo **kurl**neet
astringent	**egy borotvatapasz-timsót**	æd^y **baw**rawtvotoppos-teemshawt
bath essence	**egy fürdősampont**	æd^y **fewr**durshompawnt
bath salts	**fürdősót**	**fewr**durshawt
cologne	**egy kölnit**	æd^y **kurl**neet
cream	**egy krémet**	æd^y **kray**mæt
for dry/normal/ greasy skin	**száraz/normál/ zsíros bőrre**	**saa**roz/**nawr**maal/ **zhee**rawsh **burr**-ræ
cleansing cream	**egy tisztító krémet**	æd^y **tees**teetaw **kray**mæt
cuticle cream	**egy bőrkrémet**	æd^y **burr**kraymæt
foot cream	**egy lábkrémet**	æd^y **laab**kraymæt
foundation cream	**egy alapozó krémet**	æd^y **ol**loppawzaw **kray**mæt
hand cream	**egy kézkrémet**	æd^y **kayz**kraymæt
moisturizing cream	**egy nedvesítő krémet**	æd^y **næd**væsheetur **kray**mæt
night cream	**egy éjjeli krémet**	æd^y **ay**^{y}-yælee **kray**mæt
cuticle remover	**egy bőreltávolítót**	æd^y **burr**æltaavawleetawt
deodorant	**egy dezodort**	æd^y **dæ**zawdawrt
emery board	**egy anyósnyelvet**	æd^y **on**^{y}awshn^{y}ælvæt
eyeliner	**egy szemkihúzót**	æd^y **sæm**keehoozawt
eye pencil	**egy szemöldök-ceruzát**	æd^y **sæm**urldurktsæroozaat
eye shadow	**egy szemkifestőt**	æd^y **sæm**keefæshturt
face pack	**egy arcpakolást**	æd^y **orts**pokkawlaasht
face powder	**egy arcpúdert**	æd^y **orts**poodært
foot powder	**egy lábpúdert**	æd^y **laab**poodært
lipsalve	**egy ajakkrémet**	æd^y oyok-kraymæt
lipstick	**egy rúzst**	æd^y roozht
make-up kit	**egy make-up dobozt**	æd^y "make-up" **daw**bawzt
make-up	**make-up eltávolítót**	"make-up" **æl**taavaw-leetawt
make-up remover pads	**make-up eltávolító tamponokat**	"make-up" **æl**taavawleetaw **tom**pawnawkot
mascara	**egy maszkarát**	æd^y **mos**korraat
nail brush	**egy körömkefét**	æd^y **kur**rurmkæfayt
nail clippers	**egy körömvágót**	æd^y **kur**rurmvaagawt
nail file	**egy körömreszelőt**	æd^y **kur**rurmræsælurt

nail polish	**körömlakkot**	**kur**rurmlok-kawt
nail-polish remover	**körömlakk lemosót**	**kur**rurmlok **læ**mawshawt
nail scissors	**egy körömollót**	æd^{y} **kur**rurmawl-lawt
paper handkerchiefs	**papírzsebkendőt**	**pop**peerzhæbkændurt
perfume	**kölnit**	**kurl**neet
powder	**púdert**	**poo**dært
razor	**egy borotvát**	æd^{y} **baw**rawtvaat
razorblades	**borotvapengéket**	**baw**rawtvoppængaykæt
rouge	**egy rúzst**	æd^{y} roozht
shaving brush	**egy borotvaecsetet**	æd^{y} **baw**rawtvoæchætæt
shaving cream	**egy borotvakrémet**	æd^{y} **baw**rawtvokraymæt
shaving soap	**egy borotvaszap-pant**	æd^{y} **baw**rawtvossop-pont
soap	**egy szappant**	æd^{y} **sop**-pont
sun-tan cream	**egy napozókrémet**	æd^{y} **nop**pawzawkraymæt
sun-tan oil	**egy napolajat**	æd^{y} **nop**pawloyot
talcum powder	**egy hintőport**	ædy **heen**turpawrt
toilet paper	**w.c. papírt**	**way**tsay **pop**peert
toothbrush	**egy fogkefét**	æd^{y} **fawg**kæfayt
toothpaste	**egy fogkrémet**	æd^{y} **fawg**kraymæt
tweezers	**egy csipeszt**	æd^{y} **chee**pæst

For your hair

bobby pins	**hullámcsattokat**	**hool**-laamchot-tawkot
comb	**egy fésűt**	æd^{y} **fay**shewt
curlers	**hajcsavarokat**	**hoy**chovvorrawkot
dye	**hajfestéket**	**hoy**fæshtaykæt
hair brush	**egy hajkefét**	æd^{y} **hoy**kæfayt
hair pins	**hajtűket**	**hoy**tewkæt
lacquer	**egy hajlakkot**	æd^{y} **hoy**lok-kawt
oil	**egy brilantint**	æd^{y} **bree**lonteent
setting lotion	**hajlakkot**	**hoy**lok-kawt
shampoo	**egy sampont**	æd^{y} **shom**pawnt
for dry/greasy hair	**száraz/zsíros hajra**	**saa**roz/**zhee**rawsh **hoy**ro
for dandruff	**korpásodás ellen**	**kawr**paashawdaash **æl**-læn

For the baby

baby food	**bébi eledelt**	**bay**bee **æ**lædælt
bib	**egy előkét**	æd^{y} **æ**lurkayt
dummy (comforter)	**egy cumit**	æd^{y} **tsoo**meet
feeding bottle	**egy cumis üveget**	æd^{y} **tsoo**meesh **ew**vægæt
nappies (diapers)	**pelenkákat**	**pæ**lænkaakot
rubber teat	**egy cumit üvegre**	æd^{y} **tsoo**meet **ew**vægræ

Clothing

If you want to buy something specific, prepare yourself in advance. Look at the list of clothing on page 116. Get some idea of the colour, material and size you want. They're listed on the next few pages.

General

I'd like ... for a 10-year-old boy.	**Egy ...-t kérek 10 éves fiú részére.**	æd^{y} ...-t **kay**ræk 10 ayvæsh **fee**o͞o **ray**ssayræ
It's for a 6-year-old girl.	**Egy 6 éves leány részére lesz.**	æd^{y} 6 **ay**væsh **læ**aan^{y} **ray**ssayræ læs
I want something like this.	**Valami ilyet kérek.**	**vo**llommee **ee**^{y}æt **kay**ræk
I like the one in the window.	**Az tetszik, ami a kirakatban van.**	oz **tæ**tseek **o**mmee o **kee**rokkotbon von
How much is that per metre?	**Mibe kerül métere?**	**mee**bæ **kæ**rewl **may**tæræ

1 centimetre = 0.39 in.	1 in. = 2.54 cm
1 metre = 39.37 in.	1 ft. = 30.5 cm
10 metres = 32.81 ft.	1 yd. = 0.91 m

Colour

Do you have something in ...?	**Van ... színűben?**	von ... **se͞e**ne͞wbæn
I'd like something lighter/darker.	**Valami sötétebbet/ világosabbat szeretnék.**	**vo**llommee **shur**taytæb-bæt/ **vee**laagawshob-bot **sæ**rætnayk
I want something to match this.	**Valami ehhez illőt keresek.**	**vo**llommee **æh**-hæz **eel**-lu͞rt **kæ**ræshæk
I don't like the colour.	**A színe nem tetszik.**	o **se͞e**næ næm **tæt**seek

beige	**drapp**	drop
black	**fekete**	fækætæ
blue	**kék**	kayk
navy blue	**tengerkék**	**tæn**gærkayk
sky blue	**égszínkék**	**ayg**seenkayk
brown	**barna**	**bor**no
dark brown	**sötétbarna**	**shur**taytborno
light brown	**világosbarna**	**vee**laagawshborno
golden	**arany**	**o**ron^y
green	**zöld**	zurld
bottle green	**palackzöld**	**po**llotskzurld
lime green	**citromzöld**	**tseet**rawmzurld
olive green	**olivazöld**	**aw**leevozzurld
grey	**szürke**	**sewr**kæ
lilac	**lila**	**lee**lo
orange	**narancssárga**	**no**rronchshaargo
pink	**rózsaszín**	**raw**zhosseen
red	**vörös**	**vur**rursh
crimson	**karmazsinvörös**	**kor**mozheenvurrursh
purple	**bíbor**	**bee**bawr
scarlet	**skarlátvörös**	**shkor**laatvurrursh
silver	**ezüst**	æzewsht
turquoise	**türkiz**	**tewr**keez
violet	**ibolyakék**	**ee**baw^{y}okkayk
white	**fehér**	fæhayr
yellow	**sárga**	**shaar**go
golden yellow	**aranysárga**	**o**rron^{y}shaargo
lemon	**citromsárga**	**tseet**rawmshaargo
light ...	**világos ...**	**vee**laagawsh
dark ...	**sötét ...**	**shur**tayt

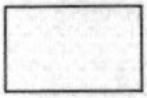
sima (**shee**mo)

csíkos (**chee**kawsh)

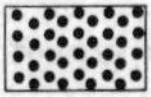
pöttyös (**purt^y**ursh)

kockás (**kawts**kaash)

mintás (**meen**taash)

Material

Have you anything in ... ?	**... anyaguk van?**	... **on^y**oggook von
Do you have any better quality?	**Valami jobb minőségü árújuk nincs?**	**vo**llommee yawb **mee**nurshaygew **aa**roo^{y}ook neench

I'd like a cotton blouse.	**Egy pamutblúzt keresek.**	æd^{y} **pom**mootbloozt **kæ**ræshæk
Is that ...?	**Az ...?**	oz
handmade	**kéziszöyésű**	**kay**zeessurvayshew
imported	**importált**	**eem**pawrtaalt
made here	**belföldi gyártású**	**bæl**furldee **d^{y}aar**taashoo
What's it made of?	**Miből van?**	**mee**burl von

cambric	**batiszt**	**bot**teest
camelhair	**teveszőr**	**tæ**væssurr
chiffon	**sifon**	**shee**fawn
corduroy	**kordbársony**	**kawrd**baarshawn^{y}
cotton	**pamut**	**pom**moot
felt	**filc**	feelts
flannel	**flanel**	**flon**næl
gabardine	**gabardin**	**gob**bordeen
lace	**csipke**	**cheep**kæ
leather	**bőr**	burr
linen	**vászon**	**vaa**ssawn
rayon	**műselyem**	**mew**shæ^{y}æm
rubber	**gumi**	**goo**mee
quilting	**tűzdelt**	**tew**zdælt
satin	**szatén**	**sot**tayn
silk	**selyem**	**shæ**^{y}æm
suede	**antilop**	**on**teelawp
taffeta	**taft**	toft
terrycloth	**frotír**	**fraw**teer
tulle	**tüll**	tewl
velvet	**bársony**	**baa**rshawn^{y}
velveteen	**gyapjúbársony**	**d^{y}op**yoobaarshawn^{y}
wool	**gyapjú**	**d^{y}op**yoo
worsted	**kamgarn-szövet**	**kom**gorn-survæt

Is it ...?	**Ez ...?**	æz
colourfast	**színtartó**	**seen**tortaw
crease-proof	**gyűrődésmentes**	**d^{y}ew**rurdayshmæntæsh
easy-care	**tiszta könnyen kezelhető**	**tees**to **kurn**^{y}æn **kæ**zælhætur
pure cotton	**tiszta pamut**	**tees**to **pom**moot
shrink-resistant	**méret tartó**	**may**ræt **tor**taw
synthetic	**műanyag**	**mew**on^{y}og
wash-and-wear	**nem kell vasalni**	næm kæl **vo**sholnee

Sizes

In Europe, sizes vary somewhat from country to country, and even within one country, so these charts must be taken as an approximate guide only.

Ladies

	Dresses/Suits						
American	8	10	12	14	16	18	20
British	30	32	34	36	38	40	42
Continental	36	38	40	42	44	46	48

	Stockings					
American / British	8	8½	9	9½	10	10½
Continental	0	1	2	3	4	5

	Shoes			
American	6	7	8	9
British	4½	5½	6½	7½
Continental	37	38	40	41

Gentlemen

	Suits/Overcoats					
American / British	36	38	40	42	44	46
Continental	46	48	50	52	54	56

	Shirts			
American / British	15	16	17	18
Continental	38	41	43	45

	Shoes								
American / British	5	6	7	8	8½	9	9½	10	11
Continental	38	39	41	42	43	43	44	44	45

A good fit?

I take size 38.	**38-ast kérek.**	38-osht **kay**ræk
May I try it on?	**Felpróbálhatom?**	**fæl**prawbaalhottawm
It fits very well.	**Nagyon jól áll.**	**nod**^{y}awn **yawl** aal
It's too ...	**Túl ...**	tool
short/long tight/loose	**rövid/hosszú** **feszes/bő**	rurveed/**haws**-soo fæsæsh/bur
How long will it take to alter?	**Meddig tart az átalakítása?**	**mæd**-deeg tort oz **aat**-ollokkeetaasho

Clothes and accessories

I'd like a/an/some ...	**Szeretnék ...**	særætnayk
anorak	**egy anorákot**	æd^{y} onnawraakawt
bath robe	**egy fürdőköpenyt**	æd^{y} fewrdurkurpæn^{y}t
blazer	**egy blézert**	æd^{y} blayzært
blouse	**egy blúzt**	æd^{y} bloozt
bra	**egy melltartót**	æd^{y} mæltortawt
braces	**egy nadrágtartót**	æd^{y} nodraagtortawt
briefs	**egy rövid alsónadrágot**	æd^{y} rurveed olshaw-nodraagawt
cap	**egy sapkát**	æd^{y} shopkaat
cardigan	**egy kardigánt**	æd^{y} kordeegaant
coat	**egy kabátot**	æd^{y} kobbaatawt
dress	**egy ruhát**	æd^{y} roohaat
dressing gown	**egy pongyolát**	æd^{y} pawnd^{y}awlaat
evening gown	**egy estélyi ruhát**	æd^{y} æshtay^{y}ee roohaat
frock	**egy öltönyt**	æd^{y} urlturn^{y}t
fur coat	**egy szőrmekabátot**	æd^{y} surrmækobbaatawt
gloves	**egy pár kesztyűt**	æd^{y} paar kæst^{y}ewt
handkerchief	**egy zsebkendőt**	æd^{y} zhæbkændurt
hat	**egy kalapot**	æd^{y} kolloppawt
house coat	**egy házikabátot**	æd^{y} haazeekobbaatawt
jacket	**egy zakót**	æd^{y} zokkawt
jeans	**egy farmernadrágot**	æd^{y} formærnodraagawt
jersey	**egy kötöttkabátot**	æd^{y} kurturtkobbaatawt
jumper	**egy pulóvert**	æd^{y} poolawvært
leather trousers	**egy bőrnadrágot**	æd^{y} burrnodraagawt
lingerie	**valami alsónemüt**	vollommee olshawnæmewt
mackintosh	**egy esőkabátot**	æd^{y} æshurkobbaatawt
nightdress	**egy hálóinget**	æd^{y} haalaweengæt
overcoat	**egy felöltőt**	æd^{y} fælurlturt
panties	**egy harisnyanadrágot**	æd^{y} horreeshn^{y}o-nodraagawt
pants	**egy nadrágot**	æd^{y} nodraagawt
pants suit	**egy nadrágkosztümöt**	æd^{y} nodraagkawstewmurt
pantyhose	**egy harisnyanadrágot**	æd^{y} horreeshn^{y}o-nodraagawt
pullover	**egy pulóvert**	æd^{y} poolawvært
pyjamas	**egy pizsamát**	æd^{y} peezhommaat
raincoat	**egy esőkabátot**	æd^{y} æshurkobbaatawt
scarf	**egy sálat**	æd^{y} shaalot
shirt	**egy inget**	æd^{y} eengæt
shorts	**egy sortot**	æd^{y} shawrtawt
skirt	**egy szoknyát**	æd^{y} sawkn^{y}aat

slip	**egy alsószoknyát**	æd^{y} **olshawsawkn^{y}aat**
socks	**egy pár zoknit**	æd^{y} paar **zawkneet**
sports jacket	**egy sportkabátot**	æd^{y} **shpawrt**kobbaatawt
stockings	**egy pár harisnyát**	æd^{y} paar **horreeshn^{y}aat**
suit (man's)	**egy férfiöltönyt**	æd^{y} **fayr**feeurlturn^{y}t
suit (woman's)	**egy női ruhát**	æd^{y} **nur**-ee **roohaat**
suspenders (Am.)	**egy nadrágtartót**	æd^{y} **nodraagtortawt**
sweater	**egy pulóvert**	æd^{y} **poolaw**vært
swimsuit	**egy fürdőruhát**	æd^{y} **fewrdur**roohaat
tie	**egy nyakkendőt**	æd^{y} **n^{y}ok**-kændurt
tights	**egy harisnya-nadrágot**	æd^{y} **horreeshn^{y}o**-nodraagawt
topcoat	**egy nagykabátot**	æd^{y} **nod^{y}**kobbaatawt
track suit	**egy tréningruhát**	æd^{y} **trayneengroohaat**
trousers	**egy nadrágot**	æd^{y} **nodraagawt**
T-shirt	**egy atléta trikót**	æd^{y} **otlayto treekawt**
undershirt	**egy trikót**	æd^{y} **treekawt**
vest (Am.)	**egy mellényt**	æd^{y} **mæl**-layn^{y}t
vest (Br.)	**egy trikót**	æd^{y} **treekawt**
waistcoat	**egy mellényt**	æd^{y} **mæl**-layn^{y}t

belt	**öv**	urv
buckle	**csatt**	chot
button	**gomb**	gawmb
collar	**gallér**	**gol**-layr
elastic	**gumi**	**goo**mee
pocket	**zseb**	zhæb
press-stud	**patentgomb**	**pot**tæntgawmb
safety pin	**biztosítótű**	**beez**tawsheetawtew
zip (zipper)	**cipzár**	**tseep**zaar

And for those handy with the needle:

crochet hook	**horgolótű**	**hawr**gawlawtew
crochet thread	**horgoló cérna**	**hawr**gawlaw **tsayr**no
knitting needles	**kötőtűk**	**kur**turtewk
sewing cotton	**varrófonál**	**vor**-rawfawnaal
sewing needles	**varrótűk**	**vor**-rawtewk
sewing thread	**varrócérna**	**vor**-rawtsayrno
thimble	**gyűszű**	**d^{y}ew**ssew
wool	**gyapjú**	**d^{y}o**pyoo

Shoes

I'd like a pair of ...	**Szeretnék egy pár ...**	særætnayk æd^y paar
boots	**csizmát**	**cheez**maat
galoshes	**sárcipőt**	**shaar**tseepu̅r̅t
hiking boots	**turista bakkancsot**	tooreeshto **bok**-konchawt
sandals	**szandált**	**son**daalt
shoes	**cipőt**	**tsee**pu̅r̅t
slippers	**papucsot**	**pop**poochawt
sneakers	**tornacipőt**	**tawr**notseepu̅r̅t
tennis shoes	**teniszcipőt**	**tæ**neestseepu̅r̅t
These are too ...	**Ez túl ...**	æz to̅o̅l
large/small	**nagy/kicsi**	nod^y/**kee**chee
narrow/wide	**keskeny/széles**	**kæsh**kæn^y/**say**læsh
Do you have the same in ...?	**Volna ugyanez ...?**	**vawl**no **ood**^yonnæz
beige/brown	**drappban/barnában**	**drop**-bon/**bor**naabon
black/white	**feketében/fehérben**	**fæ**kætaybæn/**fæ**hayrbæn
rubber/leather	**gumiból/bőrből**	**goo**meebа̅w̅l/**bu̅r̅r**bu̅r̅l
cloth/suede	**szövetből/ antilopból**	**sur**vætbu̅r̅l/**on**teelawpba̅w̅l
Is it genuine leather?	**Ez tiszta bőrből van?**	æz **tees**to **bu̅r̅r**bu̅r̅l von
I'd like ...	**Szeretnék ...**	**sær**ætnayk
pair of insoles	**egy pár talpbetétet**	æd^y paar **tolp**bætaytæt
shoe horn	**egy cipőkanalat**	æd^y **tsee**pu̅r̅konnollot
shoe laces	**egy pár cipőfűzőt**	æd^y paar **tsee**pu̅r̅fe̅w̅zu̅r̅t
shoe polish	**egy doboz cipőkrémet**	æd^y **daw**bawz **tsee**pu̅r̅-kraymæt
shoe trees	**néhány kaptafát**	**nay**haan^y **kop**toffaat

Shoe repairs

Can you repair these shoes?	**Meg tudná javítani ezt a cipőt?**	mæg **tood**naa **yo**vve̅e̅tonnee æst o **tsee**pu̅r̅t
I want them soled and heeled.	**Talpaltatni és sarkaltatni szeretném.**	**tol**poltotnee aysh **shor**-koltotnee særætnaym
When will they be ready?	**Mikorra lesz kész?**	**mee**kawr-ro læss kayss

Electrical appliances and accessories

In Hungary, 220 volts, 50 cps, AC current is universal. Plugs are different from American and British ones, so you'll need to have the plugs changed on any appliances you bring from home.

I'd like a plug for this.	**Ehhez kérek egy dugaszt.**	**æh**-hæz **kay**ræk æd^{y} **doo**gost
Do you have a battery for this?	**Van ehhez elemjük?**	von **æh**-hæz **æ**læmyewk
This is broken. Can you repair it?	**Eltört. Meg-tudják javítani?**	**æ**lturt. **mæg**tood^{y}aak yovv$\overline{ee}$tonnee
When will it be ready?	**Mikor lesz kész?**	**mee**kawr læss kayss
I'd like a/an/some ...	**Szeretnék ...**	**sæ**rætnayk
adaptor	**egy adaptert**	æd^{y} **od**doptært
amplifier	**egy erősítőt**	æd^{y} **æ**r$\overline{ur}$sh$\overline{ee}$t$\overline{ur}$t
blender	**egy keverőt**	æd^{y} **kæ**vær$\overline{ur}$t
bulb	**egy villanykörtét**	æd^{y} **veel**-lon^{y}kurrtayt
calculator	**egy kalkulátort**	æd^{y} **kol**koolaatawrt
clock	**egy órát**	æd^{y} **$\overline{aw}$**raat
alarm clock	**egy ébresztőórát**	æd^{y} **ay**bræst$\overline{ur}$$\overline{aw}$raat
wall clock	**egy faliórát**	æd^{y} **fol**lee$\overline{aw}$raat
extension cord	**egy hosszabbítót**	æd^{y} **haws**-sob-b$\overline{ee}$t$\overline{aw}$t
hair dryer	**egy hajszárítót**	æd^{y} **hoy**saar$\overline{ee}$t$\overline{aw}$t
iron	**egy vasalót**	æd^{y} **vo**sholl$\overline{aw}$t
kettle	**egy fazekat**	æd^{y} **foz**zækot
plug	**egy dugaszt**	æd^{y} **doo**gost
radio	**egy rádiót**	æd^{y} **raa**deea$\overline{w}$t
car radio	**egy autórádiót**	æd^{y} **oo**oot$\overline{aw}$raadee$\overline{aw}$t
portable radio	**egy hordozható rádiót**	æd^{y} **hawr**dawz-hott$\overline{aw}$ **raa**dee$\overline{aw}$t
record player	**egy lemezjátszót**	æd^{y} **læ**mæzyaats$\overline{aw}$t
shaver	**egy borotvát**	æd^{y} **baw**rawtvaat
speakers	**hangfalakat**	**hong**follokkot
tape recorder	**egy magnetofont**	æd^{y} **mog**nætawfawnt
cassette tape recorder	**egy kazettás magnót**	æd^{y} **koz**zæt-taash **mog**n$\overline{aw}$t
television set	**egy tévékészüléket**	æd^{y} **tay**vaykayssewlaykæt
portable TV set	**egy hordozható tévét**	æd^{y} **hawr**dawz-hott$\overline{aw}$ **tay**vayt
toaster	**egy kenyérpirítót**	æd^{y} **kæn**^{y}ayrpeer$\overline{ee}$t$\overline{aw}$t
transformer	**egy transzformátort**	æd^{y} **trons**fawrmaatawrt

Record shop

Do you have any records by ...?	**Van ...-tól/-től valamilyen lemezük?***	von ...-tawl/-turl **vollo**-meeʸæn **læ**mæzewk
May I listen to this record/ cassette?	**Meghallgathatnám ezt a lemezt/ kazettát?**	**mæ**gholgot-hotnaam æst o **læ**mæzt/**ko**zzæt-taat
I want a cassette.	**Egy kazettát kérek.**	ædʸ **ko**zzæt-taat **kay**ræk
I'd like a new stylus.	**Egy új gramofontűt kérek.**	ædʸ ooʸ **grom**mawfawntewt **kay**ræk

LP (33 rpm)	**nagylemez**	**nod**ʸlæmæz
EP (45 rpm)	**kislemez**	**keesh**læmæz
mono	**mono**	**maw**naw
stereo	**sztereo**	**stæ**ræaw

chamber music	**kamara zene**	**kom**morro **zæ**næ
classical music	**klasszikus zene**	**klos**-seekoosh **zæ**næ
folk music	**népzene**	**nayp**zænæ
instrumental music	**zenekari muzsika**	**zæ**nækorree **moo**zheeko
jazz	**dzsessz**	dzhæs
light music	**könnyűzene**	**kurn**ʸewzænæ
orchestral music	**zenekari darab**	**zæ**nækorree **dor**rob
pop music	**popzene**	**pawp**zænæ
rock music	**rockzene**	**rawk**zænæ
sacred music	**egyházi zene**	**æd**ʸhaazee **zæ**næ

Here are the names of a few popular recording artists (surnames first, Hungarian style):

Bende Zsolt
Házy Erzsébet
Koncz Zsuzsa
Kovács Kati
Sass Sylvia
Zalatnai Sarolta

* See Grammar section for word endings.

Hairdresser's—Beauty salon

Hairdressers' work usually from 7 a.m. to 9 p.m., Monday–Friday, and from 7 a.m. to 7 p.m., Saturday.

Is there a ladies' hairdresser/beauty salon in the hotel?	**Van a szállódában fodrászat/ kozmetikai szalon?**	von o **saal**-lawdaabon **faw**draassot/**kawz**mæteeko-ee **so**llawn
Can I make an appointment for (Friday)?	**Mikor jöhetek (pénteken)?**	**mee**kawr **yur**hætæk (**payn**tækæn)
I'd like a shampoo and set.	**Hajmosást kérek berakással.**	**hoy**mawshaasht **kay**ræk **bæ**rokkaash-shol

in a bun	**befonva**	**bæ**fawnvo
with curls	**fürtösítve**	**fewr**tursheetvæ
a cut	**hajvágás**	**hoy**vaagash
with a fringe	**lófarokkal**	**law**forrawk-kol
page-boy style	**fiúsra vágva**	**fee**ooshro **vaag**vo
a permanent wave	**tartós hullám**	**tor**tawsh **hool**-laam

I want a ...	**Kérek egy ...**	**kay**ræk æd[y]
bleach	**szőkítést**	**sur**keetaysht
blow-dry	**hajszárítást**	**hoy**ssaareetasht
colour rinse	**bemosást**	**bæ**mawshaasht
cut and set	**hajvágást és berakást**	**hoy**vaagaasht aysh **bæ**rokkaasht
dye	**festést**	**fæsh**taysht
shampoo	**hajmosást**	**hoy**mawshaasht
for dry hair	**száraz hajra**	**saa**roz **hoy**ro
for greasy hair	**zsíros hajra**	**zhee**rawsh **hoy**ro
tint	**színezést**	**see**næzaysht
the same colour	**ugyanilyen színűre**	**ood**[y]onnee[y]æn **see**newræ
a darker colour	**sötétebb színre**	**shur**taytæb **seen**ræ
a lighter colour	**világosabb színre**	**vee**laagawshob **seen**ræ
Do you have a colour chart?	**Van színtáblájuk?**	von **seen**taablaa[y]ook
I don't want any hair-spray.	**Hajlakkot nem kérek.**	**hoy**lok-kawt næm **kay**ræk
I want a ...	**Kérek egy ...**	**kay**ræk æd[y]
face pack	**arcpakolást**	**orts**pokkawlaasht
manicure	**manikűrt**	**mon**neekewrt
pedicure	**pedikűrt**	**pæ**deekewrt

DAYS OF THE WEEK: see page 181

Under the hair dryer, you might want to say:

It's too hot.	**Ez túl forró.**	æz to̅o̅l **fawr**-ra̅w̅
A bit warmer, please.	**Egy kissé forróbbra kérem.**	æd^{y} **keesh**-shay **fawr**-ra̅w̅bro **kay**ræm
Do you have any magazines?	**Van valami olvasnivalójuk?**	von **vol**lommee **awl**voshneevolla̅w̅^{y}ook

At the barber's

I'm in a hurry.	**Sietek.**	**shee**ætæk
I'd like a shave.	**Egy borotválást kérek.**	æd^{y} **baw**rawtvaalaasht **kay**ræk
I want a haircut, please.	**Egy hajvágást kérek.**	æd^{y} **hoy**vaagaasht **kay**ræk
Cut it short, please.	**Rövidre kérem.**	**rur**veedræ **kay**ræm
Don't cut it too short.	**Ne vágja túl rövidre.**	næ **vaag**yo to̅o̅l **rur**-veedræ
A razor cut, please.	**Egy borotva-hajvágást kérek.**	æd^{y} **baw**rawto-hoyvaa-gaasht **kay**ræk
Don't use the electric clippers.	**Ne használja a villanyborotvát.**	næ **hos**naalyo o **veel**-lon^{y}bawrawtvaat
That's enough off.	**Már eleget levett.**	maar ælægæt **læ**væt
A little more off the ...	**Még egy kicsit le lehet venni ...**	mayg æd^{y} **kee**cheet læ **læ**hæt **væn**-nee
back	**hátul**	**haa**tool
neck	**a nyaknál**	o **n^{y}ok**naal
sides	**kétoldalt**	**kay**tawldolt
top	**felül**	**fæ**lewl
I'd like some hair lotion.	**Hajszeszt kérek.**	**hoy**sæst **kay**ræk
Please don't use any oil.	**Kérem, ne használjon olajat.**	**kay**ræm næ **hos**naal-yawn **aw**loyot
Would you please trim my ...?	**Kérem, vágja le a ...**	**kay**ræm **vaag**yo læ o
beard	**szakállamat**	**sok**kaal-lommot
moustache	**bajuszomat**	**bo**yoossawmot
sideboards (sideburns)	**pajeszomat**	**po**yæssawmot

TIPPING: see page 1

Jeweller's—Watchmaker's

Major department stores, some small shops and private craftsmen sell costume jewellery, watches and items of folk art. The sale of gold and silver objects as well as precious stones is limited to branches of the *Óra és Ékszerbolt* chain and Intertourist shops. You may have to pay in hard currency.

Can you repair this watch?	**Meg tudják ezt az órát javítani?**	mæg **tood^{y}aak** æst oz awraat yovveetonnee
It's too slow.	**Sokat késik.**	**shaw**kot **kay**sheek
It's too fast.	**Nagyon siet.**	**nod^y**awn **shee**æt
The … is broken.	**Eltört …**	**æl**turrt
glass	**az üvegje**	oz **ew**vægyæ
spring	**a rugója**	o **roo**gaw^{y}o
strap	**a szíja**	o **see**^{y}o
winder	**a felhúzója**	o **fæl**hoozaw^{y}o
The battery is flat.	**Kimerült az elem.**	**kee**mærewlt oz **æl**æm
I want this watch cleaned.	**Szeretném az órát kitisztíttatni.**	**sær**ætnaym oz **aw**raat **kee**teesteet-totnee
When will it be ready?	**Mikorra lesz kész?**	**mee**kawr-ro læss kayss
Could I see that?	**Megnézhetném?**	**mæg**nayz-hætnaym
I'm just looking round.	**Csak nézelödök.**	chok **nay**zælurdurk
I'd like a small present for …	**Valami szerény ajándékot szeretnék … részére.**	**vol**lommee **sær**ayn^y **oy**aandaykawt **sær**ætnayk … **rays**sayræ
I don't want anything too expensive.	**Nem túl drágára gondolok.**	næm tool **draa**gaaro **gawn**dawlawk
I'd like something …	**Valami … szeretnék.**	**vol**lommee … **sær**ætnayk
better	**jobbat**	**yawb**-bot
cheaper	**olcsóbbat**	**awl**chawb-bot
simpler	**egyszerűbbet**	**æd^y**særewb-bæt
Is this sterling silver?	**Ez valódi ezüst?**	æz **vol**lawdee **æ**zewsht
How many carats is this?	**Ez hány karátos?**	æz haan^y **kor**raatawsh

Look up the name of the article you wish to buy in the following list. The lists on the next page will tell you what it's made of.

I'd like a/an/some ...	**Szeretnék ...**	særætnayk
bangle	**egy karperecet**	æd^{y} korpærætsæt
bead necklace	**egy gyöngynyakéket**	æd^{y} d^{y}urnd^{y}n^{y}okkaykæt
bracelet	**egy karkötőt**	æd^{y} korkurtur̄t
brooch	**egy brost**	æd^{y} brawsht
buckle	**egy csattot**	æd^{y} chot-tawt
chain	**egy nyakláncot**	æd^{y} n^{y}oklaantsawt
cigarette case	**egy cigaretta-tárcát**	æd^{y} tseegorræt-tottaartsaat
cigarette lighter	**egy öngyújtót**	æd^{y} urnd^{y}oo^{y}tawt
clock	**egy órát**	æd^{y} awraat
alarm clock	**egy ébresztőórát**	æd^{y} aybræstur-awraat
electric alarm clock	**egy villany ébresztőorát**	æd^{y} veel-lon^{y} aybræstur-awraat
kitchen clock	**egy konyhai órát**	æd^{y} kawn^{y}ho-ee awraat
wall clock	**egy faliórát**	æd^{y} folleeawraat
costume jewellery	**divatékszert**	deevottayksært
cross	**egy keresztet**	æd^{y} kæræstæt
cuff links	**inggombot**	eeng-gawmbawt
cutlery	**evőeszközt**	ævur-æskurzt
ear clips	**fülcsiptetőt**	fewlcheeptætur̄t
earings	**fülbevalót**	fewlbævollawt
jewel box	**egy ékszeres dobozt**	æd^{y} ayksæræsh dawbawzt
music box	**egy zenedobozt**	æd^{y} zænædawbawzt
napkin ring	**egy szalvéta gyűrűt**	æd^{y} solvayto d^{y}ewrewt
necklace	**egy nyakláncot**	æd^{y} n^{y}oklaantsawt
pendant	**egy függőt**	æd^{y} fewg-gurt
pin	**egy tűt**	æd^{y} tewt
powder compact	**egy púdertartót**	æd^{y} poodærtortawt
ring	**egy gyűrűt**	æd^{y} d^{y}ewrewt
engagement ring	**egy eljegyzési-gyűrűt**	æd^{y} ælyæd^{y}zayshee-d^{y}ewrewt
signet ring	**egy pecsétgyűrűt**	æd^{y} pæchaytd^{y}ewrewt
wedding ring	**egy házassági gyűrűt**	æd^{y} haazosh-shaaghee d^{y}ewrewt
rosary	**egy olvasót**	æd^{y} awlvoshawt
serviette ring	**egy szalvéta gyűrűt**	æd^{y} solvayto d^{y}ewrewt
silverware	**valami ezüst tárgyat**	vollommee æzewsht taard^{y}ot
snuff box	**egy dohány szelencét**	æd^{y} dawhaan^{y} sælæn-tsayt
tie pin	**egy nyakkendő tűt**	æd^{y} n^{y}ok-kændur tewt

watch	**egy órát**	æd^y **$\overline{aw}$**raat
pocket watch	**egy zsebórát**	æd^y **zhæ**b$\overline{aw}$raat
quartz watch	**egy kvartz órát**	æd^y kvorts **$\overline{aw}$**raat
stopwatch	**egy stopperórát**	æd^y **shtawp**-pær$\overline{aw}$raat
wristwatch	**egy karórát**	æd^y **kor**r$\overline{aw}$raat
watch strap	**egy óraszíjat**	æd^y **$\overline{aw}$**ross$\overline{ee}$^{y}ot
What kind of stone is this?	**Ez milyen kő?**	æz **mee**^{y}æn k$\overline{ur}$

amethyst	**ametiszt**	ommæteest
diamond	**gyémánt**	**d^{y}ay**maant
emerald	**smaragd**	**shmor**rogd
pearl	**igazgyöngy**	**ee**gozd^{y}urnd^y
ruby	**rubin**	**roo**been
sapphire	**zafir**	**zof**feer
tiger's-eye	**macskaszem (kvarc)**	**moch**kossæm (kvorts)
topaz	**topáz**	**taw**paaz
turquoise	**türkiz**	**tewr**keez

What's it made of?	**Miből van?**	**mee**b$\overline{ur}$l von

alabaster	**alabástrom**	**ol**lobaashtrawm
amber	**borostyánkő**	**baw**rawsht^{y}aank$\overline{ur}$
brass	**sárgaréz**	**shaar**gorrayz
copper	**réz**	rayz
coral	**korál**	**kaw**raal
crystal	**kristály**	**kreesh**taa^y
ebony	**ébenfa**	**ay**bænfo
enamel	**zománc**	**zaw**maants
glass	**üveg**	**ew**væg
cut glass	**csiszolt üveg**	**chee**ssawlt **ew**væg
gold	**arany**	**or**ron^y
gold plate	**aranyfüst**	**or**ron^{y}fewsht
ivory	**elefántcsont**	ælæfaantchawnt
jade	**ékszer**	**ayk**sær
mother-of-pearl	**gyöngyház**	**d^y**urnd^{y}haaz
nickel silver	**alpakka**	**ol**pok-ko
pewter	**ón**	$\overline{aw}$n
platinum	**platina**	**plot**teeno
silver	**ezüst**	æzewsht
silver plate	**ezüstlemez**	æzewshtlæmæz
stainless steel	**rozsdamentes acél**	**rawzh**domæntæsh otsayl

Laundry—Dry cleaning

If your hotel doesn't have its own laundry or dry-cleaning service, you'll have to go to a *Patyolat* (**pot**^{y}awlot), an establishment which handles both laundry and dry cleaning. It may take some time, but it will certainly be quite inexpensive. Some of these shops offer express service for removing spots and stains while you wait.

Where's the nearest ...?	**Hol találom a legközelebbi ...?**	hawl **to**llaalawm o **læg**-kurzælæb-bee
dry cleaner	**száraz vegytisztítót**	**saa**roz **væd**^{y}teestēētāwt
laundry	**mosodát**	**maw**shawdaat
I want these clothes ...	**Ezeket a ruhákat akarom ...**	**æ**zækæt o **roo**haakot **ok**korrawm
cleaned	**kitisztíttatni**	**kee**teestēēt-totnee
washed and ironed	**kimosatni és kivasaltatni**	**kee**mawshotnee aysh **kee**vosholtotnee
When will it be ready?	**Mikor lesz kész?**	**mee**kawr læss kayss
I need it ...	**... szükségem van rájuk.**	... **sewk**shaygæm von **raa**^{y}ook
today	**Mára**	**maa**ro
tomorrow	**Holnapra**	**hawl**nopro
before Friday	**Péntekre**	**payn**tækræ
as soon as possible	**Minél hamarabb**	**mee**nayl **ho**mmorrob
Can you mend this?	**Kijavítanák?**	**kee**yovvēētonnaak
Can you sew on this button?	**Felvarrná ezt a gombot?**	**fæl**vornaa æst o **gawm**bawt
Can you get this stain out?	**Kivennék ezt a foltot?**	**kee**væn-nayk æst o **fawl**tawt
Can this be invisibly mended?	**Meg lehet ezt láthatatlanul javítani?**	mæg **læ**hæt æst **laa**thotlonnool **yo**vvēētonnee
Is my laundry ready?	**Kész van a mosnivalóm?**	kayss von o **mawsh**neevollāwm
My name is ...	**... vagyok.**	... **vod**^{y}awk
This isn't mine.	**Ez nem az enyém.**	æz næm oz æn^{y}aym
There's one piece missing.	**Egy darab hiányzik.**	æd^y **do**rrob **hee**aan^{y}zeek

DAYS OF THE WEEK: see page 181

SHOPPING GUIDE

Photography

I want an inexpensive camera.	**Egy olcsó fényképezőgépet keresek.**	æd^y **awl**chaw **fayn^y**kaypæzurgaypæt **kæ**ræshæk
Do you sell home-movie cameras?	**Filmfelvevőjük van?**	**feelm**fælvævur-yewrk
Show me the one in the window.	**Mutassa meg a kirakatban lévőt.**	**moo**tosh-sho mæg o **kee**rokkotbon **lay**vurt
I'd like to have some passport photos taken.	**Néhány útlevélfényképet szeretnék készíttetni.**	**nay**haan^y **oo**tlævaylfayn^{y}kaypæt **sæ**rætnayk **kay**sseetætnee

Film

It would be advisable to take some film with you to Hungary since some sizes are not available (Polaroid and 127).

I'd like a film for this camera.	**Ebbe a gépbe való filmet kérek.**	**æb**-bæ o **gayp**bæ **vol**law **feel**mæt **kay**ræk
black-and-white film	**fekete-fehér film**	**fæ**kætæ **fæ**hayr feelm
colour film	**színes film**	**see**næsh feelm
slide film	**dia-film**	**dee**o-feelm
cartridge	**filmpatron**	**feelm**potrawn
cassette	**kazetta**	**koz**zæt-to
roll film	**tekercsfilm**	**tæ**kærchfeelm
120	**százhúsz**	**saaz**hooss
135	**százharmincöt**	**saaz**hormeentsurt
single 8	**normál nyolc milliméteres**	**nawr**maal n^{y}awlts **mee**leemaytæræsh
super 8	**szuper nyolc milliméteres**	**soo**pær n^{y}awlts **mee**leemaytæræsh
20/36 exposures	**húsz/harmincöt képes**	**hooss/hor**meentsurt **kay**pæsh
this size	**ez a méret**	æz o **may**ræt
this ASA/DIN number	**ez az ASA/DIN cikkszám**	æz oz **o**sho/deen **tseek**saam
artificial light type	**mesterséges fényérzékeny**	**mæsh**tærshaygæsh **fayn^y**ayrzaykæn^y
daylight type	**nappali fényre érzékeny**	**nop**-pollee **fayn^y**ræ **ayr**zaykæn^y
fine grain	**finomszemcsés**	**fee**nawmsæmchaysh
high speed	**nagy érzékenységű**	nod^y **ayr**zaykæn^{y}shaygew

NUMBERS: page 175

Processing

How long will it take you to process this film?	**Mennyi ideig tart az előhívás?**	mæn^{y}ee **ee**dæeeg tort oz ælurheevaash
How much will it cost?	**Mennyibe kerül?**	mæn^{y}eebæ **kæ**rewl
with a glossy/matt finish	**fényes/matt kikészítéssel**	**fayn^{y}**æsh/mot **kee**kay-sseetaysh-shæl
with/without border	**széllel/szél nélkül**	**sayl**-læl/sayl **nayl**kewl
Will you please enlarge this?	**Kérem ezt kinagyítani.**	**kay**ræm æst **kee**nod^{y}ee-tonnee

Accessories

I want a/some ...	**Kérek ...**	**kay**ræk
cable release	**egy kábeles kioldót**	æd^{y} **kaa**bælæsh **kee**-awldawt
filter	**egy szűrőt**	æd^{y} **sew**rurt
red/yellow	**vöröset/sárgát**	**vur**rurshæt/**shaar**gaat
ultraviolet	**ultraviolát**	**ool**trovveeawlaat
flash bulbs	**néhány vaku-izzót**	**nay**haan^{y} **vok**koo-**eez**-zawt
flash cubes	**néhány vaku-kockát**	**nay**haan^{y} **vok**koo-**kawts**kaat
lens	**egy lencsét**	æd^{y} **læn**chayt
lens cap	**egy lencsevédőt**	æd^{y} **læn**chævaydurt
light meter	**egy fénymérőt**	æd^{y} **fayn^{y}**mayrurt
telephoto lens	**egy teleobjektívet**	æd^{y} **tæ**læawbyækteevæt

Repairs

This camera doesn't work. Can you repair it?	**Ez a gép elromlott. Meg tudják javítani?**	æz o gayp **æl**rawmlawt. mæg **tood^{y}**aak **yo**vveetonnee
The film is jammed.	**Beszorult a film.**	**bæ**sawroolt o feelm
There's something wrong with the ...	**... nem működik.**	... næm **mew**kurdeek
exposure counter	**A kioldás számláló**	o **kee**awldaash **saam**laalaw
film winder	**A filmtekerő**	o **feelm**tækærur
light meter	**A fénymérő**	o **fayn^{y}**mayrur
rangefinder	**A távolság beállító**	o **taa**vawlshaag **bæ**aal-leetaw
shutter	**A zár**	o zaar

Provisions

Here's a basic list of food and drink that you might want on a picnic or for the occasional meal in your hotel room.

I'd like some …	**Kérnék …**	**kayr**nayk
apple juice	**almalét**	**ol**mollayt
apples	**almát**	**ol**maat
bananas	**banánt**	**bo**nnaant
beer	**sört**	shurrt
biscuits (Br.)	**kekszet**	**kæk**sæt
bread	**kenyeret**	**kæn**^{y}æræt
butter	**vajat**	**vo**yot
cake	**süteményt**	**shew**tæmayn^{y}t
candy	**édességet**	**ay**dæsh-shaygæt
cheese	**sajtot**	**shoy**tawt
chocolate	**csokoládét**	**chaw**kawlaadayt
coffee	**kávét**	**kaa**vayt
cola drink	**kólát**	**ka̅w̅**laat
cold meat (a selection)	**felvágottat**	**fæl**vaagawt-tot
cookies	**kekszet**	**kæk**sæt
cooking fat	**főzőzsírt**	**fu̅r̅**zu̅r̅he̅e̅rt
crackers	**ropogós pálcát**	**raw**pawga̅w̅sh **paal**tsaat
cream	**krémet**	**kray**mæt
cucumbers	**uborkát**	**oo**bawrkaat
eggs	**tojást**	**taw**^{y}aasht
flour	**lisztet**	**lees**tæt
frankfurters	**virslit**	**veersh**leet
grapefruit	**grépfrutot**	**grayp**frootawt
grapefruit juice	**grépfrut levet**	**grayp**froot **læ**væt
ham	**sonkát**	**shawn**kaat
ice-cream	**fagylaltot**	**fod**^{y}loltawt
lemons	**citromot**	**tsee**trawmawt
lettuce	**fejes salátát**	**fæ**^{y}æsh **shol**laataat
liver sausage	**májas hurkát**	**maa**^{y}osh **hoor**kaat
milk	**tejet**	**tæ**^{y}æt
mineral water	**ásványvizet**	**aash**vaan^{y}veezæt
mustard	**mustárt**	**moosh**taart
oil	**olajat**	**aw**loyot
orange juice	**narancslevet**	**no**rronchlævæt
oranges	**narancsot**	**no**rronchawt
pepper	**borsot**	**bawr**shawt
pickles	**ecetes uborkát**	**æ**tsætæsh **oo**bawrkaat
potato crisps (chips)	**burgonya csipszet**	**boor**gawn^{y}o **cheep**sæt
potatoes	**burgonyát**	**boor**gawn^{y}aat

rolls	**péksüteményt**	**payk**shewtæmayn^{y}t
salad	**salátát**	**sho**llaataat
salami	**szalámit**	**so**llaameet
salt	**sót**	sha̅w̅t
sandwiches	**szendvicset**	**sænd**veechæt
sausages	**kolbászt**	**kawl**baast
spaghetti	**spagettit**	**shpo**ggæt-teet
sugar	**cukrot**	**tsook**rawt
sweets	**édességet**	**ay**dæsh-shaygæt
tea	**teát**	**tæ**aat
tomato juice	**paradicsomlevet**	**po**rroddeechawmlævæt
tomatoes	**paradicsomot**	**po**rroddeechawmawt
yoghurt	**joghurtot**	**yawg**hoortawt

basket	**egy kosarat**	æd^{y} **kaw**shorrot
bottle	**egy üveget**	æd^{y} **ew**vægæt
bottle opener	**egy üvegnyitót**	æd^{y} **ew**vægn^{y}eeta̅w̅t
box	**egy dobozt**	æd^{y} **daw**bawzt
corkscrew	**egy dugóhúzót**	æd^{y} **doo**ga̅w̅ho̅o̅za̅w̅t
matches	**gyufát**	**d^{y}oo**faat
plastic bag	**egy plasztik zacskót**	æd^{y} **plos**teek **zoch**ka̅w̅t
shopping bag	**egy bevásár-lótáskát**	æd^{y} **bæ**vaashaarla̅w̅-taashkaat
tin	**egy konzervet**	æd^{y} **kawn**zærvæt
tin (can) opener	**egy konzervnyitót**	æd^{y} **kawn**zærvn^{y}eeta̅w̅t
tinfoil	**alufóliát**	**o**lloofa̅w̅leeaat
tube of ...	**egy tubus ...-t**	æd^{y} **too**boosh ...-t

Weights and measures

1 kilogram or kilo (kg) = 1000 grams (g)

100 g = 3.5 oz.	½ kg = 1.1 lb.
200 g = 7.0 oz.	1 kg = 2.2 lb.

1 oz. = 28.35 g
1 lb. = 453.60 g

1 litre (l) = 10 decilitres (dl) or 100 centilitres (cl) or 1000 millilitres (ml)

1 l = 0.88 imp. quarts = 1.06 U.S. quarts
1 dl = approx. ⅕ pint
2 dl = approx. ⅓ pint

1 imp. quart = 1.14 l	1 U.S. quart = 0.95 l
1 imp. gallon = 4.55 l	1 U.S. gallon = 3.8 l

Souvenirs

Hungary is a land full of fascination for souvenir- and gift-hunters. At centres throughout the country the ancient traditions of woodcarving, embroidery, weaving, pottery and other folk arts are alive and flourishing. Modern designs are found alongside age-old motifs.

Other good buys include regional costumes, local paintings, gramophone records and picture books, not to forget the many excellent local wines, fruit brandies and foodstuffs.

If you are looking for the ultimate executive toy for your boss, try the pocket-sized Hungarian "magic cube". It's a variegated cube made up of interlocking elements which you must twist around in an attempt to line up all the squares of the same colour on the same face. The endless permutations can drive even advanced mathematicians to either distraction or obsession.

carpet	**szőnyeg**	s$\overline{ur}$n^{y}æg
carved bowl	**faragott váza**	forroggawt vaazo
carved box	**faragott doboz**	forroggawt dawbawz
carved walking-stick	**faragott sétapálca**	forroggawt shaytoppaaltso
embroidered blouse	**hímzett blúz**	h$\overline{ee}$mzæt bl$\overline{oo}$z
embroidered tablecloth	**hímzett asztalterítő**	h$\overline{ee}$mzæt ostoltæreet$\overline{ur}$
embroidery (petit point)	**hímzés**	h$\overline{ee}$mzaysh
fruit brandy	**gyümölcspálinka**	d^{y}ewmurlchpaaleenko
apricot brandy	**barack pálinka**	borrotsk paaleenko
cherry brandy	**cseresznye pálinka**	chæræsn^{y}æ paaleenko
plum brandy	**szilva pálinka**	seelvo paaleenko
gramophone record	**gramofonlemez**	grommawfawnlæmæz
handicrafts	**kézmüipari termék**	kayzmeweeporree tærmayk
Herend china	**herendi porcellán**	hærændee pawrtsælaan
magic cube	**bűvös kocka**	b$\overline{ew}$vursh kotsko
picture book	**képes kalauz**	kaypæsh kollo-ooz
pottery	**fazekastárgyak**	fozækoshtaard^{y}ok
rug	**szőnyeg**	s$\overline{ur}$n^{y}æg
rustic chair	**faragott szék**	forroggawt sayk
rustic jugs	**falusi kancsók**	follooshee konch$\overline{aw}$k
szűr (Hungarian cape)	**szűr**	s$\overline{ew}$r
Tokay wine	**tokaji bor**	tawkoyee bawr

Tobacconist

Cigarettes, cigars and tobacco are on sale in *Dohánybolt* (**daw**haan^{y}bawlt) and *Trafik* (**tro**ffeek) shops, in all *ÁBC* (**aa**baytsay) and other department stores, and at most hotel counters. Intertourist branches also sell smokers' supplies, including foreign brands of cigarettes, against hard currency. Local cigarettes can be bought in packets of twenty or by the carton of 200. There are no cigarette vending machines. Smoking is strictly prohibited in all public transport vehicles with the exception of trains, which have smokers' compartments. Cinemas, theatres and concert halls also ban smoking.

A packet of cigarettes, please.	**Kérek egy csomag cigarettát.**	**kay**ræk æd^y **chaw**mog **tsee**gorræt-taat
I'd like a/an/some ...	**Kérek ...**	**kay**ræk
cigar	**egy szivart**	æd^y **see**vort
cigars	**néhány szivart**	**nay**haan^y **see**vort
cigarette case	**egy cigaretta tárcát**	æd^y **tsee**gorræt-to **taar**tsaat
cigarette holder	**egy szipkát**	æd^y **seep**kaat
cigarette lighter	**egy öngyújtót**	æd^y **urnd**^{y}oo^{y}taawt
flints	**néhány tűzkövet**	**nay**haan^y **tew**zkurvæt
lighter	**egy öngyújtót**	æd^y **urnd**^{y}ootaawt
lighter fluid	**öngyújtó benzint**	**urnd**^{y}oo^{y}taw **bæn**zeent
lighter gas	**öngyújtó gázt**	**urnd**^{y}oo^{y}taw gaast
matches	**gyufát**	**d^{y}oo**faat
packet of ...	**egy csomag ...-t**	æd^y **chaw**mog ...-t
pipe	**egy pipát**	æd^y **pee**paat
pipe cleaners	**néhány pipatísztítót**	**nay**haan^y **pee**potteesteetaawt
pipe rack	**egy pipatartót**	æd^y **pee**pottortaawt
pipe tobacco	**pipadohányt**	**pee**poddawhaan^{y}t
pipe tool	**egy pipapiszkálót**	æd^y **pee**poppeeskaalaawt
tobacco pouch	**egy dohányszelencét**	æd^y **daw**haan^{y}sælæntsayt
Do you have any ...?	**Van Önöknek ...?**	von **ur**nurknæk
American cigarettes	**amerikai cigarettájuk**	**om**mæreeko-ee **tsee**gorræt-taa^{y}ook
British cigarettes	**angol cigarettájuk**	**on**gawl **tsee**gorræt-taa^{y}ook
menthol cigarettes	**mentolos cigarettájuk**	**mæn**tawlawsh **tsee**gorræt-taa^{y}ook

I'll take 2 packets.	**2 csomaggal kérek.**	2 **chaw**mog-gol **kay**ræk
I'd like a carton, please.	**Egy kartonnal kérek.**	æd^y **kor**tawn-nol **kay**ræk
A box of matches, please.	**Egy doboz gyufát kérek.**	æd^y **daw**bawz **d^{y}oo**faat **kay**ræk

filter-tipped	**szűrőbetétes**	**sew**rurbætaytæsh
without filter	**szűrő nélküli**	**sew**rur **nayl**kewlee
light tobacco	**könnyű dohány**	**kurn^{y}ew daw**haan^y
dark tobacco	**nehéz dohány**	**næ**hayz **daw**haan^y

While we're on the subject of cigarettes:

Do you mind if I smoke?	**Nem zavarja, ha dohányzom?**	næm **zov**voryo ho **daw**-haan^{y}zawm
Would you like a cigarette.	**Parancsol egy cigarettát?**	**por**ronchawl æd^y **tsee**gorræt-taat
Have one of mine.	**Válasszon az enyémből.**	**vaa**loss-sawn oz æn^{y}aym-burl
Try one of these.	**Próbálja ki ezt.**	**praw**baalyo kee æst
They're very mild.	**Nagyon gyengék.**	**nod^y**awn **d^{y}æn**gayk
They're a bit strong.	**Egy kissé erősek.**	æd^y **keesh**-shay **æ**rurshæk

And if somebody offers you one:

Thank you.	**Köszönöm.**	**kur**surnurm
No, thanks.	**Nem kérem.**	næm **kay**ræm
I don't smoke.	**Nem dohányzom.**	næm **daw**haan^{y}zawm
I'm trying to give it up.	**Le akarok szokni a dohányzásról.**	læ okkorawk **sawk**nee o **daw**haan^{y}zaashrawl
I've given it up.	**Felhagytam a dohányzással.**	**fæl**hod^{y}tom o **daw**haan^y-zaash-shol

DOHÁNYZÓ
SMOKING ALLOWED

TILOS A DOHÁNYZÁS
NO SMOKING

Your money: banks—currency

Official foreign exchange facilities can be found at: branches of the Hungarian National Bank *(Magyar Nemzeti Bank)* the National Savings Bank *(Országos Takarékpénztár—O.T.P.)* and the Hungarian Foreign Trade Bank *(Magyar Külkereskedelmi Bank)*, most hotels, motels, larger campsites and tourist agencies. Some department stores and speciality shops also operate currency exchange counters.

Banking hours are generally from 9 a.m. to 5 p.m., Monday to Friday, and 9 a.m. to 2 p.m., Saturday. Keep all exchange slips. Remember to take your passport with you.

At larger exchange offices some staff usually speak English.

The unit of Hungarian currency is the *Forint* (**faw**reent), abbreviated *Ft.* It is divided into 100 *fillér* (**feel**-layr). Here are the different banknotes and coins in circulation:

Banknotes: 10, 20, 50, 100, 500 and 1000 Forints.
Coins: 10, 20 and 50 fillérs; 1, 2, 5, 10 and 20 Forints.

Visitors may take any amount of foreign currency or traveller's cheques into or out of the country, but check before leaving with your home travel agency on possible currency registration requirements. The import and export of local currency is limited to Ft. 100.

Note that there are restrictions on the amount of forints that may be re-exchanged when leaving the country. Remember to keep the official exchange slips you were issued at the time of the original transaction.

Most internationally recognized traveller's cheques and credit cards are accepted by official currency exchange agencies. A considerable number of tourist-oriented establishments (hotels, restaurants, shops, etc.) also take them—just look for the signs on the door.

Where?

Where's the nearest ...?	**Hol a legköze-lebbi ...?**	hawl o **læg**kurzælæb-bee
bank	**bank**	bonk
exchange office	**valuta beváltó hely**	**vol**looto **bæ**vaaltaw hæ^{y}
Where can I cash a traveller's cheque (check)?	**Hol lehet traveller's csekket beváltani?**	hawl **læ**hæt **trov**væl-lærs **chæk**-kæt **bæ**vaaltonnee

At the counter

I'd like to change some ...	**Szeretnék ... beváltaní.**	**sæ**rætnayk ... **bæ**vaal-tonnee
Austrian schillings	**osztrák shillinget**	**os**traak **sheel**-leengæt
Canadian dollars	**kanadai dollárt**	**kon**noddo-ee **dawl**-laart
German marks	**nyugatnémet márkát**	**n^{y}oo**gotnaymæt **maar**kaat
pounds sterling	**angol fontot**	**on**gawl **fawn**tawt
U.S. dollars	**amerikai dollárt**	**om**mæreeko-ee **dawl**-laart
What's the exchange rate?	**Mi az átváltási árfolyam?**	mee oz **aat**vaaltaashee **aar**faw^{y}om
I'd like to cash a traveller's cheque (check).	**Egy traveller's csekket szeretnék beváltani.**	**æd^{y} trov**væl-lærs **chæk**-kæt **sæ**rætnayk **bæ**vaal-tonnee
Can you cash a personal cheque?	**Személyes csekket elfogadnak?**	**sæ**may^{y}æsh **chæk**-kæt **æl**fawgodnok
What rate of commission do you charge?	**Mennyi az átváltási jutalék?**	**mæn^{y}**ee oz **aat**vaaltaa-shee **yoo**tollayk
How long will it take to clear?	**Meddig tart a csekk ellenőrzése?**	**mæd**-deeg tort o chæk **æl**-lænurrzayshæ
Can you wire my bank at home?	**Táviratoznának a bankomnak?**	**taa**veerottawznaanok o **bon**kawmnok
I have ...	**Rendelkezem ...**	**ræn**dælkæzæm
a credit card	**hitelkártyával**	**hee**tælkaart^{y}aavol
an introduction	**ajánló levéllel**	**oy**aanlaw **læ**vayl-læl
a letter of credit	**hitellevéllel**	**hee**tæl-lævayl-læl
I'm expecting some money from home.	**Hazulról várok átutalást.**	**hoz**zoolrawl **vaa**rawk **aa**tootollaasht
Has it arrived yet?	**Megjött már?**	**mæg**yurt maar

Please give me 5000 forints in large denominations and 100 forints in small change.	**5000 forintot kérek nagy címletekben, továbbá 100 forintot apróban.**	5000 **faw**reentawt **kay**ræk nod^{y} **tsēē**mlætækbæn **tawl**-vaab-baa 100 **faw**reentawt opr$\overline{aw}$bon
I'd like some small change.	**Aprót szeretnék.**	opr$\overline{aw}$t særætnayk
Could you please check that again?	**Lenne szíves újra ellenőrizni?**	**læn**-næ **sēē**væsh **ōō**^{y}ro **æl**-læn$\overline{ur}$reeznee
Could I have an exchange slip, please?	**Kaphatnék egy elismervényt?**	**kop**hotnayk æd^{y} **æ**leeshmærvayn^{y}t

Depositing

I want to credit this to my account.	**Ezt az összeget szeretném a számlámra befizetni.**	æst oz **urs**-sægæt særætnaym o **saam**laamro **bæ**feezætnee
I'd like to pay this amount into Mr. ...'s account.	**Ezt az összeget ... úr számlájára szeretném befizetni.**	æst oz **urs**-sægæt ... **ōō**r **saam**laa^{y}aaro **sæ**rætnaym **bæ**feezætnee
Where should I sign?	**Hol írjam alá?**	hawl **ēē**ryom **ol**laa

Currency converter

In a world of floating currencies, we can offer no more than this do-it-yourself chart. You can obtain details of current exchange rates from any bank or tourist agency.

	£	$
50 fillér		
1 forint		
2 forint		
5 forint		
10 forint		
15 forint		
20 forint		
50 forint		
100 forint		

NUMBERS: see page 175

At the post office

The offices of the Hungarian postal authority *(Magyar Posta)* are open from 8 a.m. to 4 p.m., Monday–Friday, and from 8 a.m. to 1 p.m., Saturday. Main municipal and regional post offices work from 7 a.m. to 8 p.m., Monday–Saturday, sometimes with a skeleton service in the morning on Sundays and public holidays. Post offices handle mail, telephone, telegraphic and telex services, but not international money transfers.

In Budapest, a special international post, telegraph and telex office operates at the corner of Petofi Sándor utca and Martinelli-tér. It is open from 7 a.m. to 9 p.m., Monday-Friday, until 7 p.m., Saturday, and in the morning only on Sundays and public holidays.

Registered, airmail and express (special-delivery) services are available. Postal and telegraph charges, which are quite low compared with those practised in most western European countries, may be paid in forints.

Postage stamps are also on sale in tobacconists' shops. Mailboxes are red.

Few post office counter staff speak foreign languages.

Where's the nearest post office?	**Hol a legközelebbi postahivatal?**	hawl o **læg**kurzælæb-bee **pawsh**toheevottol
What time does the post office ...?	**Mikor ... a postahivatal?**	**mee**kawr ... o **pawsh**toheevottol
open	**nyit**	n^{y}eet
close	**zár**	zaar
Which counter do I go to for stamps?	**Melyik ablaknál kapok bélyegeket?**	**mæ**^{y}eek **ob**loknaal **kop**pok **bay**^{y}ægækæt
I want some stamps.	**Bélyegeket kérek.**	**bay**^{y}ægækæt **kay**ræk
I want ... 5-Ft. stamps.	**... darab 5 forintos címletet.**	... **dor**rob 5 **faw**reentawsh **tsee**mlætæt

What's the postage for a letter/postcard to ...?	**Mennyibe kerül egy levél/képeslap postadíja ...?**	mæn^{y}eebæ **kæ**rewl æd^{y} lævayl/**kay**pæshlop **pawsh**toddēēyo
Great Britain	**Angliába**	**on**gleeaabo
the U.S.A.	**az Egyesült Allamokba**	os æd^{y}æsewlt **aal**-lommawkbo
I want to send this parcel.	**Szeretném feladni ezt a csomagot.**	særætnaym **fæ**lodnee æst o **chaw**moggawt
I'd like to send this ...	**... szeretném feladni.**	... særætnaym **fæ**lodnee
airmail	**Légipostán**	**lay**gheepawshtaan
express (special delivery)	**Expressz**	**æx**præs
registered	**Ajánlva**	**oy**aanlvo
Where's the mailbox?	**Hol a postaláda?**	hawl o **pawsh**tollaado
Do I have to fill in a customs declaration form?	**Vámnyilatkozatot ki kell töltenem?**	**vaam**n^{y}eelotkawzottawt kee kæl **turl**tænæm
Where's the poste restante (general delivery)?	**Hol a «poste restante» szolgálat?**	hawl o pawst **ræs**tont **sawl**gaalot
Is there any mail for me? My name is ...	**Van posta a részemre? ... vagyok.**	von **pawsh**to o **ray**ssæmræ. ... **vod**^{y}awk

BÉLYEGEK	**STAMPS**
CSOMAGFELADÁS	**PARCELS**
TÁVIRATOK	**TELEGRAMS**

Telegrams

Where's the telegram counter?	**Hol lehet táviratot feladni?**	hawl læhæt **taa**veerottawt **fæ**lodnee
I'd like to send a telegram.	**Táviratot szeretnék feladni.**	**taa**veerottawt særætnayk **fæ**lodnee
May I have a form, please?	**Kaphatok egy táviró-blankettát?**	**kop**hottawk æd^{y} **taa**vee-rāw-**blon**kæt-taat
When will the telegram be delivered?	**Mikor kézbesítik a táviratot?**	**mee**kawr **kayz**bæshēēteek o **taa**veerottawt

PLACE NAMES: see page 174

Telephoning

Apart from local calls, direct dialling facilities are still the exception rather than the rule in Hungary. Among hotels, only a few five-star establishments can be reached automatically. However, modernization is proceeding apace, and each year brings an expansion of the automatic telephone network.

Local calls can be made from street pay phones. Long-distance connections are best made through your hotel switchboard operator or at a post office.

To phone abroad you'll have to ask your hotel operator to put the call through for you or go to a major post office. In Budapest you may use the convenient facilities of the international telecommunications centre at the corner of Petőfi Sándor utca and Martinelli-tér.

Where's the telephone?	**Hol a telefon?**	hawl o **tæ**læfawn
Where's the nearest telephone booth?	**Hol a legközelebbi telefonfülke?**	hawl o **læg**kurzælæb-bee **tæ**læfawnfewlkæ
May I use your phone?	**Használhatom a telefonját?**	**hos**naalhottawm o **tæ**læfawnyaat
Do you have a telephone directory for ...?	**Van ...-i telefonkönyvük?**	von ...-ee **tæ**læfawn-kurn^{y}vewk
Can you help me get this number?	**Segítene felhívni ezt a számot?**	**sh**æghēētænæ **f**ælhēēvnee æst o **saa**mawt

Operator

Do you speak English?	**Beszél angolul?**	**b**æsayl **on**gawlool
Hello, I want Boston 123-456.	**Halló! A Boston 123-456-os számot kérem kapcsolni.**	**hol**-la̅w̅. o **baws**tawn 123-456 awsh **saa**mawt **kay**ræm **kop**chawlnee
Can I dial direct?	**Lehet közvetlenül tárcsázni?**	**l**æhæt **kurz**vætlænewl **taar**chaaznee

NUMBERS: see page 175

I want to place a personal (person-to-person) call.	**Személyes beszélgetést szeretnék rendelni.**	sæmay^{y}æsh **bæ**saylgætaysht **sær**ætnayk **ræn**dælnee
A transferred-charge (collect) call, please.	**«R» beszélgetést kérek.**	"ær" **bæ**saylgætaysht **kay**ræk
Please tell me the cost of the call when I'm finished.	**A beszélgetés végén legyen szíves közölni a költséget.**	o **bæ**saylgætaysh **vay**gayn **læd**^{y}æn **seevæsh** **kur**zurlnee o **kurlt**shayghæt

Speaking

Hello, this is ... speaking.	**Halló, itt ... beszél.**	**hol**-law eet ... **bæ**sayl
Would you put me through to ...?	**Kapcsolná ...-t?**	**kop**chawlnaa ...-t
I want to speak to Mr./Mrs. ...	**... úrral/úrnövel szeretnék beszélni.**	... **oor**-rol/**oor**nurvæl **sær**ætnayk **bæ**saylnee
I want extension ...	**A ...-es melléket kérem.**	o ...-æsh **mæl**-laykæt **kay**ræm
Is that ...?	**Ön ...?**	urn
Please speak more slowly.	**Legyen szíves, mondja lassabban.**	**læd**^{y}æn **see**væsh **mawnd**^{y}o **losh**-shob-bon

Telephone alphabet

A	**Aladár**	**ol**loddaar	N	**Nándor**	**naan**dawr
Á	**Ágota**	**aa**gawto	O	**Olga**	**awl**go
B	**Balázs**	**bol**laazh	Ö	**Ödön**	**ur**durn
C	**Cecília**	**tsæt**seeleeo	P	**Péter**	**pay**tær
D	**Dénes**	**day**næsh	Q	**Kú**	koo
E	**Erzsébet**	**ær**zhaybæt	R	**Róbert**	**raw**bært
É	**Éva**	**ay**vo	S	**Sándor**	**shaan**dawr
F	**Ferenc**	**fæ**rænts	T	**Tivadar**	**tee**voddor
G	**Gábor**	**gaa**bawr	U	**Ubul**	**oo**bool
H	**Helén**	**hæ**layn	Ü	**Üröm**	**ew**rurm
I	**Ilona**	**ee**lawno	V	**Vilma**	**veel**mo
J	**József**	**yaw**zhæf	W	**duplavé**	**doo**plovvay
K	**Károly**	**kaa**raw^{y}	X	**iksz**	eeks
L	**László**	**laas**law	Y	**ipszilon**	**eep**seelawn
M	**Mónika**	**maw**neeko	Z	**Zorán**	**zaw**raan

Bad luck

Operator, you gave me a wrong number.	**Központ! Rossz számot adott meg nekem.**	**kurz**pawnt. rawss **saa**mawt oddawt mæg **næ**kæm
Operator, we've been cut off.	**Központ! Megszakadt a beszélgetés.**	**kurz**pawnt. **mæg**sokkodt o **bæ**saylgætaysh
Would you please try again later?	**Kérem, később legyen szíves újra felhívni.**	**kay**ræm **kay**shurb **læd**^{Y}æn **see**væsh **oo**^{Y}ro **fæl**heevnee

Not there

When will he/she be back?	**Mikor lesz benn az illető?**	**mee**kawr læs bæn oz **eel**lætur
Will you tell him/her I called? My name is ...	**Kérem, értesítse, hogy kerestem. ... vagyok.**	**kay**ræm **ayr**tæsheetshæ hawd^{Y} **kæ**ræshtæm. ... **vod**^{Y}awk
Would you please take a message?	**Átadná az üzenetet?**	**aa**todnaa oz **ew**zænætæt

Önt keresik telefonon.	There's a phone call for you.
Melyik számot hívja?	What number are you calling?
Kérem, tartsa a vonalat.	Please hold the line.
Foglalt a vonal.	The line is busy.
Nem veszik fel.	There's no answer.
Téves számot hív.	You've got the wrong number.
A telefon nem működik.	The phone is out of order.
Az illető jelenleg nincs benn.	He/She is out at the moment.

Charges

What was the cost of that call?	**Mibe kerül a beszélgetés?**	**mee**bæ **kæ**rewl o **bæ**saylgætaysh
I want to pay for the call.	**Ki szeretném fizetni a telefonbeszélgetés díját.**	kee **sæ**rætnaym **fee**zætnee o **tæ**læfawnbæsaylgætaysh **dee**yaat

The car

Filling station

We'll start this section by considering your possible needs at a filling station.

Petrol (gasoline), oil and diesel fuel are sold by the litre. Fuel generally comes in three octane ratings—98, 92, 86—and unleaded (rare). Most filling stations will change your oil and wash your car, but they are rarely equipped for handling any repairs.

Since spare parts for Western-built vehicles are extremely difficult to obtain, it's advisable at least to take a set of some basic items with you (gaskets, fan belt, etc.) when driving to Hungary. A wise precaution is to have your car thoroughly serviced before leaving home.

Where's the nearest filling station?	**Hol a legközelebbi töltőállomás?**	hawl o **læg**kurzælæb-bee **turl**tūr-aal-lawmaash
I'd like 30 litres of ...	**30 liter ... benzint kérek.**	30 **lee**tær ... **bæn**zeent **kay**ræk
98 octane	**extra**	**æx**tro
92 octane	**szuper**	**soo**pær
86 octane	**normál**	**nawr**maal

Fluid measures					
litres	imp. gal.	U.S. gal.	litres	imp. gal.	U.S. gal.
5	1.1	1.3	30	6.6	7.9
10	2.2	2.6	35	7.7	9.2
15	3.3	4.0	40	8.8	10.6
20	4.4	5.3	45	9.9	11.9
25	5.5	6.6	50	11.0	13.2

TIPPING: see page 1

Give me ... forints' worth of petrol (gas), please.	**Kérek ... forintért benzint.**	kay**ræk** ... **faw**reentayrt **bæn**zeent
Fill the tank, please.	**Tele kérem.**	**tæ**læ **kay**ræm
Please check the oil and water.	**Kérem, ellenőrizze az olajszintet és a hűtővizet.**	**kay**ræm **æl**-lænūrreez-zæ oz **aw**loyseentæt aysh o **hēw**tūrveezæt
Give me a litre of oil.	**Egy liter motor-olajat kérek.**	æd[y] **lee**tær **maw**tawraw-loyot **kay**ræk
Top up the battery with distilled water, please.	**Kérem, töltse fel az akkumulátort desztillált vízzel.**	**kay**ræm **turlt**shæ fæl oz **ok**-koomoolaatawrt **dæ**steel-laalt **vēē**z-zæl
Would you check the brake fluid?	**Kérem, ellenőrizze a fékolajnyomást.**	**kay**ræm **æl**-lænūrreez-zæ o **fay**kawloyn[y]awmaasht
Please check the tire pressure.	**Kérem, ellenőrizze a gumikat.**	**kay**ræm **æl**-lænūrreez-zæ o **goo**meekot
1.6 front, 1.8 rear.	**1 egész 6 elöl, 1 egész 8 hátul.**	æd[y] **æ**gayss hot **æ**lurl æd[y] **æ**gayss n[y]awlts **haa**tool
Please check the spare tire, too.	**Kérem a tartalék-kereket is ellenőrizni.**	**kay**ræm o **tor**tollayk-kæ-rækæt eesh **æl**-lænūrreeznee

Tire pressure

lb./sq.in.	kg./cm²	lb./sq.in.	kg./cm²
10	0.7	26	1.8
12	0.8	27	1.9
15	1.1	28	2.0
18	1.3	30	2.1
20	1.4	33	2.3
21	1.5	36	2.5
23	1.6	38	2.7
24	1.7	40	2.8

Note: In Hungary, tire pressure is measured in kilograms per square centimetre. The following conversion chart will make sure your tires get the treatment they deserve. You can just show this panel to the filling station attendant and point to the pressures you need.

NUMBERS: page 175

Can you mend this puncture (fix this flat)?	**Kérem ezt a defektes gumit megjavítani.**	**kay**ræm æst o **dæ**fæktæsh **goo**meet **mæg**yovēētonnee
Would you please change this tire?	**Kérem ezt az abroncsot kicserélni.**	**kay**ræm æst oz **ob**rawnchawt **kee**chæraylnee
Would you please change the oil?	**Egy olajcserét kérek.**	æd^y **aw**loychærayt **kay**ræk
Would you clean the windscreen (windshield)?	**Lemosná a szélvédőt?**	**læ**mawshnaa o **sayl**vaydūrt

Miles into kilometres										
1 mile = 1.609 kilometres (km)										
miles	10	20	30	40	50	60	70	80	90	100
km	16	32	48	64	80	97	113	129	145	161

Kilometres into miles													
1 kilometre (km) = 0.62 miles													
km	10	20	30	40	50	60	70	80	90	100	110	120	130
miles	6	12	19	25	31	37	44	50	56	62	68	75	81

Have you any windscreen scrapers?	**Van szélvédő tisztítójuk?**	von **sayl**vaydūr **tees**tēētāw^yook
Can you sell me some antifreeze?	**Van fagyásgátló folyadékjuk?**	von **fod**^yaashgaatlāw **faw**^yoddaykyook
Could you give me small change for this?	**Adna ezért aprót?**	**od**no æzayrt **op**rāwt
Have you a road map of this area?	**Van a környékről útitérképük?**	von o **kurrn**^yaykrūrl **ōō**teetayrkaypewk
May I use your phone?	**Használhatom a telefonját?**	**hos**naalhottawm o **tæ**læfawnyaat
Where are the toilets?	**Hol a W.C.?**	hawl o **vay**tsay

Asking the way—Street directions

Excuse me.	**Elnézést.**	æ**l**nayzaysht
Do you speak English?	**Beszél ön angolul?**	**b**æsayl urn **on**gawlool
Could you tell me the way to ...?	**Elmagyarázná az utat ...-ba/-be/ -ra/-re?***	**æl**mod^{y}orraaznaa oz **oo**tot ...-bo/-bæ/-ro/-ræ
How do I get to ...?	**Hogy jutok el ...-ba/-be/-ra/-re?***	hawd^{y} **yoo**tawk æl ...-bo/-bæ/-ro/-ræ
Where does this road lead to?	**Ez az út hova vezet?**	æz oz o͞ot **haw**vo **v**æzæt
Can you show me on the map where I am?	**Megmutatná ezen a térképen, hogy hol vagyok?**	**mæg**moototnaa æzæn o **tayr**kaypæn hawd^{y} hawl **vod**^{y}awk
How far is it to ... from here?	**Innen milyen messze van ...?**	**een**-næn **mee**^{y}æn **mæs**-sæ von
How far is the next town?	**Milyen messze van a legközelebbí város?**	**mee**^{y}æn **mæs**-sæ von o **læg**kurzælæb-bee **vaa**rawsh
Where can I find this address?	**Hogy jutok el erre címre?**	hawd^{y} **yoo**tawk æl **ær**-ræ o **tse͞em**ræ
Where's this?	**Ez merre van?**	æz **mær**-ræ von

Nem jó irányban megy.	You're on the wrong road.
Egyenesen tovább előre.	Go straight ahead.
Balra/Jobbra van, arra lenn.	It's down there on the left/right.
Menjen az első/második keresztútig.	Go to the first/second crossroads.
A közlekedési lámpánál forduljon balra/jobbra.	Turn left/right at the traffic lights.

Can you show me on the map where ... is?	**Megmutatná a tér-képen, hogy hol ...?**	**mæg**moototnaa o **tayr**kay-pæn hawd^{y} hawl
Are we on the right road for ...?	**Jó úton vagyunk ... felé?**	ya͞w **oo**tawn **vod**^{y}oonk ... **fæ**lay

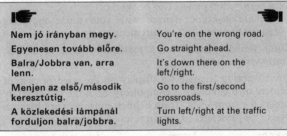

* See Grammar section for word endings.

In the rest of this section we'll be more closely concerned with driving conditions in Hungary and the car itself. We've divided it into two parts:

Part A contains general advice on motoring in Hungary. It would be advisable to read through it in advance.

Part B is concerned with the practical details of accidents and breakdowns. It includes a list of car parts and of things that may go wrong with them. All you have to do is to show it to the garage mechanic and get him to point to the items required.

Part A

Customs—Documentation—Other requirements

You will need the following documents in order to drive in Hungary:

- passport and visa
- valid driving licence
- car registration papers (log book)
- adequate insurance (check with your home motoring organization on latest requirements)

Motor vehicles must bear a nationality plate or sticker, clearly visible at the rear.

A red warning triangle for display on the road in case of accident or breakdown is compulsory. So is the use of safety belts in the front seats. Crash helmets must be worn by both driver and passenger of motorcycles and scooters.

Here's my ...	**Tessék ...**	**tæsh**-shayk
driving licence	**a jogosítványom**	o **yaw**gawshēētvaanʸawm
insurance certificate	**a biztosítási kötvényem**	o **beez**tawshēētaashee **kurt**vaynʸæm
passport	**az útlevelem**	oz **ōō**tlævælæm
registration (log) book	**a gépkocsim okmányai**	o **gayp**kawcheem **awk**maanʸo-ee

CUSTOMS, see also page 22

I've nothing to declare.	**Nincs elvámolni valóm.**	neench ælvaamawlnee voll$\overline{aw}$m
Where can I get a visa?	**Hol kapok vízumot?**	hawl koppawk v$\overline{ee}$zoomawt

Driving—Roads

In Hungary you drive on the right and pass on the left. Go carefully until you have had time to take the measure of the local drivers—the accident rate is one of Europe's highest.

Hungary's motorways (expressways) are well maintained and toll-free. Emergency telephones for use in case of breakdown or accident are located every two kilometres (about 1¼ miles) along these roads.

Other roads are well maintained but out in the countryside not always very wide. Roads are numbered.

Traffic lights have the familiar red, yellow and green colours. You'll probably notice that the yellow stays lit longer than you're used to—but nevertheless, you are supposed to wait until it changes to green before moving off. The green light flashes several times before changing to yellow. At night, traffic lights work on a single flashing yellow, advising all drivers to pay great attention at the crossroads.

You must always stop at railway level crossings. These points are indicated by flashing red and white lights. At bridges, the vehicle closest to the approach, or already on the bridge, has priority.

Pedestrian crossings are marked with white stripes and are illuminated at night. Pedestrians have absolute priority on these crossings at all times.

Winter tires or chains are not compulsory, but driving during the November–March period without them is hazardous.

For help in case of breakdown, see page 151.

Roadsigns—Signposts

Roadsigns used in Hungary are mainly the international pictographs that are also seen on roads throughout western Europe. Some of the more important signs are shown on pages 160–161. Since they are mostly self-explanatory, they are hardly ever supplemented with written notices.

When a signboard has a smaller plate under it bearing a figure in metres, this means that the directive indicated by the roadsign only becomes effective after you have covered the distance shown.

Motorways are indicated by green signs, and other main roads by dark-blue shields. Minor roads and country lanes have signposts bearing black lettering on a white background. Signposting is generally clear.

Speed limits and some other special regulations

Speed limits for cars are: 120 kilometres per hour (75 miles per hour) on motorways, 80 kph (50 mph) on other roads outside city limits and 60 kph (37 mph) within residential areas.

Buses, heavy good vehicles, cars towing caravans (trailers) and motorcycles are restricted to 90 kph (56 mph), 70 kph (43 mph) and 50 kph (31 mph), respectively, on the three types of road specified above.

At night within residential areas, drive with your sidelights only.

If you intend to drive, don't touch a drop of alcohol: the zero limit for blood alcohol content is strictly enforced. If you are caught driving under the influence of alcohol there will be no mitigating circumstances. Penalties range from a very heavy fine to loss of your driving licence, and if you have been the cause of an accident while under the influence of drink, you are likely to end up with a stiff prison sentence.

Police

The police are normally lenient with foreign drivers, but don't push your luck. They are particularly vigilant about alcohol (see above), speeding and illegal parking in urban areas.

I'm sorry, Officer, I didn't see the sign.	**Sajnálom, uram, nem vettem észre a jelzőtáblát.**	**shoy**naalawm **oo**rom næm **væt**-tæm **ays**ræ o **yæl**z$\overline{ur}$taablaat
The light was green.	**Zöldet mutatott a lámpa.**	**zurl**dæt **moo**totawt o **laam**po
How much is the fine?	**Mennyi a büntetés?**	**mæn**^{y}ee o **bewn**tætaysh
Excuse me, my car has broken down.	**Elnézését kérem. Meghibásodott a gépkocsim.**	**æl**nayzayshayt **kay**ræm. **mæg**heebaashawdawt o **gayp**kawcheem

Parking

On the street, park your car in the direction of the traffic flow. Do not park at bus, tram (streetcar) or trolley-bus stops or at taxi ranks. Zigzag markings painted on the road surface and "no parking" signs indicate other areas where parking is prohibited. If your car has been parked in such a way as to impede traffic, it will be towed away by the police.

Budapest has parking meters, which take 1- and 5-forint coins, and guarded parking lots where you must purchase your ticket in advance.

Is there a car park in the neighbourhood?	**Van a környéken, gépkocsi parkoló?**	von o **kurrn**^{y}aykæn **gayp**kawchee **por**kawl$\overline{aw}$
Excuse me, may I park here?	**Elnézést, szabad itt parkolnom?**	**æl**nayzaysht **sob**bod eet **por**kawlnawm
What's the charge for parking here?	**Mennyi itt a parkolási díj?**	**mæn**^{y}ee eet o **por**kawlaa-shee d$\overline{ee}$^{y}
Excuse me, have you some forint coins for the parking meter?	**Elnézést kérek, volna néhány egy-forintosa a parkoló órába?**	**æl**nayzaysht **kay**ræk **vawl**no **nay**haan^{y} **æd**^{y}faw-reentawsho o **por**kawl$\overline{aw}$ $\overline{aw}$raabo

Part B

Accidents

This section is confined to immediate aid. The legal problems of responsibility and settlement can be taken care of at a later stage. Your first concern will be for the injured.

Is anyone hurt?	**Megsérült valaki?**	**mæg**shayrewlt **voll**okkee
Don't move.	**Ne mozogjon!**	næ **maw**zawgyawn
It's all right, don't worry.	**Nincs semmi baj, ne aggódjon.**	neench **shæm**-mee boy næ **og**-gāwd^y^awn
Where's the nearest telephone?	**Hol a legközelebbi telefon?**	hawl o **læg**kurzælæb-bee **tæ**læfawn
May I use your telephone? There's been an accident.	**Használhatom a telefonját? Baleset történt.**	**hos**naalhottawm o **tæ**læfawnyaat. **boll**æshæt **turr**taynt
Call a doctor/an ambulance quickly.	**Kérem, azonnal hívjon orvost/ mentőket!**	**kay**ræm **oz**zawn-nol **hēēv**yawn **awr**vawsht/**mæn**tūrkæt
There are people injured.	**Többen megsérültek.**	**turb**-bæn **mæg**shayrewltæk

Police—Exchange of information

Please call the police.	**Kérem, hívja a rendőrséget.**	**kay**ræm **hēē**vyo o **ræn**dūrrshaygæt
There's been an accident.	**Baleset történt.**	**boll**æshæt **turr**taynt
It's about 3 kilometres from ...	**...-tól/-től körülbelül 3 kilométernyire.***	...-tāwl-tūrl **kurr**ewlbælewl 3 **kee**lawmaytærn^y^eeræ
I'm on the Vienna–Budapest road ... of Győr.	**A Bécs–budapesti országúton vagyok Győrtől ...**	a baych **boo**doppæshtee **awr**saagōōtawn **vod**^y^awk **d**^y^**ūr**rtūrl
north/south east/west	**északra/délre keletre/nyugatra**	**ays**sokro/**day**lræ **kæ**lætræ/**n**^y^**oo**gotro

* See Grammar section for word endings.

DOCTOR: see page 162

Here's my name and address.	**Tessék a nevem és a címem.**	tæsh-shayk o nævæm aysh o tseemæm
Would you mind acting as a witness?	**Vállalná a tanuskodást?**	vaalolnaa o tonnooshkaw-daasht
I'd like an interpreter.	**Kérek tolmácsot.**	kayræk tawlmaachawt

B-r-e-a-k-d-o-w-n

Remember to put out a red warning triangle if the car is out of action or impeding traffic. It should be placed 50 metres behind your vehicle.

On all major roads, all year round, any driver may call for a "yellow angel"—one of the patrol cars of the Hungarian Automobile Club *(Magyar Autóklub)*. They do quick repairs at moderate prices, though they won't have any important spare parts for Western models.

This section is divided into four parts:

1 On the road
You ask where the nearest garage is.

2 At the garage
You tell the mechanic what's wrong.

3 Finding the trouble
He tells you what he thinks is the trouble.

4 Getting it repaired
You tell him to repair it and, once that's over, settle the account (or argue about it).

Phase 1—On the road

Where's the nearest garage?	**Hol a legközelebbi javítóműhely?**	hawl o lægkurzælæb-bee yovveetawmewhæ^y
What's the telephone number of the nearest garage/"yellow angel" post?	**Mi a telefonszáma a legközelebbi javítóműhelynek/ «sárga angyal» szolgálatnak?**	mee o tælæfawnsaamo o lægkurzælæb-bee yovveetawmewhæ^ynæk/ shaargo ond^yol sawlgaa-lotnok

TELEPHONE: see page 139

May I use your telephone?	**Használhatom a telefonját?**	**haws**naalhottawm o tælæfawnyaat
I've had a breakdown at ...	**...-nál/-nél elromlott a kocsim.***	...-naal/-nayl **æl**rawmlawt o **kaw**cheem
Can you send a mechanic?	**Küldene egy szerelőt?**	**kewl**dænæ æd^{y} særælurt
Can you send a breakdown truck?	**Tudna küldeni egy szervizkocsit?**	**too**dno **kewl**dænee æd^{y} **sær**veezkawcheet
How long will you be?	**Meddig tart?**	**mæd**-deeg tort
Shouldn't we call the police?	**Nem szükséges a rendőrséget kihívni?**	næm **sewk**shaygæsh o **ræn**durshaygæt **kee**heevnee

Phase 2—At the garage

Can you help me?	**Segítene?**	**shæ**gheetænæ
I don't know what's wrong with it.	**Nem tudom, mije romlott el.**	næm **too**dawm **mee**^{y}æ **rawm**lawt æl
I think there's something wrong with the ...	**Azt hiszem, ... elromlott.**	ost **hees**sæm ... **æl**rawmlawt
battery	**az akkumulátor**	oz **ok**-koomoolaatawr
brakes	**a fék**	o fayk
bulbs	**az izzók**	oz **eez**-zawk
cables	**a vezetékek**	o **væ**zætaykæk
carburettor	**a karburátor**	o **kor**booraatawr
clutch	**a kuplung**	o **koo**ploong
contact	**az érintkezés**	oz **ay**reentkæzaysh
cooling system	**a hűtőberendezés**	o **hew**turbæræendæzaysh
dipswitch (dimmer switch)	**a reflektor-kapcsoló**	o **ræ**flæktawr-kopchawlaw
dynamo	**a dinamó**	o **dee**nommaw
electrical system	**az elektromos berendezés**	oz **æ**læktrawmawsh bæraendæzaysh
engine	**a motor**	o **maw**tawr
exhaust pipe	**a kipuffogó**	o **kee**poof-fawgaw
fan	**a ventillátor**	o **væn**teel-laatawr
filter	**a szűrő**	o **sew**rur

* See Grammar section for word endings.

fuel pump	**az üzemanyag-szivatyú**	oz ewzæmonyogseevotyoo
fuel tank	**az üzemanyagtartály**	oz ewzæmonyogtortaay
gear shift	**a sebességváltó kar**	o shæbæsh-shaygvaaltaw kor
generator	**a dinamó**	o deenommaw
handbrake	**a kézifék**	o kayzeefayk
headlights	**a fényszórók**	o faynysawrawk
heating	**a fűtés**	o fewtaysh
horn	**a kürt**	o kewrt
ignition system	**a gyujtás**	o dyooytaash
indicator	**az irányjelző**	oz eeraanyyælzur
lights	**a lámpák**	o laampaak
backup lights	**a hátrameneti lámpák**	o haatrommænætee laampaak
brake lights	**a féklámpák**	o fayklaampaak
rear lights	**a hátsóvilágítás**	o haatshawveelaa-gheetaash
reversing lights	**a hátrameneti lámpák**	o haatrommænætee laampaak
sidelights	**a városi világítás**	o vaarawshee veelaagheetaash
tail lights	**a hátsóvilágítás**	o haatshawveelaa-gheetaash
lines (cables)	**a vezetékek**	o væzætaykæk
lubrication system	**a fékbetétek**	o faykbætaytæk
parking brake	**a kézifék**	o kayzeefayk
radiator	**a vízhűtő**	o veezhewtur
seat	**az ülés**	oz ewlaysh
sliding roof	**a tolótető**	o tawlawtætur
spark plugs	**a gyújtógyertya**	o dyooytawdyærtyo
speedometer	**a sebességmérő**	o shæbæsh-shaygmayrur
starter	**az önindító**	oz urneendeetaw
steering	**a kormánymű**	o kawrmaanymew
suspension	**a felfüggesztés**	o fælfewg-gæstaysh
transmission	**a sebességváltó-áttétel**	o shæbæsh-shaygvaaltaw-aat-taytæl
turn signal	**az irányjelző**	oz eeraanyyælzur
wheels	**a kerekek**	o kærækæk
wipers	**az ablaktörlők**	oz oblokturrlurk

LEFT	RIGHT
BALRA	**JOBBRA**
(bolro)	(yawbro)

FRONT	REAR
ELÖL	**HÁTUL**
(ælurl)	(haatool)

It's …

blowing	**ereszt**	ær**æst**
broken	**eltört**	**æl**turrt
burnt	**kiégett**	**kee**aygæt
cracked	**megrepedt**	**mæg**ræpædt
defective	**hibás**	**hee**baash
disconnected	**szétszakadt**	**sayt**sokkodt
dry	**száraz**	**saa**roz
frozen	**befagyott**	**bæ**fod^{y}awt
jammed	**beszorult**	**bæ**sawroolt
knocking	**kopog**	**kaw**pawg
leaking	**folyik**	**faw**^{y}eek
loose	**meglazult**	**mæg**lozzoolt
misfiring	**rossz a gyújtása**	rawss o **d**^{y}**oo**^{y}taasho
noisy	**hangos**	**hon**gawsh
not working	**nem működik**	næm **mew**kurdeek
overheating	**túlmelegszik**	**tool**mælægseek
short-circuiting	**zárlatos**	**zaar**lottawsh
slack	**laza**	**loz**zo
slipping	**csúszik**	**choo**sseek
stuck	**beszorult**	**bæ**sawroolt
vibrating	**beremeg**	**bæ**ræmæg
weak	**gyenge**	**d**^{y}**æn**gæ
worn	**elkopott**	**æl**kawpawt
The car won't start.	**Nem indul.**	næm **een**dool
It's locked and the keys are inside.	**Be van zárva és a kulcsok belül vannak.**	bæ von **zaar**vo aysh o **kool**chawk **bæ**lewl **von**-nok
The battery is flat.	**Az akkumulátor kimerült.**	oz **ok**-koomoolaatawr **kee**mærewlt
The fan belt is too slack.	**A ventillátor-szíj nagyon laza.**	o **væn**teel-laatawr **see**^{y} **nod**^{y}awn **loz**zo
I want my car serviced and lubricated.	**Karbantartást és zsírzást kérek.**	**kor**bontortaasht aysh **zhee**rzaasht **kay**ræk
The idling needs adjusting.	**Az alapjáratot be kell állítani.**	oz **ol**lopyaarottawt bæ kæl **aal**-leetonnee
The pedals need adjusting.	**A pedált szükséges beállítani.**	o **pæ**daalt **sewk**shaygæsh **bæ**aal-leetonnee
The steering wheel is vibrating.	**A kormánykerék beremeg.**	o **kawr**maan^{y}kærayk **bæ**ræmæg
The wipers are smearing.	**Az ablaktörlők maszatolnak.**	oz **ob**lokturrlurk **mos**sottawlnok

Now that you've explained what's wrong:

How long will it take to repair?	**Meddig tart a javítás?**	**mæd**-deeg tort o **yovvēē**-taash
Can you give me a ride into town?	**Elvinne a városba?**	ælveen-næ o **vaarawshbo**
Could you get me a taxi?	**Hívna nekem egy taxit?**	**hēēvno** nækæm æd^y **toxeet**
Is there a hotel nearby?	**Van a környéken szálloda?**	von o **kurn**^yaykæn **saal**-lawdo

Phase 3—Finding the trouble

If you don't know what's wrong with the car, it's up to the mechanic to find the trouble. You can ask him what has to be repaired by handing him the book and pointing to the Hungarian text below.

Kérem, tekintse végig a következő, ábécé sorrendben összeállított listát és mutasson rá a meghibásodott tételre. Ha az ügyfele a hiba okát is tudni kívánja, válassza ki a megfelelő kifejezést a következő listából (eltört, zárlatos stb.).*

adagoló	injection pump
akkumulátor	battery
akkumulátor cellák	battery cells
automata sebességváltó	automatic transmission
betét	lining
csapágy	bearing
csapszeg	stems
csatlakozó	connection
desztillált víz	distilled water
dinamó	dynamo, generator
dugattyú	piston
dugattyú gyűrű	piston ring
elosztó kábel	distributor leads

* Please look at the following alphabetical list and point to the defective item. If your customer wants to know what's wrong with it, pick the applicable term from the next list (broken, short-circuited, etc.).

érintkezési pont	contact
felfüggesztés	suspension
felfüggesztő gyűrű	suspension ring
felfüggesztő rugó	suspension spring
fék	brakes
fékdob	brake drum
fékpofa	brake shoes
féktárcsa	brake disc
fogastengely	rack and pinion
fogazás	teething
főcsapágy	main bearing
főtengely	camshaft
függesztőmű	stabilizer
gyertya	spark plug
gyertyakábel	plug leads
gyújtás	ignition
gyűrű	ring
hajtómű	transmission
henger	cylinder
hengerfej	cylinder head
hengerfej tömítés	cylinder head gasket
hűtőberendezés	cooling system
illesztés	joints
indító motor	starter motor
karburátor	carburettor
kardánház	crankcase
kardántengely	crankshaft
kardán vezérlés	universal joint
kábel	cable
kondenzátor	capacitor
kormány	steering column
kormánymű	steering system
kuplung	clutch
kuplung pedál	clutch pedal
lengéscsillapító	shock absorber
légrugózás	pneumatic suspension
légszűrő	air filter
membrán	diaphragm
motor	engine
motorház	engine block
olajszivattyú	oil pump
olajszűrő	oil filter
radiátor	radiator
reflektor kapcsoló	dipswitch (dimmer switch)
rugók	springs
sebességváltó	gearbox

szelep emelő	tappet
szeleptest	valve
szivattyú	pump
szűrő	filter
tengely	shaft
termosztát	thermostat
úszó	float
üzemanyag szivattyú	petrol (gas) pump
üzemanyag szűrő	petrol (gas) filter
ventillátor	fan
ventillátor szíj	fan belt
villamos berendezés	electrical system
vízszivattyú	water pump

A következő lista azokat a kifejezéseket tartalmazza, amelyek a hibákat és a kijavítás módját magyarázzák meg.*

alacsony	low
áteresztés	blowing
beállítani	to adjust
becsiszolni	to grind in
befagyott	frozen
beszorult	jammed, stuck
csúszás	sliding
defekt	puncture
elégett	burnt
elgörbült	deformed, bent, warped
elkopott	chipped, worn
eltört	broken
feltölteni	to charge
folyás	leaking
gyenge	weak
gyors	quick
gyújtáshibás	misfiring
hegeszteni	to weld
hibás	defective
holtjáték	play
kicserélni	to change, replace
kiegyensúlyozni	to balance
kiereszteni	to bleed
kiégett	blown
kiszerelni	to strip down
kiugrott	cracked

* The following list contains words which describe what's wrong as well as what may need to be done.

kopogás	knocking
laza	slack, loose
magas	high
meghúzni	to tighten
meglazítani	to loosen
megrozsdásodott	corroded
piszkos	dirty
rezgés	vibration
rövid	short
száraz	dry
széntelenítení	to decarbonize
szétment	disconnected
túlmelegedés	overheating
újrabélelni	to reline
üres	empty
zárlatos	short-circuited
zsírozni	to grease

Phase 4—Getting it repaired

Have you found the trouble?	**Megvan a hiba?**	**mæg**von o **hee**bo
Is it serious?	**Komoly?**	**kaw**maw^{y}
Can you repair it?	**Meg tudják javítani?**	mæg **tood**^{y}aak yovvēētonnee
Can you repair it at once?	**Meg tudják rögtön javítani?**	mæg **tood**^{y}aak **rurg**turn yovvēētonnee
What's it going to cost?	**Mennyibe kerül?**	**mæn**^{y}eebæ **kæ**rewl
Do you have the necessary spares?	**Van alkatrészük hozzá?**	von **ol**kotrayssewk **hawz**-zaa

What if he says "no"?

Why can't you do it?	**Miért nem tudják megjavítani?**	**mee**ayrt næm **tood**^{y}aak **mæg**yovvēētonnee
Is it essential to have that part?	**Feltétlenül szükséges az az alkatrész?**	**fæl**taylænewl **sewk**shaygæsh oz oz **ol**kotrayss
How long is it going to take to get the spare parts?	**Meddig tart beszerezni az alkatrészeket?**	**mæd**-deeg tort **bæ**sæ-ræznee oz **ol**kotrayssækæt

Where's the nearest garage that can repair it?	**Hol a legközelebbi szerviz, ahol meg tudják javítani?**	hawl o **læg**kurzælæb-bee **sær**veez **o**hawl mæg **tood**^{y}aak **yo**vvēētonnee
Can you fix it so that I can get as far as ...?	**Rendbe tudják annyira hozni, hogy ...-ig eljuthassak vele?**	**rænd**bæ **tood**^{y}aak **on**^{y}eero **hawz**nee hawd^{y} ...-eeg **æl**yoot-hosh-shok **væ**læ

If you're really stuck, ask if you can leave the car at the garage. Don't forget to empty it of valuables. Contact the Hungarian Automobile Association or hire another car.

Settling the bill

Is everything all right?	**Minden rendben?**	**meen**dæn **rænd**bæn
How much do I owe you?	**Mennyivel tartozom?**	**mæn**^{y}eevæl **tor**tawzawm
Do you accept traveller's cheques (checks)?	**Traveller's csekket elfogadnak?**	**tro**vvæl-lærs **chæk**-kæt **æl**fawgodnok
Can I pay with this credit card?	**Fizethetek ezzel a hitelkártyával?**	**fee**zæt-hætæk **æz**-zæl o **hee**tælkaart^{y}aavol
Do you accept foreign money?	**Külföldi valutát elfogadnak?**	**kewl**furldee **vol**lootaat **æl**fawgodnok
I have to change some money.	**Pénzt kell váltanom.**	paynzt kæl **vaal**tonnawm
Thanks very much for your help.	**Köszönöm szépen a segítségét.**	**kur**surnurm **say**pæn o **shæ**ghēētshaygayt

But you may feel that the workmanship is sloppy or that you're paying for work not done. In that case, get the bill itemized. If necessary have it translated before you pay.

I'd like to check the bill first.	**Először szeretném ellenőrizni a számlát.**	**æ**lūrssurr **sæ**rætnaym **æl**-lænūrreeznee o **saam**laat
Will you itemize the work done?	**Részleteznék az elvégzett munkát?**	**rays**lætæznayk oz **æl**vaygzæt **moon**kaat

CAR—REPAIRS

Some international road signs

No vehicles

No entry

No overtaking (passing)

Oncoming traffic has priority

Maximum speed limit

No parking

Caution

Intersection

Dangerous bend (curve)

Road narrows

Intersection with secondary road

Two-way traffic

Dangerous hill

Uneven road

Falling rocks

Give way (yield)

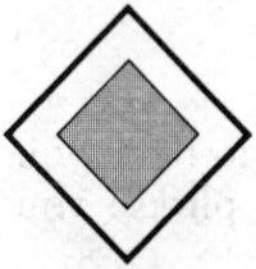

Main road, thoroughfare

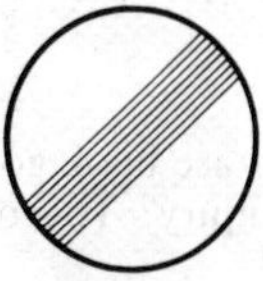

End of restriction

One-way traffic

Traffic goes this way

Roundabout (rotary)

Bicycles only

Pedestrians only

Minimum speed limit

Keep right (left if symbol reversed)

Parking

Hospital

Motorway (expressway)

Motor vehicles only

Filling station

No through road

Doctor

Frankly, how much use is a phrase book going to be to you in case of serious illness or injury? The only phrase you need in such an emergency is:

Get a doctor quickly!	**Kérem, azonnal hívjon orvost!**	**kay**ræm **ozzawn**-nol **hēē**vyawn **awr**vawsht

But there are minor aches and pains, ailments and irritations, that can upset the best planned trip. Here we can help you—and, perhaps, the doctor.

Some doctors may speak a little English. At any rate, they are likely to know enough medical terminology in English for your needs. But suppose there's something the doctor cannot explain because of language difficulties? We've thought of that. As you'll see, this section has been arranged to enable you and the doctor to communicate. From page 165 to page 171, you'll find your part of the dialogue on the upper half of each page—the doctor's is on the lower half.

The whole section is divided into three parts: illness, wounds, nervous tension. Page 171 is concerned with prescriptions and fees. The phrases on pages 172 and 173 will be of help to you at the dentist's or the optician's.

General

Can you get me a doctor?	**Tudna hívni orvost?**	**tood**no **hēē**vnee **awr**vawsht
Is there a doctor here who speaks English?	**Van angolul beszélő orvosuk?**	von **on**gawlool **bæ**saylūr **awr**vawshook
Where's the surgery (doctor's office)?	**Hol az orvosi rendelő?**	hawl oz **awr**vawshee **rænd**ælūr
What are the surgery (office) hours?	**Mikor rendel?**	**mee**kawr **rænd**æl
Could the doctor come to see me here?	**Kihívható az orvos hozzám?**	**kee**hēēvhottāw oz **awr**vawsh **hawz**-zaam

PHARMACY: see page 108

The Hungarian National Health Service, widely known by its abbreviation *Sz. T. K.* (**æs**taykaa), or the special emergency squad *Mentők* (**mæn**tu̅r̅k) provide all necessary help, including hospitalization, in case of emergency. Medical standards are in general very high. Most doctors and dentists also have private practices, and many foreigners go to Hungary to enjoy private medical and dental care at relatively low cost.

Symptoms

Use this section to tell the doctor what's wrong. Basically, what he'll require to know is:

What?	(ache, pain, bruise, etc.)
Where?	(arm, stomach, etc.)
How long?	(have you had the trouble)

Before you visit the doctor find out the answers to these questions by glancing through the pages that follow. In this way you'll save time.

Parts of the body

ankle	**boka**	**baw**ko
appendix	**vakbél**	**vok**bayl
arm	**kar**	**kor**
artery	**ütőér**	**ewtu̅r̅**-ayr
back	**hát**	haat
bladder	**hólyag**	**ha̅w̅**^{y}og
blood	**vér**	vayr
bone	**csont**	chawnt
bowels	**has**	hosh
breast	**mell**	mæl
cheek	**arc**	orts
chest	**mellkas**	**mæl**kosh
chin	**áll**	aal
collar-bone	**kulcs-csont**	**koolch**-chawnt
ear	**fül**	fewl
elbow	**könyök**	**kurn**^{y}urk
eye	**szem**	sæm
face	**arc**	orts
finger	**ujj**	oo^{y}

foot	**lábfej**	**laab**fæ^{y}
forehead	**homlok**	**hawm**lawk
genitals	**nemi szervek**	næmee **sær**væk
gland	**mirigy**	**meereed**^{y}
hair	**haj**	hoy
hand	**kéz**	kayz
head	**fej**	fæ^{y}
heart	**szív**	s$\overline{ee}$v
heel	**sarok**	**shor**rawk
hip	**csípő**	**ch$\overline{ee}$**p$\overline{ur}$
intestines	**belek**	**bæ**læk
jaw	**állkapocs**	**aal**koppawch
joint	**ízület**	**$\overline{ee}$**zewlæt
kidney	**vese**	**væ**shæ
knee	**térd**	tayrd
knee-cap	**térdkalács**	**tayrd**kollaach
leg	**láb**	laab
lip	**ajak**	**oy**ok
liver	**máj**	maa^{y}
lung	**tüdő**	**tew**d$\overline{ur}$
mouth	**száj**	saa^{y}
muscle	**izom**	**ee**zawm
neck	**nyak**	n^{y}ok
nerve	**ideg**	**ee**dæg
nervous system	**idegrendszer**	**ee**dægrændsær
nose	**orr**	awr
rib	**borda**	**baw**rdo
shoulder	**váll**	vaal
skin	**bőr**	b$\overline{ur}$r
spine	**hátgerinc**	**haat**gæreents
stomach	**gyomor**	**d^{y}aw**mawr
tendon	**ín**	$\overline{ee}$n
thigh	**comb**	tsawmb
throat	**torok**	**taw**rawk
thumb	**hüvelyk**	**hew**væ^{y}k
toe	**lábujj**	**laa**boo^{y}
tongue	**nyelv**	n^{y}ælv
tonsils	**mandula**	**mon**doolo
urine	**vizelet**	**vee**zælæt
vein	**ér**	ayr
wrist	**csukló**	**chook**l$\overline{aw}$

LEFT/ON THE LEFT SIDE
BAL/A BALOLDALON
(bol/o **bol**lawldollawn)

RIGHT/ON THE RIGHT SIDE
JOBB/A JOBB OLDALON
(yawb/o yawb **awl**dollawn)

PATIENT

Part 1—Illness

I'm not feeling well.	**Rosszul érzem magam.**	rawss-sool ayrzæm moggom
I'm ill.	**Beteg vagyok.**	bætæg vod^{y}awk
I've got a pain here.	**Itt fáj valami.**	eet faa^{y} vollommee
I've got a fever.	**Lázas vagyok.**	laazosh vod^{y}awk
I've got a ...	**Fáj a ...**	faa^{y} o
backache	**hátam**	haatom
headache	**fejem**	fæ^{y}æm
sore throat	**torkom**	tawrkawm
stomachache	**gyomrom**	d^{y}awmrawm
I've been vomiting.	**Hánytam.**	haan^{y}tom
I'm constipated.	**Szorulásom van.**	sawroolaashawm vawn

DOCTOR

Első rész—Betegség

Mi a panasza?	What's the trouble?
Hol fáj?	Where does it hurt?
Milyen fájdalmat érez?	What kind of pain is it?
tompa/éles/lüktető **állandó/változó**	dull/sharp/throbbing constant/on and off
Mióta érzi így magát?	How long have you been feeling like this?
Tűrje fel az ingujját.	Roll up your sleeve, please.
Kérem vetközzön le (derékig).	Please undress (down to the waist).

PATIENT

I feel dizzy.	**Szédülök.**	**say**dewlurk
I feel faint.	**Gyengének érzem magamat.**	**d^{y}æn**gaynæk **ayr**zæm **mog**gommot
I feel shivery.	**Ráz a hideg.**	raaz o **hee**dæg
I feel nauseous.	**Hányingerem van.**	**haan^{y}**eengæræm von
I've got ... degrees temperature.	**... fok lázam van.**	... fawk **laa**zom von
I've got (a/an) ...		
asthma	**Asztmás vagyok.**	**ost**maash **vod^{y}**awk
bronchitis	**Bronhitiszem van.**	**brawn**heeteessæm von
cold	**Meg vagyok fázva.**	mæg **vod^{y}**awk **faa**zvo
cough	**Köhögök.**	**kur**hurgurk
cramps	**Görcsölök.**	**gurr**churlurk
diarrhoea	**Megy a hasam.**	mæd^{y} o **ho**shom
earache	**A fülem fáj.**	o **few**læm faa^{y}
haemorrhoids	**Aranyerem van.**	**or**ron^{y}æræm von
hayfever	**Szénanáthám van.**	**say**nonnaat-haam von
heartburn	**Gyomorégésem van.**	**d^{y}aw**mawraygayshæm von

DOCTOR

Kérem, feküdjön le ide.	Please lie down over there.
Nyissa ki a száját.	Open your mouth.
Sóhajtson mélyeket.	Breathe deeply.
Köhögjön kérem.	Cough, please.
Megmérem a vérnyomását/a lázát.	I'll take your blood pressure/ temperature.
Először van ilyen állapotban?	Is this the first time you've had this?
Adok egy injekciót.	I'll give you an injection.
Vér/Széklet/Vizelet mintára van szükségem.	I want a specimen of your blood/stools/urine.
... napig ágyban kell maradnia.	You must stay in bed for ... days.

PATIENT

hernia	**Sérvem van.**	shayrvæm von
indigestion	**Gyomorrontásom van.**	d^{y}awmawr-rawntaashawm von
an itch	**Viszketegségem van.**	veeskætægshaygæm von
nosebleed	**Vérzik az orrom.**	vayrzeek oz awr-rawm
palpitations	**Szívdobogásom van.**	s$\overline{\text{ee}}$vdawbawgaashawm von
period pains	**Menstruálok.**	mænshtrooaalawk
rash	**Kiütéses vagyok.**	keeewtayshæsh vod^{y}awk
rheumatism	**Reumás vagyok.**	ræoomaash vod^{y}awk
shivers	**Ráz a hideg.**	raaz o heedæg
stiff neck	**Nyakmerevedésem van.**	n^{y}okmærævædayshæm von
sunstroke	**Napszúrásom van.**	nops$\overline{\text{oo}}$raashawm von
ulcer	**Fekélyem van.**	fækay^{y}æm von
It's nothing serious, I hope.	**Remélem, semmi komoly.**	ræmaylæm shæm-mee kawmaw^{y}
Is it contagious?	**Fertőző?**	fært$\overline{\text{ur}}$z$\overline{\text{ur}}$
I'd like you to prescribe some medicine for me.	**Kérem írjon fel a részemre néhány orvosságot.**	kayræm $\overline{\text{ee}}$ryawn fæl o rayssæmræ nayhaan^{y} awrvawsh-shaagawt

---

DOCTOR

Semmi komoly.	It's nothing serious.
Önnek ...	You've got ...
ételmérgezése	food poisoning
gyomorhurutja van	gastritis
... gyulladása van	inflammation of ...
hólyaggyulladása	cystitis
homloküreggyulladása van	sinusitis
influenzája van	flu
ízületi gyulladás	arthritis
középfültő gyulladása van	inflammation of the middle ear
megfązásos hasmenése	gastric flu
tüdőgyulladása van	pneumonia
vakbélgyulladása	appendicitis
veseköve van	biliary colics
Önnek szakorvoshoz kell mennie.	I want you to see a specialist.

PATIENT

I'm a diabetic.	**Cukorbeteg vagyok.**	**tsoo**kawrbætæg **vod^{y}awk**
I've a cardiac condition.	**Szívbántalmaim vannak.**	**s$\overline{ee}$**vbaantolmo-eem **von**-nok
I had a heart attack ... years ago.	**... évvel ezelőt szívrohamom volt.**	... **ayv**-væl **æ**zæl$\overline{ur}$t **s$\overline{ee}$**vrawhommawm **vawlt**
I'm allergic to ...	**Allergiás vagyok ...-ra/-re.***	**ol**-lærgheeaash **vod^{y}awk** ...-ro/-ræ
This is my usual medicine.	**Ezt a gyógyszert szoktam szedni.**	æst o **d$^{y}\overline{aw}$d^{y}**sært **sawk**tom **sæd**nee
I need this medicine.	**Erre a gyógyszerre van szükségem.**	**ær**-ræ o **d$^{y}\overline{aw}$d^{y}**sær-ræ von **sewk**shaygæm
I'm expecting a baby.	**Terhes vagyok.**	**tær**hæsh **vod^{y}awk**
I'm in my ... month.	**A ...-dik hónapban vagyok.**	o ...-deek **h$\overline{aw}$**nopbon **vod^{y}awk**
Can I travel?	**Utaznom szabad?**	**oo**toznawm **sob**bod

DOCTOR

Milyen adag inzulint kap?	What dose of insulin are you taking?
Injekcióban, vagy szájon át?	Injection or oral?
Hogy kezelik jelenleg?	What treatment are you having?
Milyen gyógyszert szed?	What medicine are you taking?
Általában mennyit szed?	What's your normal dose?
(Enyhe) szívrohama volt.	You've had a (mild) heart attack.
...-t Magyarországon nem használjuk. Ez hasonló.	We don't use ... in Hungary. This is similar.
Mikorra esedékes a szülés?	When is the baby due?
...-ig nem utazhat.	You can't travel until ...

* See Grammar section for word endings.

PATIENT

Part 2—Wounds

Could you have a look at this ...?	**Megvizsgálná ezt a ...?**	mægveezhgaalnaa æst o
bite	**harapást**	horroppaasht
blister	**hólyagot**	haw^{Y}oggawt
boil	**kelést**	kælaysht
bruise	**zúzódást**	zoozawdaasht
burn	**égést**	aygaysht
cut	**vágást**	vaagaasht
graze	**horzsolást**	hawrzhawlaasht
insect bite	**rovarcsípést**	rawvorcheepaysht
lump	**csomót**	chawmawt
rash	**kiütést**	keeewtaysht
sore	**sebet**	shæbæt
sting	**csípést**	cheepaysht
swelling	**daganatot**	doggonnottawt
wound	**sebet**	shæbæt
I can't move ... It hurts.	**Nem tudok mozogni a ... Fáj.**	næm toodawk mawzawgnee o ... faa^{Y}

DOCTOR

2. rész—Sebesülés

(Nem) fertőzött.	It's (not) infected.
Porckorongsérve/Isiásza van.	You've got a slipped disc/sciatica.
Meg kell önt röntgeneztetnem.	I'd like you to have an X-ray.
Ez ...	It's ...
eltört/kiugrott	broken/dislocated
elszakadt/kificamodott	torn/sprained
Izomrándulása van.	You've pulled a muscle.
Antiszeptikumot/ Fájdalomcsillapítót adok Önnek.	I'll give you an antiseptic/a painkiller.
Tetanusz ellen már oltották?	Have you been vaccinated against tetanus?
Kérem, hogy ... nap múlva jöjjön vissza.	I'd like you to come back in ... days.

PARTS OF THE BODY: see page 163

PATIENT

Part 3—Nervous tension

I'm in a nervous state.	**Ideges vagyok.**	eedægæsh vod^{y}awk
I'm feeling depressed.	**Depressziós a hangulatom.**	dæpræs-see$\overline{aw}$sh o hongoolottawm
I'm suffering from anxiety.	**Izgatott vagyok.**	eezgottawt vod^{y}awk
I can't eat.	**Nem tudok enni.**	næm toodawk æn-nee
I can't sleep.	**Nem tudok aludni.**	næm toodawk olloodnee
Can you prescribe ...?	**Felírna valami ...?**	fæl$\overline{ee}$rno vollommee
an antidepressant	**depresszió elleni szert**	dæpræs-see$\overline{aw}$ æl-lænee sært
some sleeping pills	**altatót**	oltott$\overline{aw}$t
a tranquillizer	**nyugtatót**	n^{y}oogtott$\overline{aw}$t
I don't want anything too strong.	**Kérem, ne adjon túl erős orvosságot.**	kayræm næ odyawn t$\overline{oo}$l ær$\overline{ur}$sh awrvawsh-shaagawt

---

DOCTOR

3. rész—Idefeszültség

Ön idegfeszültségben szenved.	You're suffering from nervous tension.
Pihenésre van szüksége.	You need a rest.
Milyen gyógyszert szedett eddig?	What pills have you been taking?
Naponta hányat?	How many a day?
Mióta érzi így magát?	How long have you been feeling like this?
Felírok néhány tablettát.	I'll prescribe some pills.
Adok Önnek nyugtatót/ altatót.	I'll give you a tranquillizer/ some sleeping pills.
Ezzel kihúzza amíg hazaér.	This will see you through until you get home.

PATIENT

Prescription and dosage

What kind of medicine is this?	**Ez milyen orvosság?**	æz **mee^{y}æn awrvawsh-shaag**
How many times a day should I take it?	**Naponta hányszor szedjem?**	noppawnto **haan^{y}sawr sæd^{y}æm**
Must I swallow them whole?	**Egészben kell lenyelnem?**	ægaysbæn kæl **læn^{y}ælnæm**

Fee

How much do I owe you?	**Mennyivel tartozom?**	mæn^{y}eevæl **tortawzawm**
Do I pay you know or will you send me your bill?	**Most fizessek, vagy elküldi a számláját?**	mawsht **feezæsh-shæk** vod^{y} ælkewldee o **saamlaa^{y}aat**
May I have a receipt for my health insurance?	**Kaphatok egy elismervényt a biztosítóm részére?**	**kop**hottawk æd^{y} **æl**eeshmærvayn^{y}t o **beez**tawsheetawm **rayssayræ**

DOCTOR

Gyógyszerfelírás és adagolás

Ebből az orvosságból ... kávéskanállal szedjen.	Take ... teaspoons of this medicine.
... tablettát vegyen be minden ...-ik órában egy pohár vízzel.	Take ... pills with a glass of water every ... hours.
minden étkezés előtt	before each meal
minden étkezés után	after each meal
reggelente/esténként	in the morning/at night
mikor fájdalmai vannak	in case of pain
... napig	for ... days

Tiszteletdíj

Tudna most fizetni?	Can you pay me now, please?
Elküldöm Önnek a számlát.	I'll send you the bill.

NUMBERS: page 175

Dentist

Can you recommend a good dentist?	**Ajánlana egy jó fogorvost?**	oyaanlonno æd^{y} y$\overline{aw}$ **fawg**awrvawsht
Can I make an (urgent) appointment to see Doctor ...?	**(Sürgősen) mikor kereshetem fel doktor ...-t?**	(**shewr**g$\overline{ur}$shæn) **mee**kawr **kæ**ræshhætæm fæl **dawk**tawr ...-t
Can't you possibly make it earlier than that?	**Nem lehetne hamarabb?**	næm **læ**hætnæ **hom**morrob
I've a toothache.	**Fáj a fogam.**	faa^{y} o **faw**gom
I've an abscess.	**Tályogos a fogam.**	**taa**^{y}awgawsh o **faw**gom
This tooth hurts.	**Ez a fogam fáj.**	æz o **faw**gom faa^{y}
at the top	**fent**	fænt
at the bottom	**lent**	lænt
in the front	**elöl**	**æ**lurl
at the back	**hátul**	**haa**tool
Can you fix it up temporarily?	**Ideiglenesen rendbe tudná hozni?**	**ee**dæeeglænæshæn **rænd**bæ **tood**naa **hawz**nee
Please give me a local anaesthetic.	**Kérem, adjon helyi érzéstelenítést.**	**kay**ræm **od**^{y}awn **hæ**^{y}ee **ayr**zayshtælæn$\overline{ee}$taysht
I don't want it extracted.	**Nem akarom kihúzatni.**	næm **ok**korrawm **kee**h$\overline{oo}$zotnee
I've lost a filling.	**Kiesett egy tömítésem.**	**kee**æshæt æd^{y} **tur**m$\overline{ee}$tayshæm
The gum is ...	**... az ínyem.**	... oz **$\overline{ee}$**n^{y}æm
bleeding	**Vérzik**	**vayr**zeek
sore	**Sebes**	**shæ**bæsh

Dentures

I've broken my denture.	**Eltörtem a műfogsoromat.**	**æl**turrtæm o **m$\overline{ew}$**fawgshawrawmot
Can you repair this denture?	**Meg tudná javítani?**	mæg **tood**naa **yov**v$\overline{ee}$tonnee
When will it be ready?	**Mikor lesz kész?**	**mee**kawr læss kayss

Optician

Where can I find an optician?	**Hol találok egy optikust?**	hawl **toll**aalawk æd^{y} **awp**teekoosht
I've broken my glasses.	**Eltörtem a szemüvegemet.**	**æl**turrtæm o **sæ**mewvægæmæt
Can you repair them for me?	**Meg tudná javítani?**	mæg **tood**naa **yov**veetonnee
When will they be ready?	**Mikor lesz kész?**	**mee**kawr læss kayss
Can you change the lenses?	**Ki tudja cserélni az üvegeket?**	kee **tood**^{y}o **chæ**raylnee oz **ew**vægækæt
I'd like tinted lenses.	**Színes üveget szeretnék.**	**see**næsh **ew**vægæt **sæ**rætnayk
I'd like to have my eyesight checked.	**Szeretném megvizsgáltatni a szememet.**	**sæ**rætnaym **mæg**veezhgaaltotnee o **sæ**mæmæt
I'm short-sighted/ long-sighted.	**Rövidlátó/ Távolbalátó vagyok.**	**rur**veedlaataw/**taa**vawlbolaataw **vod**^{y}awk
I'd like a spectacle case.	**Egy szemüvegtartót kérnék.**	æd^{y} **sæ**mewvægtortawt **kayr**nayk
I've lost a contact lens.	**Elvesztettem az egyik kontakt üvegemet.**	**æl**væstæt-tæm oz **æd**^{y}eek **kawn**tokt **ew**vægæmæt
I've hard/soft lenses.	**Kemény/Puha lencséim vannak.**	**kæ**mayn^{y}/**poo**ho **læn**chayeem **von**-nok
Could you give me another lens?	**Tudna másik lencsét adni?**	**tood**no **maa**sheek **læn**chayt **od**nee
Have you got some liquid for contact lenses?	**Van kontakt lencséhez szemcseppjük?**	von **kawn**tokt **læn**chayhæz **sæm**chæpyewk
A small/large bottle, please.	**Egy kis/nagy üveggel kérek.**	æd^{y} keesh/nod^{y} **ew**væg-gæl **kay**ræk
I'd like a pair of sunglasses.	**Egy napszemüveget kérek.**	æd^{y} **nop**sæmewvægæt **kay**ræk
May I look in a mirror?	**Megnézhetem magam a tükörben?**	**mæg**nayz-hætæm **mog**gom o **tew**kurrbæn
I'd like a pair of binoculars.	**Egy távcsövet kérnék.**	æd^{y} **taav**churvæt **kayr**nayk
How much do I owe you?	**Mennyivel tartozom?**	**mæn**^{y}eevæl **tor**tawzawm

Reference section

Hungarian cities

Budapest	**bood**oppæsht
Debrecen	**dæ**brætsæn
Győr	d^{y}ūūrr
Pécs	paych
Szeged	**sæ**gæd

Countries

Austria	**Ausztria**	oostreeo
Belgium	**Belgium**	**bæl**gheeoom
Canada	**Kanada**	**kon**noddo
Czechoslovakia	**Csehszlovákia**	**chæh**slawvaakeeo
East Germany	**Német Demokratikus Köztársaság**	**nay**mæt **dæ**mawkrottee-koosh **kurz**taarshoshaag
England	**Anglia**	**ong**leeo
Finland	**Finnország**	**feen**awrsaag
France	**Franciaország**	**front**seeo-awrsaag
Great Britain	**Nagybritánia**	**nod**^{y}breetaaneeo
Hungary	**Magyarország**	**mod**^{y}orawrsaag
Ireland	**Írország**	**ēē**rawrsaag
Italy	**Olaszország**	**aw**lossawrsaag
Japan	**Japán**	**yop**paan
Netherlands	**Hollandia**	**hawl**-londeeo
New Zealand	**Újzéland**	**ōō**^{y}zaylond
Poland	**Lengyelország**	**lænd**^{y}ælawrsaag
Scotland	**Skócia**	**shkāw**tseeo
Soviet Union	**Szovjetunió**	**saw**vyætooneeāw
Sweden	**Svédország**	**svay**dawrsaag
Switzerland	**Svájc**	shvaa^{y}ts
United States	**Egyesült Államok**	**æd**^{y}æshewlt **aal**-lommawk
Wales	**Vélsz**	væls
West Germany	**Nyugatnémetország**	**n**^{y}oogotnaymætawrsaawg
Yugoslavia	**Jugoszlávia**	**yoo**gawslaaveeo

... and continents

Africa	**Afrika**	**of**reeko
Asia	**Ázsia**	**aa**zheeo
Australia	**Ausztrália**	**oo**ostraaleeo
Europe	**Európa**	**æ**oorāwpo
North America	**Északamerika**	**ays**sokkommæreeko
South America	**Délamerika**	**day**lommæreeko

Numbers

0	**nulla**	**nool**-lo
1	**egy**	æd^{y}
2	**kettő**	**kæt**-tūr
3	**három**	**haa**rawm
4	**négy**	nayd^{y}
5	**öt**	urt
6	**hat**	hot
7	**hét**	hayt
8	**nyolc**	n^{y}awlts
9	**kilenc**	**kee**lænts
10	**tíz**	tēēz
11	**tizenegy**	**tee**zænæd^{y}
12	**tizenkettő**	**tee**zænkæt-tūr
13	**tizenhárom**	**tee**zænhaarawm
14	**tizennégy**	**tee**zæn-nayd^{y}
15	**tizenöt**	**tee**zænurt
16	**tizenhat**	**tee**zænhot
17	**tizenhét**	**tee**zænhayt
18	**tizennyolc**	**tee**zæn-n^{y}awlts
19	**tizenkilenc**	**tee**zænkeelænts
20	**húsz**	hōōss
21	**huszonegy**	**hoo**ssawnæd^{y}
22	**huszonkettő**	**hoo**ssawnkæt-tūr
23	**huszonhárom**	**hoo**ssawnhaarawm
24	**huszonnégy**	**hoo**ssawn-nayd^{y}
25	**huszonöt**	**hoo**ssawnurt
26	**huszonhat**	**hoo**ssawnhot
27	**huszonhét**	**hoo**ssawnhayt
28	**huszonnyolc**	**hoo**ssawn-n^{y}awlts
29	**huszonkilenc**	**hoo**ssawnkeelænts
30	**harminc**	**hor**meents
31	**harmincegy**	**hor**meentsæd^{y}
32	**harminckettő**	**hor**meentskæt-tūr
33	**harminchárom**	**hor**meentshaarawm
40	**negyven**	**næd**^{y}væn
41	**negyvenegy**	**næd**^{y}vænæd^{y}
42	**negyvenkettő**	**næd**^{y}vænkæt-tūr
43	**negyvenhárom**	**næd**^{y}vænhaarawm
50	**ötven**	**urt**væn
51	**ötvenegy**	**urt**vænæd^{y}
52	**ötvenkettő**	**urt**vænkæt-tūr
53	**ötvenhárom**	**urt**vænhaarawm
60	**hatvan**	**hot**von
61	**hatvanegy**	**hot**vonnæd^{y}

62	**hatvankettő**	hotvonkæt-tūr
63	**hatvanhárom**	hotvonhaarawm
70	**hetven**	hætvæn
71	**hetvenegy**	hætvænæd^{y}
72	**hetvenkettő**	hætvænkæt-tūr
73	**hetvenhárom**	hætvænhaarawm
80	**nyolcvan**	n^{y}awltsvon
81	**nyolcvanegy**	n^{y}awltsvonnæd^{y}
82	**nyolcvankettő**	n^{y}awltsvonkæt-tūr
83	**nyolcvanhárom**	n^{y}awltsvonhaarawm
90	**kilencven**	keelæntsvæn
91	**kilencvenegy**	keelæntsvænæd^{y}
92	**kilencvenkettő**	keelæntsvænkæt-tūr
93	**kilencvenhárom**	keelæntsvænhaarawm
100	**egyszáz**	æd^{y}saaz
101	**százegy**	saazæd^{y}
102	**százkettő**	saazkæt-tūr
103	**százhárom**	saazhaarawm
110	**száztíz**	saaztēēz
120	**százhúsz**	saazhōōss
130	**százharminc**	saazhormeents
140	**száznegyven**	saaznæd^{y}væn
150	**százötven**	saazurtvæn
160	**százhatvan**	saazhotvon
170	**százhetven**	saazhætvæn
180	**száznyolcvan**	saazn^{y}awltsvon
190	**százkilencven**	saazkeelæntsvæn
200	**kettőszáz**	kæt-tūrsaaz
300	**háromszáz**	haarawmsaaz
400	**négyszáz**	nayd^{y}saaz
500	**ötszáz**	urtsaaz
600	**hatszáz**	hotsaaz
700	**hétszáz**	haytsaaz
800	**nyolcszáz**	n^{y}awlts-saaz
900	**kilencszáz**	keelænts-saaz
1000	**egyezer**	æd^{y}æzær
1100	**ezeregyszáz**	æzæræd^{y}saaz
1200	**ezerkettőszáz**	æzærkæt-tūrsaaz
1300	**ezerháromszáz**	æzærhaarawmsaaz
2000	**kétezer**	kaytæzær
5000	**ötezer**	urtæzær
10,000	**tízezer**	tēēzæzær
50,000	**ötvenezer**	urtvænæzær
100,000	**százezer**	saazæzær
1,000,000	**egymillió**	æd^{y}meel-leeāw

first	**első**	ælshūr
second	**második**	maashawdeek
third	**harmadik**	hormoddeek
fourth	**negyedik**	næd^{y}ædeek
fifth	**ötödik**	urturdeek
sixth	**hatodik**	hottawdeek
seventh	**hetedik**	hætædeek
eighth	**nyolcadik**	n^{y}awltsoddeek
ninth	**kilencedik**	keelæntsædeek
tenth	**tizedik**	teezædeek
hundredth	**századik**	saazoddeek
thousandth	**ezredik**	æzrædeek
once	**egyszer**	æd^{y}sær
twice	**kétszer**	kaytsær
three times	**háromszor**	haarawmsawr
half	**fél**	fayl
half of ...	**a ... fele**	o ... fælæ
a quarter	**egy negyed**	æd^{y} næd^{y}æd
a third	**egy harmad**	æd^{y} hormod
a pair of ...	**egy pár ...**	æd^{y} paar
a dozen	**egy tucat**	æd^{y} tootsot
half a dozen	**féltucat**	fayltootsot
the 19th century	**a tizenkilencedik század**	o teezækeelæntsædeek saazod
in the 20th century	**a huszadik században**	o hoossoddeek saazodbon
How old are you?	**Hány éves?**	haan^{y} ayvæsh
I'm 26.	**26 éves vagyok.**	26 ayvæsh vod^{y}awk
When's your birthday?	**Mikor van a születésnapja?**	meekawr von o sewlætayshnopyo
I was born in ...	**...-ban/-ben születtem.**	...-bon/-bæn sewlættæm
1986	**ezerkilencszáz-nyolcvanhat**	æzærkeelænts-saaz-n^{y}awltsvonhot
1997	**ezerkilencszáz-kilencvenhét**	æzærkeelænts-saaz-keelæntsvænhayt
1998		

Time

tizenkettő óra múlt tizenöt perccel
(**tee**zænkæt-t$\overline{\text{ur}}$ **$\overline{\text{aw}}$**ro m$\overline{\text{oo}}$lt **tee**zænurt **pærts**-tsæl)

egy óra múlt húsz perccel
(æd[y] **$\overline{\text{aw}}$**ro m$\overline{\text{oo}}$lt h$\overline{\text{oo}}$ss **pærts**-tsæl)

fél négy*
(fayl nayd[y])

négy óra harmincöt perc
(nayd[y] **$\overline{\text{aw}}$**ro **hor**meen-tsurt pærts)

hat óra lesz húsz perc múlva
(hot **$\overline{\text{aw}}$**ro læs h$\overline{\text{oo}}$ss pærts **m$\overline{\text{oo}}$**lvo)

háromnegyed hét
(**haa**rawmnæd[y]æd hayt)

öt perc múlva kilenc óra
(urt pærts **m$\overline{\text{oo}}$**lvo **kee**lænts **$\overline{\text{aw}}$**ro)

tíz óra
(t$\overline{\text{ee}}$z **$\overline{\text{aw}}$**ro)

tizenegy óra múlt öt perccel
(**tee**zænæd[y] **$\overline{\text{aw}}$**ro m$\overline{\text{oo}}$lt urt **pærts**-tsæl)

* literally "half *to* four".

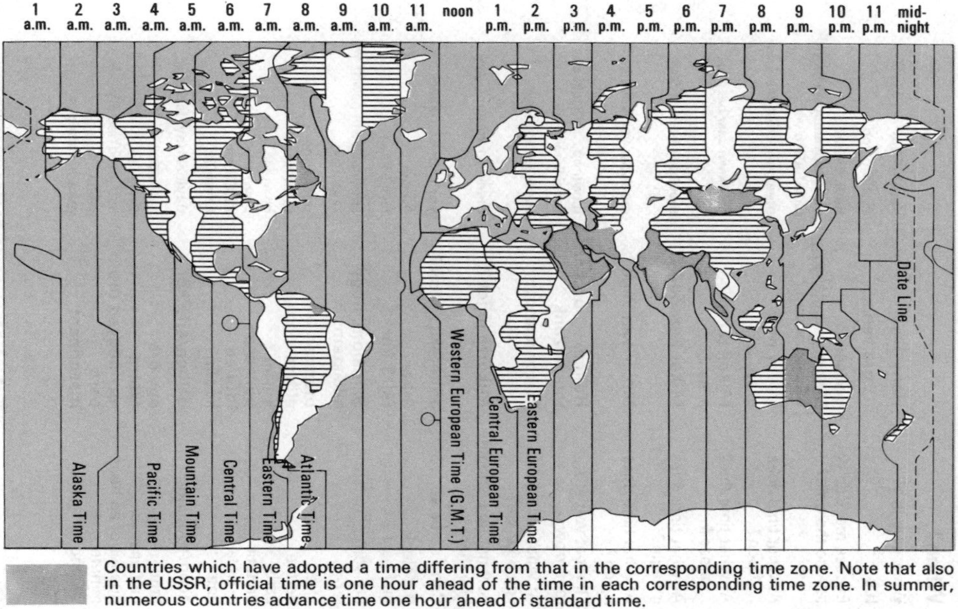

Countries which have adopted a time differing from that in the corresponding time zone. Note that also in the USSR, official time is one hour ahead of the time in each corresponding time zone. In summer, numerous countries advance time one hour ahead of standard time.

When?

What time is it?	**Hány óra?**	haan^y $\overline{aw}$ro
It's ...	**... óra van.**	... $\overline{aw}$ro von
Excuse me. Can you tell me the time?	**Bocsánat. Megmondaná hogy hány óra van?**	bawchaanot. mægmawndonnaa hawd^y haan^y $\overline{aw}$ro von
At what time does ... open?	**Mikor nyit a/az ...?**	meekawr n^{y}eet zaar o/oz
At what time does ... close?	**Mikor zár be a/az ...?**	meekawr zaar bæ o/oz
At what time does it begin?	**Mikor kezdődik?**	meekawr kæzd$\overline{ur}$deek
At what time does it end?	**Mikor van vége?**	meekawr von vaygæ
I'll meet you at ... tomorrow.	**Holnap ... órakor találkozunk.**	hawlnop ... $\overline{aw}$rokkawr tollaalkawzoonk
At what time will you be there?	**Mikor lesz ott?**	meekawr læs awt
At what time should I be there?	**Mikorra jöjjek?**	meekawr-ro yur^y-yæk
Can I come at ...?	**Jöhetek ... -kor?**	yurhætæk ...-kawr
9 o'clock	**9-kor**	9-kawr
half past 2	**fél-3-kor**	fayl 3-kawr
I'm sorry, I'm late.	**Sajnálom, hogy elkéstem.**	shoynaalawm hawd^y ælkayshtæm
after	**utánna**	ootaan-no
before	**előtte**	æl$\overline{ur}$t-tæ
early	**korán**	kawraan
on time	**pontosan**	pawntawshon
in time	**időben**	eed$\overline{ur}$bæn
late	**későn**	kaysh$\overline{ur}$n
noon/midnight	**délben/éjfélkor**	daylbæn/ay^{y}faylkawr
hour	**egy óra**	æd^y $\overline{aw}$ro
half an hour	**félóra**	fayl$\overline{aw}$ro
quarter of an hour	**egy negyed óra**	æd^y næd^{y}æd $\overline{aw}$ro
minute	**perc**	pærts
second	**másodperc**	maashawdpærts

Days

What day is it today?	**Ma milyen nap van?**	mo **mee**^{Y}æn nop von
It's ...	**... van.**	... von
Sunday	**Vasárnap***	**vo**shaarnop
Monday	**Hétfő**	**hayt**fu̅r̅
Tuesday	**Kedd**	kæd
Wednesday	**Szerda**	**sær**do
Thursday	**Csütörtök**	**chew**turrturk
Friday	**Péntek**	**payn**tæk
Saturday	**Szombat**	**sawm**bot
in the morning	**reggel**	**ræg**-gæl
at noon	**délben**	**dayl**bæn
in the afternoon	**délután**	**day**lootaan
in the evening	**este**	**æsh**tæ
at night	**éjjel**	**ay**^{Y}-yæl
at midnight	**éjfélkor**	**ay**^{Y}faylkawr
the day before yesterday	**tegnapelőtt**	**tæg**nopælu̅r̅t
yesterday	**tegnap**	**tæg**nop
today	**ma**	mo
tomorrow	**holnap**	**hawl**nop
the day after tomorrow	**holnapután**	**hawl**noppootaan
the day before	**az előző nap**	oz **æ**lu̅r̅zu̅r̅ nop
the next day	**a következő nap**	o **kur**vætkæzu̅r̅ nop
two days ago	**két nappal ezelőtt**	kayt **nop**-pol **æ**zælu̅r̅t
in three days' time	**három nap múlva**	**haa**rawm nop **mo̅o̅l**vo
last week	**a múlt héten**	o **mo̅o̅lt hay**tæn
this week	**ezen a héten**	**æ**zæn o **hay**tæn
next week	**a jövő héten**	o **yur**vu̅r̅ **hay**tæn
birthday	**születésnap**	**sew**lætayshnop
day	**nap**	nop
holiday	**ünnepnap**	**ewn**-næpnop
holidays	**szabadság**	**sob**bodshaag
month	**hónap**	**ha̅w̅**nop
week	**hét**	hayt
week-end	**hétvége**	**hayt**vaygæ
working day	**munkanap**	**moon**konnop
year	**év**	ayv

* Note that, except when they appear at the beginning of a sentence, the names of days and months are not capitalized in Hungarian.

Months

January	**január***	yonnooaar
February	**február**	fæbrooaar
March	**március**	martseeoosh
April	**április**	aapreeleesh
May	**május**	maa^{y}oosh
June	**június**	yo͞oneeoosh
July	**július**	yo͞oleeoosh
August	**augusztus**	ooogoostoosh
September	**szeptember**	sæptæmbær
October	**október**	awkta͞wbær
November	**november**	nawvæmbær
December	**december**	dætsæmbær
since June	**június óta**	yo͞oneeoosh a͞wto
in August	**augusztusban**	ooogoostooshbon
3 months ago	**3 hónappal ezelőtt**	3 ha͞wnop-pol æzælu͞rt
last month	**a múlt hónapban**	o mo͞olt ha͞wnopbon
next month	**a következő hónapban**	o kurvætkæzu͞r ha͞wnop-bon
the month before	**az előző hónapban**	oz ælu͞rzu͞r ha͞wnopbon
the following month	**a következő hónapban**	o kurvætkæzu͞r ha͞wnopbon

Letter headings are written thus:

Budapest, May 24, 19..	**Budapest 19.. május 24**

Seasons

spring	**tavasz**	tovvoss
summer	**nyár**	n^{y}aar
autumn	**ősz**	u͞rss
winter	**tél**	tayl
in spring	**tavasszal**	tovvos-sol
in summer	**nyáron**	n^{y}aarawn
in autumn	**ősszel**	u͞rs-sæl
in winter	**télen**	taylæn

---

* Note that the names of days and months are not capitalized in Hungarian.

Public holidays

January 1	**Újév**	New Year's Day
April 4	**A felszabadulás ünnepe**	Liberation Day
May 1	**A munka ünnepe**	Labour Day
August 20	**Az alkotmány napja**	Constitution Day
November 7	**A forradalom ünnepe**	Revolution Day
December 25	**Karácsony első napja**	Christmas Day
December 26	**Karácsony második napja**	Boxing Day
Movable:	**Húsvét hétfő**	Easter Monday

The year round

Here are the average monthly temperatures in Fahrenheit and centigrade for some centres in Hungary:

	Budapest		Lake Balaton		Mountains	
	°F	°C	°F	°C	°F	°C
January	34	1	37	3	18	– 8
February	34	1	32	0	14	–10
March	46	8	48	9	32	0
April	52	11	55	13	43	6
May	59	15	61	16	50	10
June	66	19	68	20	57	14
July	68	20	75	24	59	15
August	66	19	73	23	55	13
September	61	16	64	18	50	10
October	54	12	59	15	48	9
November	37	3	45	7	28	– 2
December	36	2	39	4	21	– 6

Common abbreviations

áll.	**állami**	state
ált.	**általános**	general
bek.	**bekezdés**	paragraph
B.N.V.	**Budapesti Nemzetközi Vásár**	Budapest International Fair
Bp.	**Budapest**	Budapest
db/drb.	**darab**	piece
d.e.	**délelőtt**	a.m.
d. u.	**délután**	p.m.
et.	**elvtárs**	comrade
évf.	**évfolyam**	year
f.é.	**folyó év**	this year
f.h.	**folyó hó**	this month
fmh	**feltételes megállóhely**	request stop
főv.	**fővárosi**	metropolitan
fsz.	**földszint**	ground floor
gk.	**gépkocsi**	car
gy.v.	**gyorsvonat**	express train
hat.eng.	**hatóságilag engedélyezett**	licensed
IBUSZ	**Idegenforgalmi Ügynökség**	Ibusz Tourist Agency
kb.	**körülbelül**	approximately
K.B.	**Központi Bizottság**	Central Committee
KEOKH	**Külföldieket Ellenőrző Országos Központ**	Foreigners' Registration Office
Közért	**élelmiszerüzlet**	food shop trust
LE	**lóerő**	horsepower
MALÉV	**Magyar Légiforgalmi Vállalat**	Hungarian Airlines
MÁV	**Magyar Államvasutak**	Hungarian State Railways
M.N.B.	**Magyar Nemzeti Bank**	Hungarian National Bank
M.T.I.	**Magyar Távirati Iroda**	Hungarian Telegraphic Services
p.u.	**pályaudvar**	railway station
röv.	**rövidítés**	abbreviation
s.k.	**sajátkezüleg**	in one's own hand
stb.	**és a többi**	etc.
szt.	**szent**	saint
távb.	**telefon**	telephone
T.c.	**Tisztelt Cím!**	Sir, Madam (polite, written)
u.	**utca, út**	street
u.a.	**ugyanaz**	the same, idem
u.n.	**úgynevezett**	so called
v.á.	**vasútállomás**	railway station

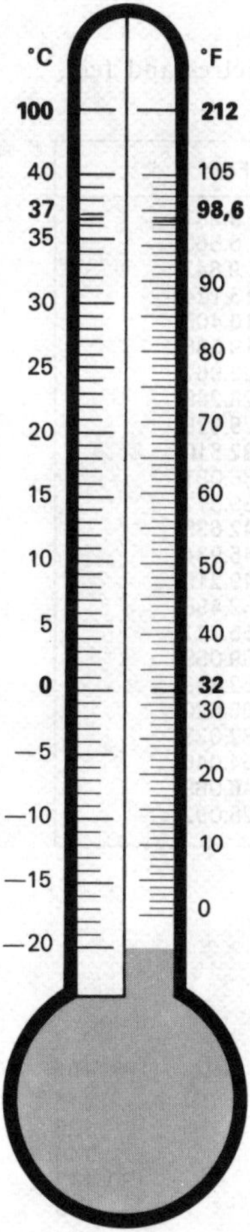

Conversion tables

Centimetres and inches

To change centimetres into inches, multiply by .39.

To change inches into centimetres, multiply by 2.54.

	in.	feet	yards
1 mm	0.039	0.003	0.001
1 cm	0.39	0.03	0.01
1 dm	3.94	0.32	0.10
1 m	39.40	3.28	1.09

	mm	cm	m
1 in.	25.4	2.54	0.025
1 ft.	304.8	30.48	0.305
1 yd.	914.4	91.44	0.914

(32 metres = 35 yards)

Temperature

To convert centigrade into degrees Fahrenheit, multiply centigrade by 1.8 and add 32.

To convert degrees Fahrenheit into centigrade, subtract 32 from Fahrenheit and divide by 1.8.

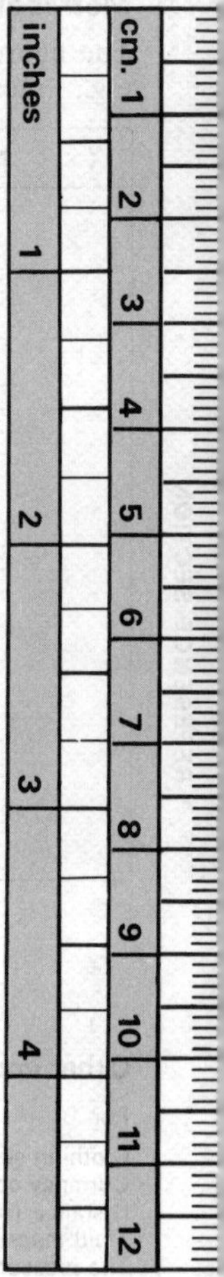

Metres and feet

The figure in the middle stands for both metres and feet, e.g., 1 metre = 3.28 ft. and 1 foot = 0.30 m.

Metres		Feet
0.30	**1**	3.281
0.61	**2**	6.563
0.91	**3**	9.843
1.22	**4**	13.124
1.52	**5**	16.403
1.83	**6**	19.686
2.13	**7**	22.967
2.44	**8**	26.248
2.74	**9**	29.629
3.05	**10**	32.810
3.35	**11**	36.091
3.66	**12**	39.372
3.96	**13**	42.635
4.27	**14**	45.934
4.57	**15**	49.215
4.88	**16**	52.496
5.18	**17**	55.777
5.49	**18**	59.058
5.79	**19**	62.339
6.10	**20**	65.620
7.62	**25**	82.023
15.24	**50**	164.046
22.86	**75**	246.069
30.48	**100**	328.092

Other conversion charts

For	see page
Clothing sizes	115
Currency converter	136
Distance (miles-kilometres)	144
Fluid measures	130, 142
Tire pressure	143

Weight conversion

The figure in the middle stands for both kilograms and pounds, e.g., 1 kilogram = 2.205 lb. and 1 pound = 0.45 kilograms.

Kilograms (kg.)		Avoirdupois pounds
0.45	**1**	2.205
0.91	**2**	4.409
1.36	**3**	6.614
1.81	**4**	8.818
2.27	**5**	11.023
2.72	**6**	13.227
3.17	**7**	15.432
3.62	**8**	17.636
4.08	**9**	19.841
4.53	**10**	22.045
6.80	**15**	33.068
9.06	**20**	44.089
11.33	**25**	55.113
22.65	**50**	110.225
34.02	**75**	165.338
45.30	**100**	220.450

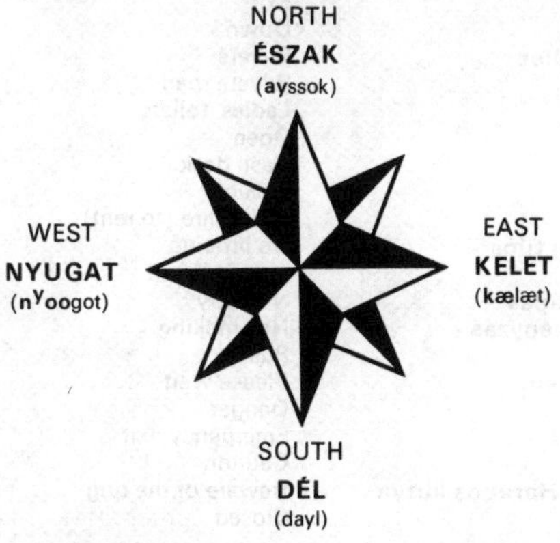

What does that sign mean?

You're sure to encounter some of these signs or notices on your trip:

A bejáratot kérjük szabadon hagyni	Do not block the entrance
Átjárás tilos	Trespassers will be prosecuted
Bejárat	Entrance
Belépés díjtalan	Admission free
Dohányzó	Smoking allowed
Eladó	For sale
Elfogyott	Sold out
Érintése tilos	Do not touch
Fáradjon be	Enter without knocking
Fel	Up
Felvilágosítás	Information
Férfi W.C.	Men's toilets
Foglalt	Reserved, occupied
Forró	Hot
Halálveszély	Danger of death
Hideg	Cold
Húzni	Pull
Kérem, csengessen	Please ring
Kiadó	To let
Kiárusítás	Sale
Kijárat	Exit
Le	Down
Magánterület	Private
Magánút	Private road
Női W.C.	Ladies' toilets
Nyitva	Open
Pénztáros	Cash desk
Szabad	Vacant
... kiadó	... for hire (to rent)
Szemetelni tilos	No littering
... tilos	... prohibited
Tilos a belépés	No entry
Tilos a dohányzás	No smoking
Tólni	Push
Várjon kérem	Please wait
Veszély	Danger
Vészkijárat	Emergency exit
Vigyázat	Caution
Vigyázat! Harapós kutya	Beware of the dog
Zárva	Closed

REFERENCE SECTION

Emergency

By the time the emergency is upon you it's too late to turn to this page to find the Hungarian for "Call the police". So have a look at this short list beforehand—and, if you want to be on the safe side, learn the expressions shown in capitals.

Be quick	**Gyorsan**	d^{y}awrshon
Call the police	**Hívja a rendőrséget**	heevyo o rændurrshaygæt
CAREFUL	**ÓVATOSAN**	awvottawshon
Come here	**Jöjjön ide**	yur^{y}-yurn eedæ
Come in	**Szabad**	sobbod
Consulate	**Konzulátus**	kawnzoolaatoosh
Danger	**Veszély**	væsay^{y}
Embassy	**Nagykövetség**	nod^{y}kurvætshayg
FIRE	**TŰZ**	tewz
GET A DOCTOR	**HÍVJON ORVOST**	heevyawn awrvawsht
Get help quickly	**Hozzon gyorsan segítséget**	hawz-zon d^{y}awrshon shægheetshaygæt
Go away	**Távozzék**	taavawz-zayk
HELP	**SEGÍTSÉG**	shægheetshayg
I'm ill	**Beteg vagyok**	bætæg vod^{y}awk
I'm lost	**Eltévedtem**	æltayvædtæm
Keep your hands to yourself	**Ne fogdosson**	næ fawgdawsh-shawn
Leave me alone	**Hagyjon békét**	hod^{y}yawn baykayt
Lie down	**Feküdjön le**	fækewdyurn læ
Listen	**Figyeljen**	feed^{y}ælyæn
Look	**Nézzen körül**	nayz-zæn kurrewl
Look out	**Vigyázat**	veed^{y}aazot
POLICE	**RENDŐRSÉG**	rændurrshayg
STOP	**MEGÁLLNI**	mægaalnee
Stop, or I'll scream	**Hagyjon békét, vagy kiáltok**	hod^{y}awn baykayt vod^{y} keeaaltawk
Stop that man	**Állítsák meg azt az embert**	aal-leetshaak mæg ost oz æmbært
STOP THIEF	**FOGJÁK MEG TOLVAJ**	fawgyaak mæg tawlvoy

Emergency telephone numbers:

Ambulance	04	**Mentők**
Fire	05	**Tűzoltók**
Police	07	**Rendőrség**

CAR ACCIDENTS: see page 150

Index

Quick reference page

Yes/No.	**Igen/Nem.**	**ee**gæn/næm
Please.	**Kérem.**	**kay**ræm
Thank you.	**Köszönöm.**	**kur**surnurm
Excuse me.	**Bocsásson meg.**	**baw**chaash-shawn mæg
I'm sorry.	**Sajnálom.**	**shoy**naalawn
Waiter/Waitress, please!	**Pincér/Pincérnő, kérem!**	**peen**tsayr/**peen**tsayrn$\overline{ur}$ **kay**ræm
How much is that?	**Mennyibe kerül?**	**mæn**^{y}eebæ **kæ**rewl
Where are the toilets?	**Hol a W.C.?**	hawl o **vay**tsay

Toilets

FÉRFI W.C. (**fayr**fee **vay**tsay)	**NŐI W.C.** (**n$\overline{ur}$**ee **vay**tsay)

Please, could you tell me ...?	**Kérem, meg tudná mondani, hogy ...?**	**kay**ræm mæg **tood**naa **mawn**donnee hawd^{y}
where/when/why	**hol/mikor/miért**	hawl/**mee**kawr/**mee**ayrt
What time is it?	**Hány óra van?**	haan^{y} $\overline{aw}$ro von
Help me, please.	**Segítene kérem.**	**shæ**gh$\overline{ee}$tænæ **kay**ræm
Where's the ... consulate/embassy?	**Hol ... Konzulátus/ Nagykövetség?**	hawl ... **kawn**zoolaatoosh/ **nod**^{y}kurvætshayg
American	**az amerikai**	oz **om**mæreeko-ee
British	**az angol**	oz **on**gawl
Canadian	**a kanadai**	o **kon**noddo-ee
What does this mean?	**Ez mit jelent?**	æz meet **yæ**lænt
I don't understand.	**Nem értem.**	næm **ayr**tæm
Do you speak English?	**Beszél angolul?**	**bæ**sayl **on**gawlool